SOME OF THE DO-IT-YOURSELF BUSINESS IDEAS, TIPS, AND PLANS IN THIS BOOK...

... can be started on less than $10!

See RECYCLED REFUNDS (page 60), HOW TO HAND-LETTER FOR CASH (page 292), or A NICE LITTLE CEMENT BUSINESS (page 90).

... could help you break into publishing or broadcasting!

See HOW TO BE A CARTOONIST (page 296), PAY THE RENT WITH A GUIDEBOOK (page 270), and BE A ONE-MAN OR ONE-WOMAN RADIO NETWORK (page 92).

... offer a fun way to make a quick $250!

See GARAGE SALES CAN BE VERY GOOD (page 56).

... tell how to make typing at home really pay off!

See A $12,000-A-YEAR HOME TYPING BUSINESS (page 2), START A HOME STENO SERVICE (page 14), and THE BEST HOME TYPING BUSINESS OF ALL (page 30).

... can be operated out of a kitchen or spare room!

See START YOUR OWN CANDY FACTORY (page 100), THERE'S GOLD IN THEM THAR TWILLS (page 114), or OUR FAMILY UPHOLSTERY BUSINESS (page 122).

... might put you into a downtown store of your own!

See HOW I STARTED A SILVER SHOP (page 197), MY PAPERBACK BOOK EXCHANGE BUYS ME BOTH LEISURE AND PROFIT (page 210), and YOU CAN MAKE FIRST-CLASS PROFITS WITH A SECONDHAND BUSINESS (page 160).

... will let you come and go as you please!

See TEMPORARY WORK CAN BE A PERMANENT CAREER (page 360), THE GOOD LIFE (page 322), or GET PAID FOR TAKING A FREE VACATION (page 338).

... can help you earn a lot of money fast!

See UNDERGROUND MOVING (page 258).

IT'S ALL HERE! EVERY "TRADE SECRET" AND ALL THE "INSIDE INFORMATION" YOU'LL EVER NEED TO

AND EXCITING

BUSINESSES AND "SHI

INTO PROFITABLE O

D1455539

CREDITS

Research for this book was done by Kenny Hodges, Diane Kaczor, Jim Ed Morgans, John Shuttleworth, Ed Vitale, and the authors whose names appear on some of the articles contained herein.

Copy written and proofread by Kenny Hodges, Diane Kaczor, Terry Krautwurst, and Jim Ed Morgans under the direction of John Shuttleworth.

Typesetting by Jerry Collins and Julia Pridgen under the direction of Lucy Wilmoth.

Layout by Kay Holmes, J.D. Neuenschwander, and Mark Wilson under the direction of Debby Flint.

Index by Karly Lubach and Jim Ed Morgans.

Superexcellent artwork by Kay Holmes.

SPECIAL ACKNOWLEDGMENTS

Some of the material in this book originally appeared in different form in the magazine, THE MOTHER EARTH NEWS, published by THE MOTHER EARTH NEWS, Inc., P.O. Box 70, Hendersonville, North Carolina 28739, and/or was used on the syndicated radio program, NEWS FROM THE MOTHER EARTH NEWS, distributed by THE MOTHER EARTH NEWS, Inc., and/or appeared in the syndicated newspaper feature, THE MOTHER EARTH NEWS, distributed by The Register and Tribune Syndicate, 715 Locust Street, Des Moines, Iowa 50304, and/or appeared in LIFESTYLE! magazine, published by THE MOTHER EARTH NEWS, Inc.

Special thanks to *Cartoon World*, P.O. Box 30367, Lincoln, Nebraska 68503, for permission to reprint "The Lonely Worker" on pages 310—315 of this book. Special thanks, also, to Arthur E. Victor for permission to reprint excerpts from *So You Want to Start a Rock Shop* on pages 136—159 of this book.

THE MOTHER EARTH NEWS®

HANDBOOK OF
HOME
BUSINESS
IDEAS AND PLANS

BY THE STAFF OF
THE MOTHER EARTH NEWS®

BANTAM BOOKS · TORONTO · LONDON · NEW YORK

THE MOTHER EARTH NEWS®
HANDBOOK OF HOME BUSINESS IDEAS AND PLANS

A Bantam Book / September 1976

Published simultaneously in the United States and Canada

Bantam Books are published by Bantam Books, Inc. Its trade-
mark, consisting of the words "Bantam Books" and the por-
trayal of a bantam, is registered in the United States Patent
Office and in other countries. Marca Registrada. Bantam
Books, Inc., 666 Fifth Avenue, New York, New York 10019.

PRINTED IN THE UNITED STATES OF AMERICA

0 9 8 7 6 5 4 3 2 1

This book

is dedicated to

a revival of

THE NEIGHBORLY SELF-RELIANCE

that softheaded

government bureaucrats

seem so determined

to kill.

TABLE OF

CONTENTS

INTRODUCTION

This, as you'll soon discover, is not your usual "home business" book. It does not vaguely promise overnight wealth in mail order. It contains no "miracle" accounts of the manner in which "a woman with an invalid husband devised a wonderful item she could manufacture at home and now she enjoys a $50,000-a-year income". It was written by no "expert" with six degrees in business administration. It is not filled with dry discussions of proper markup ratios, tax reserves, and double entry bookkeeping systems.

Instead, this book is made up almost entirely of firsthand "how I did it" articles. Articles written by the actual people who rolled up their sleeves and successfully put themselves into the 36 self-employment enterprises covered by this manual.

Only in a few cases—when the entrepreneur in question was too busy or too inexperienced with words to author a story about his or her business venture—have the rudiments of an enterprise been presented by an "outside" writer. And even then, not a shred of "theory" has been allowed to creep into the articles you're about to read. Every word, every sentence, every paragraph in this manual is based on exact, experienced fact.

And here's another surprise: No single author's word was taken as "gospel" when this book was assembled. His or her experience, ideas, and prejudices in the field in question were carefully weighed against the experiences, ideas, and prejudices of others working in the same business. And—in all cases where one or more additional individuals had something worthwhile to add to the original author's discussion of a particular do-it-yourself venture—the additions were made.

It should also be pointed out that this handbook has not been restricted by any narrow definition of the term "home business". Some people, of course, do interpret the expression to mean only those enterprises that can be set up and run from a residence. All well and good . . . and those folks will find that nearly every self-employment venture covered by this manual can be so organized and operated.

Individuals with less limited vision, however, will soon note that this guide has been organized with them in mind too. Emphasis has been placed, in certain sections, on the possibility of expanding some enterprises into the form of a "real" store. Or on taking some businesses out on the road. Or on the artistic aspects of some undertakings. Or on still other facets of yet other self-employment ventures described in the pages that follow. And, at all times, the widest possible interpretation of "home business" and "self-employment" has been used. We are interested, in other words, in helping you find exactly the way of making a livelihood that suits you best . . . and we've tried to keep every possibility—no matter how seemingly farfetched—open for your consideration.

And that raises another important point: Although some of the do-it-yourself occupations covered by this manual can be very profitable indeed, most of the entrepreneurs quoted seem to stress the emotional, spiritual, and human satisfactions of their mini-enterprises . . . instead of the sheer dollars they're making. We believe that this is a very healthy and a very adult attitude . . . and we applaud it.

Finally, just in case you should wonder why so many of the following authors briefly mention "getting back to the land", "finding employment in the country", or "putting together a grubstake so we can move to the sticks": All the success stories in this book originally appeared in either THE MOTHER EARTH NEWS® or LIFESTYLE!, two magazines devoted to helping people trade the stress and strain of modern urban life for a gentler way of living. And a sizable number of both publications' authors and readers feel that their ultimate destiny lies in a rural setting.

So. What are *you* looking for? Something you can do part time? A full-time enterprise? A business that you can work hard at for six months and then "retire" from for a year? An outlet for your creative talents? A single-person occupation where you and you alone set the hours? A moneymaking venture that you can eventually expand into a "real" store or factory? A business that will allow you to travel? Something that you can start on less than $100? A way of letting someone else take care of all the details so that you can just "freelance" a little profitable work when and where you choose?

The answers—thirty-six of 'em, in fact—to all those "home business" ideals are right here in this little book. And all for less than seven cents apiece! ⬤

TYPING
AT HOME

Survey after survey has shown that the all-time *most* popular self-employment wish throughout (at least the female half of) the civilized world is for "a little typing business I can run at home".

So let's get right down to satisfying that wish! Here are—not one, not two, and not three—*four* separate and distinct work-at-home enterprises that involve typing. Two require—in addition to a small assortment of paper, ribbons, carbons, erasers, etc.—little more than an "ordinary" standard or electric typewriter. A third can also be handled quite satisfactorily on such a machine (although you'll make more money for the same amount of work if you can rent or buy an office electric with a slightly modified "pitch"). And the fourth (presented first in the section that follows) and most profitable of all can only be set up and run with a special "typesetting" machine.

In all four cases specific recommendations are given that will help you test the business in question at absolutely minimum expense, line up your first customers or clients, keep accurate records, and otherwise run and manage your new venture.

And then, just in case you've missed one or more important points the first time around, a *fifth* experienced home typist wraps up this section of the book with an overview of the field that should be helpful no matter *what* kind of home typing business you might finally decide to enter. ●

BILL MONTANARY: A GUARANTEED, GEN-U-WINE $12,000 - A-YEAR HOME TYPING BUSINESS

One of the All-Time Great Elusive Dreams of American man- and woman-kind—ranking right up there with The Fountain of Youth and World Peace—is A Little Business at Home. In the case of the gentler sex, this dream is often further refined into A Little *Typing* Business At Home . . . and many are the ads in the back pages of the confession magazines that promise to tell—for a fee—how to establish a Profitable Home Typing Operation.

All well and good . . . *except* that those promises seldom materialize. Furthermore, the cost of the "course" involved often amounts to a fairly hefty little chunk of cash . . . especially for widows, divorcees with children, and shut-ins. In other words, most of the home typing schemes are just that: *schemes* that make a fast buck for con artists at the expense of those most desperate and least able to stand the gaff.

Well, be of good cheer, gang. Because MOTHER is now going to tell you about a guaranteed, gen-u-wine home typing business that will not only work . . . but that can net you $10,000 a year or more right from the start . . . on a part-time basis.

As might be expected, the typing we're talking about is not the ordinary garden variety. It's a specialized form of the art called _typesetting_ and—before you panic—let me add that the tools of the trade which you'll be using are actually easier and cleaner to operate than most office electric or home portable typewriters.

What's more, the primary machine and all supporting equipment and supplies you'll need to run your home typesetting business for a full year—together in one lump—are small enough to fit on a single desk or tabletop. As a final frosting on the cake—unlike the rip-off home business "courses"—you can actually try this one out for a month or more before you personally lay out one nickel . . . _and_, if you do decide to establish a typesetting operation, you can then either lease or purchase everything you'll need in any one of several very easy ways.

Sounds too good to be true, doesn't it? There's got to be a catch somewhere . . . maybe the business is just too tough for the average person to break into . . . or something.

Well, it may _sound_ too good to be true, but it _is_ true and you _can_ start cycling some of the multi-billion-dollar printing industry through your basement study or kitchen nook right now. I know one housewife in Cleveland—Myra Schneider—who has already established _her_ home typesetting operation, and she says that busting into the field is no trick at all. Matter of fact, she claims she sort of wandered in by accident.

Myra's old high school, it seems, had a reunion about two and a half years back, and her committee was given the job of putting together and printing a typeset program for the digs. Myra was put in charge of the project and she quickly learned that [1] typesetting is very expensive and [2] she could do the job herself for much less money on a rented IBM Composer.

As it turned out, the typesetting for the booklet didn't cost the high school anything at all because Myra became so intrigued with the possibilities offered by the Composer that she arranged to have one set into her home on a free demonstration. That demonstration was evidently quite successful because, with only the salesman's instructions, Myra was able to set all the type for the reunion program . . . and launch herself into a part-time business that has netted close to $1,000 a month right from the start.

Myra says, "The very next week after I composed the high school program, the printer who had worked on the booklet got a call from the man in charge of a local corporation's print shop. That man asked our printer if he knew anyone who could do a typesetting job in a hurry, and the printer recommended me. That was kind of scary because—except for the reunion booklet—I'd never done the work in my life. But when I heard the job was paying $900, I figured I'd give it a go. The work turned out well, and that one job paid several months' rent on the machine and bought me a desk and light table. The man I had done the typesetting for told another printer about me and, before I knew it, I was rolling. I decided to keep the Composer."

With each new job, word of mouth advertising for Myra's work traveled to still other potential buyers, and her new business continued to grow rapidly. It's hard to say just how much you can bank on that kind of assistance, but Myra sees no problem in starting or promoting a home composing operation.

"Look at it this way," she says. "Say you order a machine. The average delivery time is three to four weeks. You'll probably be allowed to keep a demonstrator until your unit arrives and, if you have second thoughts, you can always cancel your order right up until the Composer is delivered. So you've got a grace period in which you can typeset samples and circulate them to your potential market. If you line up just one customer who will send you $150 worth of work a month, you've covered your overhead.

"And I'll tell you, if you can't make $150 a month setting type . . . well, you shouldn't be doing it. Look at the local printers around you. Most of the smaller ones—especially all the new "quick print" shops—have no typesetting facilities and no real desire to handle that kind of work. On the other hand, their lack of composing equipment is costing them customers every day that they'd like to hold. If you can give these printers the profitable alternative of offering their customers professionally composed copy for a price nearly as low as typewritten pages, they're almost sure to accept. Really, you *have* to make a minimum of three to four hundred dollars a month with your Composer unless you completely botch every job you touch."

Well, of course, some people—those who don't type—*would* botch every job. But, as Myra says, "If you can type at all, you can use a Composer. I was an absolutely miserable typist when I began, but I still brought in the work. If you already handle a typewriter with some speed and accuracy, you'll find the Composer a breeze to use. And if you don't type at all . . . well, you can *learn* on the Composer."

By the way, Myra speaks from experience when she quotes that $300-a-month minimum figure because that was the lowest income she ever earned with her machine way back in the beginning when she charged only $5.00 an hour for her time. "I was such a poor typist," Myra says, "that I didn't feel right asking for more. Now that my composing speed is up to a more acceptable level, though, I ask—and get—$12.00 an hour. That may sound high, but my customers consider it a bargain when they find my finished jobs cost only about 20–30% of what a downtown shop gets for the same work."

It's not hard to understand—at a quoted $12.00 an hour—how Myra Schneider grosses an average $1,000 per month with her home typesetting business. Actually, she could earn much more if she tried, but she prefers to hold her "job" down to four hours a night (eight p.m. to midnight), five nights a week. "I have three preschool children," says Myra, "and I like to be with them during the day. This way I can be a full-time mother and still earn all the money—roughly $250 a week—that I want."

Myra hastens to add that, although she likes to keep her income at a constant thousand dollars per month, it doesn't always work that way. Some months her billings shoot up to $2,000, and they drop lower in others. But with almost no promotional efforts at all (in two and a half years of composing, she has spent only two days looking for work), Myra's gross income seems to average an easy $12,000 a year.

If you happen to be a person who likes to hustle or you want to put in more time than Myra, there's no reason to believe that you can't do several times that volume of business. A friend of hers, for instance, started with one machine a little over a year ago. He went out selling and now has seven people setting copy on as many Composers. The work is there if you want it.

But let's say you'd prefer a setup more like Myra's. How do you—as a housewife, retiree, or shut-in—obtain a Composer? Well, coaxing a machine out of IBM is surprisingly simple.

Call the nearest IBM office and ask for an "office machines" salesman. Tell him you want to start a home typesetting service for printers and that you want a demonstration of the IBM Composer. Within a day or—at most—two, that fellow should be knocking on your front door with a demo Composer under his arm. He'll give you enough instructions to turn you loose on the machine . . . and then he'll simply disappear for at least a week! There's no high pressure and no arm twisting. Just you and the Composer and a chance to see what it can do. If you're smart, you'll practice for a couple days and then dash off some samples to show your local printers.

If you then decide to give the business a try—but you still aren't sure that you want to commit yourself to buying a Composer—you'll find that IBM makes it very easy for you to obtain a brand new machine on a trial rental basis. In fact, if you have a well-established credit rating, you won't even be required to put down a deposit. The demonstrator will be left with you, your Composer will be ordered, and you'll pay nothing until the new machine arrives in approximately one month. Then, and only then, you'll be charged a monthly rental and maintenance fee of about $160 for a minimum of six months.

If you have no credit rating, the terms are a little stiffer:

You'll be required to put up about $480 front money to cover the last three months' rental on your contract. That's still more than fair on IBM's part when you consider that a Composer sells for a base price of $4,610! Once you keep the machine six months, by the way, that deposit is completely refunded, so—even if you go into the deal with no credit rating and have to put up the front money—you won't lose a thing if you're honest. IBM is taking all the risk.

If that's not bending over backwards to give you a good deal, the company will sweeten the pot even more at the end of one year's rental. By that time you'll have paid a total of $1,800 rent, and IBM will cheerfully apply exactly half of this—$900—toward the purchase of your Composer if you'd like to buy the machine. The $900 will be considered a down payment, and—get this—your monthly payments will then drop from $150 to only $120. Again, full maintenance is included in the contract.

Now, in effect, what this means is that IBM will virtually finance your new business with very few questions asked . . . and that's a good deal any way you look at it.

Once you get your Composer (or even the loaner) you've got nine-tenths of what you need to set up shop. The only other major piece of "professional" equipment you'll have to have is a light table, and you can make that: It's just a frame that holds a piece of frosted glass over a light. Trying to save a few bucks by cobbling a light board together is hardly worth the effort, however, because you can buy a really good, small ANCO board—just like the one Myra has—for around $50.00 from any well-stocked art supply store. It will give you outstanding service from now on, and is well worth the money.

In case you're wondering, you'll use the light board for cutting in corrections. The typed copy you send to a printer must be ready to be photographed, and no smudges or mistakes will be accepted. Since it's impossible to erase an error on camera-ready copy, it's standard practice to type a correction on a separate piece of paper and then cut or paste the correction exactly in the place of the rejected error: This is almost impossible without a light board . . . and ridiculously easy with one.

Other than a few miscellaneous straight edges, an Exacto knife, a roll of white layout tape, and some thirty-nine-cent black-ink ball-point pens (for ruling business forms), you're in business. You can get all the small items from any well-stocked art supply store.

A special desk and chair would be nice, but Myra found that a kitchen chair and card table worked quite well for her until her first check came in.

That covers your equipment. The only supplies you'll need are Composer ribbons and paper. There's no way to skimp on them and, all told, the cost of paper and ribbons will run approximately $58.00 for every $4,000–$5,000 you bill. You'll hardly feel it, in other words.

There *is* one other small selection of equipment you'll buy from time to time that I haven't mentioned . . . because your customers will do the buying for you! You'll soon learn that—no matter how many type balls, or fonts, you have— someone always wants another. When Myra runs into the problem she just pulls out the IBM catalog and lets the customer pick the typeface he *does* prefer. Then, if he OKs the purchase, Myra tacks $30.00 on his bill and orders the font especially for that job. Once the work is completed, the type ball is hers to keep, and she now has a hundred fonts that were purchased this way. That's $3,000 worth of equipment that Myra's customers were happy to buy her!

Another bit of free percentage you should know about is the free school that IBM runs for folks like you. The company will give you and *any number of people you want to break in on the Composer* sixteen hours *each* of training at no charge. That's right. Any time you want to bring a new partner or employee into the business, IBM will give them the sixteen-hour course at absolutely no charge.

In addition to good money and good hours, Myra finds that her home business offers a continuing opportunity for expansion into other satisfying areas. An increasing number of folks who come to her for typesetting request that she handle the coordination of any layout, printing, binding, and other graphic arts procedures too. Myra contracts out most of this work, of course, but she does enjoy the occasional layout assignment. "I'm not a very creative person," she says, "but this work allows me to be a little original. Using a bit from one design in my reference file and something else from another page I've clipped, I'm able to add enough of myself to make a layout that is unique and that satisfies the customer."

Yep. Typesetting at home can be a darn good business . . . but to be realistic, it has some drawbacks too. The worst of these—if you let it shake you—will be pressure. Printers and their customers are notorious for wanting jobs done *yesterday*. If you accept a rush-rush assignment, you'll probably be forced to politely but *firmly* insist that you be left completely alone while you do it.

You'll also find that your work will tend to come in spurts. Some seasons will leave you with time on your hands . . . then, suddenly, *everyone* will want a Christmas catalog or spring clearance or back-to-school sales brochure composed and printed at the same time. You'll learn to ride that roller coaster soon enough, but the real problem will be the regular customer who contacts you with a hurry-up job . . . when you're already loaded to the gills. If you turn him away he may not be back, and if you take the assignment it will mean working all night. That can be a tough decision.

Perhaps the worst drawback to home typesetting is the fact that it just won't work well at all "back of beyond" in that wilderness cabin you may have in mind. There *is* composing— and a lot of it—done by mail . . . but there's a whale of a lot more done as the result of personal contact. The nearer to an urban center you locate, in other words, the better your business will be. The ideal compromise might be setting up on an organic homestead within an hour's drive of any medium or large city in the country. You'll have access to a ready market that way . . . but most of your living will be done in the relatively tall and uncut.

Then again, you may actually prefer to live in town. Some folks do, you know. In that case—just like Myra—you'll almost certainly have it made. Myra Schneider is quite happy knocking down $12,000 a year right in the basement "office" of her suburban home. She's completely free of the downtown hassle, she works the hours she chooses, her business has helped pay for and remodel the house in which the Schneiders live . . . and Myra's done it all without once sacrificing the pleasures of parenthood.

If that sounds good to you, call IBM and check out the opportunity for yourself. You know the ground rules now, and you should be able to talk intelligently enough to an office equipment salesman to make sense. Remember that he's already in the business—so to speak—and he should know exactly which printers need outside composing help. Don't be afraid to ask for such leads . . . and double check them *before* you commit yourself to purchasing a Composer. By the time you sign the contract for your machine, your business should already be well launched. That is, if you have Myra's success . . . and there's no reason to believe that you won't.

In researching this article I asked a few printers around Cleveland if they felt Myra's luck had been exceptional. They seemed to think not. According to them, anyone offering a composing service—and making it known—is in for a share of the work. Printers are a closely knit group, and they like the home industry prices you'll be able to offer. If you can deliver quality work (the Composer makes that easy)—and do it on time—the word will quickly get around, and you should soon have more jobs looking for you than you can handle.

No doubt about it: You *can* make that dream of a Little Typing Business At Home come true. ◓

HOT VS. COLD TYPE

If you still think that all typesetting is dirty, noisy, hard work done on a cumbersome, clacking, linecasting monster like the one down at the weekly newspaper's office . . . you only know half (the outdated half) of the story.

There are two kinds of typesetting, you see: hot and cold. The old, traditional method of hot casting lead into type that is locked into a frame, mounted on a press, and otherwise physically manhandled *is* dirty, noisy, and hard work. For all the years that *letterpress* ruled the printing industry, however, it was almost the only game in town. Now, though, a faster and easier and simpler method of printing—*offset*—has changed the picture.

An offset press prints—not from heavy metal type—but

from a thin, featherweight, photographically exposed plate. And that plate can be exposed from *cold type* . . . which is nothing more than regular black images on a sheet of white paper.

It stands to reason, then, that an offset plate can be made by photographing copy produced on a regular typewriter . . . and it can. But for most jobs that's not good enough because almost all typewriters have only one typeface, cram the fat letters together while leaving large gaps between the skinny ones, index each line the same monotonous amount, and have absolutely no provisions for justifying (making the ends of the lines come out even) a column of type.

Even the IBM Selectric typewriter (the one that uses interchangeable type balls) is not the answer. True, by changing the ball, you can alter the appearance of a Selectric's copy from light to bold to italic in a number of faces . . . but those faces are all approximately the same size, the big letters are still packed in closer than the skinny ones, the vertical line indexing is always the same, there's no provision for justification, and . . . well, the finished copy *still* looks like it came off a typewriter, dang it.

What you need is a super-sophisticated typing machine: one that will space proportionally (leave a big gap for fat letters and a narrow gap for skinny ones), one that accepts a *number* of type faces of *different* sizes, one that will index a little or a lot between lines, one that can be set so that every line comes out exactly even with the ones above and below.

The machine you need, in other words, is the Selectric's big brother, the IBM Composer . . . and, although it does all these things and more, there's nothing complicated about it. Except for an extra dial or two and a couple of additional keys, the IBM Composer has exactly the same keyboard as the ordinary IBM office Selectric typewriter. In fact—of the two—the Composer has the better touch, and you'll quickly find yourself typing both faster and easier on it.

And what typing! Anything from teenie little letters only 6 points tall to type 12 points high. With and without serifs. Light, medium, bold, and italic. All proportionally spaced. Justified and unjustified. With no vertical space at all . . . or big, airy gaps between lines.

In short, the copy you produce on an IBM Composer will meet the standards of any printer who is set up to handle offset work . . . and almost every shop in this country is either so set up, or soon will be . . . or stands a good chance of going out of business. (EDITOR'S NOTE: IBM is no longer the only company in the low-cost, cold-type equipment business. Compugraphic, Photon, Addressograph-Multigraph, and others now offer "kitchen nook"-sized typesetting machines. Any printer should be able to help you contact the appropriate salesmen.)

TAPPING THE MARKET

To make any business—typesetting included—succeed, you must sometimes sell. But that doesn't necessarily mean a back-slapping, glad-handing, door-to-door effort. If you're uncomfortable "selling", you may find composing to be a very attractive business because you can introduce the service to potential buyers largely by mail. One small presentation kit, duplicated as many times as necessary and sent to prospective customers, can save you the endless time and frustration normally invested in "cold calls".

The kit should consist of three basic elements: a cover letter, your business card, and representative samples of your work. *Be brief* in your letter: Don't force a prospect to wade through an epic, because he won't. Quickly introduce yourself, list the major advantages of your service (low cost and availability), and refer to your samples. Close with the promise of a follow-up phone call to answer any questions.

With a prospect introduced to your composing service, it's up to you to learn what he thinks of it. When you call, begin your telephone conversation by referring to the letter . . . then let things take their natural course.

If a potential customer isn't interested the first time around, don't give up. Each time you increase your capabilities (by adding new type fonts to your inventory or expanding into layout work), send every buyer and possible buyer of your services a written notice. Let 'em know you're there, in other words . . . and keep on lettin' 'em know.

It's always a good bet—unless you have an "in" with a printer—to address your samples to a print shop's "Production Manager". In many cases you can obtain the production manager's name by simply calling the company and asking. If that doesn't work, use the title.

There's another—perhaps even better—way to get those jobs . . . and that's by hiring a salesman to do it for you. This is not as difficult or as expensive as it sounds if you know how to go about it.

The trick is to find a retired or semi-retired graphic arts salesman who is interested in part-time work on a commission basis. Many such folks exist and a good number of them—just like you—are looking for an opportunity to keep active and supplement their incomes.

The best way to find your representative is through a classified advertisement in the Part-Time Employment section of your local newspaper. Writing the ad is just a matter of describing the job and the person you want. In screening applicants consider sincerity, interest, experience, and contacts. An older graphic arts salesman will be hard to beat on those last two points because he'll probably know—and have dealt with—every printer in the area. Of course, you mustn't discount an eager young rep either . . . sheer fire and vinegar can make a lot of sales. Just insist that the man or woman you hire represents you honestly at all times.

Once you have a representative, don't drop the entire promotional burden into his or her lap. Help your salesman in every way possible. Make sure he understands all the details and advantages of your service. Remember, he may know the business inside out . . . but he's starting out completely unfamiliar with you. Follow his suggestions, when necessary, in preparing your sales kit. Work with your representative on a list of prospects and arrange for him to report his progress regularly.

When your salesman brings in an order, let your gratitude shine through. The folks out on the firing line get a lot of their satisfaction from the psychological end of the bargain. And the money doesn't hurt either: 10—15% should be about right on a straight commission deal, but that's negotiable for a few points either way. Pay your rep promptly when he brings you a sale if you can . . . or, if your budget is really tight, immediately upon your receipt of payment for the jobs he's brought in.

If you choose a salesman carefully and hammer out a fair working relationship, you'll both have a most satisfying situation going for you. ◐

The above article originally appeared in THE MOTHER EARTH NEWS® NO. 9 . . . along with a great deal of other live-better-for-less and self-sufficiency how-to information. For further information about the magazine—and other books and periodicals devoted to home businesses, self-sufficiency, and related subjects—please see page 367 of this handbook.

SUZETTE HADEN ELGIN:

START A HOME STENO SERVICE:

PAINLESS, PART TIME, AND PROFITABLE

If you type, if you own or can rent a typewriter (preferably electric), if you have a private telephone line, and live within or on the edge of a metropolitan area . . . there's a way of beating the 9-to-5 that I highly recommend from personal experience.

I fell into this great arrangement by accident when I happened to be at a party where three or four salesmen (traveling type) were exchanging gripes. It seemed that in the area of secretarial services these men really had problems. Their hours were long and irregular, and when they got into a town in the evening it was usually after the public stenographers had closed for the day. This forced the men to delay their departure until after the stenos opened the next morning.

The salesmen had some pitiful stories to tell about sitting until 11 o'clock waiting for a letter to get typed . . . meanwhile missing an important appointment. One and all, they complained that they didn't have enough correspondence to justify hiring a personal secretary . . . but that all other arrangements were terribly inconvenient.

It seemed to me, listening to these sad tales of woe, that I could solve the problem. So I made the salesmen an offer: If each would supply me with stationery bearing his business letterhead, he could call me whenever he got into town (unless it was some ungodly hour like three in the morning) and dictate his correspondence over the phone. He could then go on about his business without delay while I typed, signed, and mailed the letters. I would also mail a carbon of each letter to the salesman and keep a carbon in my files. I would supply typewriter ribbons, carbon paper, and other incidentals, and send the salesman one bill for my services and the postage actually used on his correspondence.

I was initially disappointed when only one man took me up on the offer . . . but, when I soon found myself with more work than I could handle, I was grateful that the others had been dubious.

The obvious reason a businessman is afraid to try such an arrangement is because he's terrified that you might be incompetent, that you'll foul up his contacts, mail out price quotations that will bankrupt him, send his letters to the wrong people, and do all the other awful things that have probably been done to him at least once in the past. Therefore, you have to suggest— as I did—that he begin by trusting you with only the very simplest and most innocuous correspondence.

For example, you might start with routine letters just to customers who are "old friends" and with whom your client is on an intimate basis. Then if you goof, he can always call the customers, explain that his secretary is an idiot . . . and no harm will be done.

With this beginning, of course, it's up to you to prove that you are trustworthy and dependable. If—indeed—you *are* good, you'll quickly become indispensable to your client even if he continues to hold his really important correspondence for another secretary "in the home office". On the other hand—if you're *not* good—you'll lose the client, he'll tell his friends, and you've had it . . . so be sure of your ability before you try.

If you don't happen to fall over a potential client for your home steno service at a party (as I did), there are several ways to find customer number one. I do *not* recommend that you advertise, however. If my experience is any indication, your biggest problem is going to be keeping your business small enough . . . not making it bigger.

I was only looking for supplemental income when I operated my service, I had just three clients . . . and that was too many. They kept recommending me to others and I kept turning those others down. Even if you want your home business to earn you a full-time living, I still recommend that you let word of mouth do your advertising for you.

There are several ways to locate that first customer. First, find out if there is a motel or hotel near you that specializes in putting up salesmen. There usually is. Explain your service nicely to the owner and ask him to refer the next salesman desperate for a secretary to you. If you're determined to advertise "just a little", get permission to put up a sign (a very small one) in the motel lobby *and then take it down the instant you have your first client.*

If this doesn't work or if you don't want to try such an approach, just inquire around. Ask the people who run the stores where you shop. Ask the neighbors. Ask your doctor. Ask the barber or the lady who does your hair . . . if somebody does your hair.

Some of these people are sure to know a traveling salesman, or have a friend who knows one . . . and even if the man you finally get in touch with can't use your services, you're in business. Because *he* will know other salesmen, and lots of them (by the way, be prepared to ignore a lot of very bad salesman jokes).

And once you've found that first potential client . . . how do you convince him to try your service? I just offered mine two free letters and told him he didn't have to pay me for any work that wasn't satisfactory . . . ever. (I think this is important. It's possible that your customer will take advantage of such a deal because there *are* stinkers in any line of business . . . but if he does, just refuse to work for him any longer. And if your client is honest with you—which is much more likely—he's certain to be impressed by the fairness of the satisfaction-guaranteed-or-no-charge arrangement.)

By the way, before you land that first customer, you'll want to make sure your service complies with the regulations of your town/city/whatever. Chances are, if you operate on a small scale and don't advertise, you won't even need a license or permit . . . but check it out anyway. You don't want to find your client, get started in business . . . and suddenly find yourself faced with a fine because you didn't fill out a form in front.

After working with client number one for a week or so, you'll find that his schedule will—in a rough, approximate sense—give you a schedule too. Let's say he usually calls and dictates for an hour on Monday nights and Thursday afternoons (the two times he's ordinarily in town and within convenient reach of a phone). That means you should always let him know in advance, if you possibly can, when you're going to have to be away from your phone at those times. In return, your customer should warn you if—say—he intends to be in town on Wednesday for a change. If his schedule is totally erratic, of course, then you'll both just have to take your chances.

There's a number of ways to set a fee for your services. You can charge a flat sum per item that you type and mail . . . or establish an hourly rate that includes dictation, mailing, filing, et al . . . or figure a monthly rate based on some hypothetical minimum number of hours or items with a specific charge for anything over those minimums.

If you work at average speed you may even prefer a combination rate of a fixed price per letter mailed, with an added hourly charge for time spent taking dictation, processing mail, etc. In my case—because I type very fast—I find an hourly fee unprofitable and I set a per-item figure. Your rates are up to you. However you decide to charge, though, remember to provide your client with an explanation of the pricing system and an approximate quote of what it will cost him for each letter.

You'll find that it's simpler for you to provide your own materials, as I've already said, and simply include their price in your fee. Remember, the image you want to present is one of total convenience . . . and you'll do that best by requiring nothing from your client except his letterhead stationery items. Be sure, too, that you always have an ample supply of these letterhead supplies on hand. Your customer certainly won't find it very convenient if his correspondence is delayed because you ran out of his stationery and envelopes.

Pay your own phone bill and figure it into your fee. Local calls, of course, will be included in overhead and you should always let your client call you long distance COLLECT so he doesn't have to struggle with coins and operators. Bill him for those conversations on an individual basis.

If you need more help in setting a fee, check into the going rate for public stenography services in your area. The contacts you make with the stenos may even increase your business. In my case, at least, I found that such services were delighted to have someone to whom they could refer customers for an occasional "after hours" job.

As careful as you'll probably be about establishing your rates, *be even more careful about keeping records* . . . for two reasons.

First, since you'll be self-employed, you'll be able to trim your taxes by deducting all business expenses and a portion of your rent and utility bills from your income. To do so, however, you'll have to have records that support your claimed income and expenses.

Don't try to get by with such makeshift strategy as jotted notes on the backs of envelopes, either. Get yourself an ordinary business ledger and keep detailed records of everything you spend, the hours you put in, the money you earn, and anything else that strikes you as pertinent. Invest a dollar in one of those tax preparation guides that you find on newsstands and pay attention to the things that *they* regard as pertinent also (you may be surprised). Make a point of getting a receipt for the stamps you buy at the post office, keeping sales slips for stationery and supplies . . . and always, always put down the date you spend or receive monies, however small. Far better, when tax time comes, to have too many records than too few.

The second—and equally important—reason for keeping records involves your client. If he calls in one heck of a hurry and says, "Here's five addresses. Just send all of them the same letter I sent Joe Murphy Furniture Manufacturing last Friday," then you need to know where to find your carbon of that letter to Murphy. If your client wants you to read him back a letter he sent somebody three months ago, you'll have to be able to find that one fast, too.

When I ran my steno service, I made myself two carbons (in addition to the carbon for my client) of everything and used a double filing system for work done. One of my copies went into an alphabetical file in the usual way and the other was kept in a daily file. That way, I had two methods of locating anything I needed.

If a customer said, "I know I sent a letter about rug samples to somebody on the third Friday in July, but I can't remember who," I pulled the daily file for that Friday and hunted through everything I did for the day. If he remembered that the letter went to Acme Rugs but had no idea when it was sent, I thumbed through the Acme Rug file. Such a double system will save you untold time and grief in the long run and will certainly add to the "total convenience" image that you want to project.

The record keeping bit is probably the only really annoying part of this business and it's the part you'll be most tempted to neglect . . . but resist the temptation. Don't be a fanatic about records, but be thorough. And while you're filing those carbons, just think about all the *nice* features your home steno business offers:

Your overhead is practically nil, you don't have to go anywhere or get sitters or buy a fancy wardrobe (or *any* wardrobe, for that matter), you can control the size of the business yourself, records are easy to keep, you don't have to be a speed worker, you can always stop in the middle of a letter and cook dinner . . . and the whole operation is very profitable.

When I did this work I was also holding down an additional full-time job . . . not recommended, but necessary at the time. Nonetheless, working only evenings and weekends, I cleared $40.00 a week. If you want to go into this full time, you should make a more than ample living wage.

As a matter of fact, I still think your biggest problem—once you land your first client—will be fighting off the customers that beat a path to your telephone. But that's a pleasant problem to have . . . good for both the morale and the budget. Other businesses should have it so good. ◐

The above article originally appeared in THE MOTHER EARTH NEWS® NO. 12 . . . along with a great deal of other live-better-for-less and self-sufficiency how-to information. For further information about the magazine—and other books and periodicals devoted to home businesses, self-sufficiency, and related subjects—please see page 367 of this handbook.

CHARLENE SONIA: HERE'S ANOTHER HOME TYPING BUSINESS THAT REALLY WORKS!

If you can type, are willing to meet some standards, can work under the pressure of a deadline, and live in or near a university or college town you can start a home business—full or part time—doing typing for students. If you turn out clean, crisp copy at some speed, the business can be a good one too: once

your reputation is established you can earn up to $500 a month.

You'll find a demand for your services because college students are required to turn in large numbers of papers, there's a general feeling that professors prefer those papers to be typed . . . and many students cannot type, cannot type well, or just don't have time to do the job. In addition to simple term papers, graduate students must often prepare a thesis as a degree requirement. This thesis must be typewritten and meet certain standards so that it can be microfilmed, xeroxed, or printed by offset. Most grad students either cannot type well enough to meet the standards for a thesis, or do not leave themselves the time to do their own typing.

THE MACHINE

Obviously, you'll need a typewriter if you expect to establish yourself in this business . . . and lucky is the person employed as a secretary by a boss who'll let her work evenings on the office IBM. If you work out such an arrangement, though, it's only fair that you conduct your moonlighting efforts with your own ribbons and paper. Keep the supply receipts, too . . . just in case someone decides to make an issue of your activities.

If you're not already employed by an understanding boss or do not otherwise have access to an office electric, you'll have to rent or purchase a machine. This will increase your overhead but will also give you more time to work and a more flexible schedule. The pros outweigh the cons, so call the nearest IBM office and arrange to rent or purchase an office electric.

Why IBM? Because, in my limited experience, there isn't a better typewriter made. The quality of its copy is high and the machine is sturdy. You can gallop up to 120 wpm on an IBM and it won't boggle, skip, or jam. (If you type for long, you'll hit 90 to 120 wpm on familiar word groups and phrases and there's nothing more exasperating than a dinky little machine that jams up and makes mistakes for you when you can already make enough by yourself.)

Brand X typewriters drive me wild. They hop across the desk and spin when I hit the return. At the end of every ten lines, I have to seize such a useless device and put it back in front of me. An IBM on a rubber typewriter mat, on the other hand, will stay in front of you and TYPE.

Ask for an IBM Selectric. Once you've used this model, you won't be able to return to a portable, standard, or electric machine of any other brand without great feelings of rage and frustration.

The Selectric has an ordinary keyboard . . . but it does not have an ordinary striking mechanism or a carriage on which the paper rides back and forth. Instead, the sheet being typed on remains stationary while a little ball on a carriage runs across the paper to strike out the lines. The balls are available in many typefaces (at $18.00 each) and, although you get one with the machine, you're sure to want two or three more eventually so that you can vary the appearance of your finished work.

The element design does make the Selectric different from any other typewriter you've ever used but you'll receive an easily understood manual with the machine. Once you read that book, it'll only take you about two seconds to master— and learn to love—the Selectric.

Where I live (near Sacramento, California), the prices on an IBM Selectric range as follows:

Rental	$30.00/month
Purchase on Time (12% interest. 24-month payment plan with 15% down.)	$25.00/month (approximately)
Lease	$30.00/month (maintenance included). The agreement is for four years and when you are done they take the typewriter back. Insane. Neither lease nor rental money applies to purchase.
Maintenance Agreement	$42.00/year (worth it . . . the IBM repairman gets $16.50 an hour, not counting parts).

You may be quoted slightly different figures in your area, but I'm sure they'll run close to the above. Whatever, it's only good business sense to be sure that you have enough capital to tide you over a slow start . . . or that you have a job lined up in advance that will cover your setup costs.

When the IBM man brings your machine, ask him for an erasure guard (a little plastic card with various-sized holes in it). He should have a mess of them in his pocket to give away free (they say "IBM" on them) and they're handy little gadgets. Just place the right size hole over an error and erase through the opening. The guard will reduce smearing, protect adjacent characters, and help you make a faster correction.

MATERIALS

Use nothing but carbon ribbons on your typewriter. A box of a dozen costs $11.15 and you can use each one only once. Why expensive carbon instead of less costly, reusable cloth? Because most people are beginning to appreciate and expect the sharper, blacker image made by the better ribbon. The carbon tape may not be thrifty, but it does produce the best possible copy for reproductive purposes. The finest work done with a cloth ribbon simply does not have the same legibility, and graduate students, especially, have begun to specify "carbon ribbon" for their papers.

About the only other materials you'll need are a ream (500 sheets) or two of 20-lb. BOND paper, several typewriter erasers, and a correction fluid such as SNOPAQUE or CORRECTETTE *(STENO-AID is also good—Ed.).* Correction fluid is white and opaque. You paint it across an error and, when the liquid dries, you can retype right over it. Used with discretion, such corrections can be detected only by paranoids. You can usually use as much of the fluid as you want on term papers and reports, but be reasonable . . . a page that weighs a pound isn't very professional.

Visit the Graduate Divisions of the universities and colleges in your area and ask for their sheets of rules and regulations regarding the typing of theses. You'll find that many schools do *not* permit use of correction fluids and specify that any erasures be almost invisible. Such strict standards must be maintained where theses are microfilmed because correction fluid will mess up the microfilming process. The rules sheets will also give you, in great detail, each school's specifications for margins, spacing, etc. Some customers bring a set of regulations along with them when they deliver their rough draft . . . but I find that it saves time and confusion if I have a rules sheet on file for each school that I deal with.

When I have a margin requirement to meet, I take a sheet of bond and mark the margins in with heavy black ink (see Fig. 1). Then I put the marked sheet behind the page I'm typing and try not to run over the lines (which show through). I also make lines three inches, two inches, and one inch above the *bottom margin* (not the bottom of the page) to warn me when I'm getting to the end of the prescribed area.

ADVERTISING

Type up a small notice offering your services. Keep it short enough to fit three or four times on a single 8-1/2 X 11 sheet of paper and have the page duplicated on a copy machine for a few cents. Then cut the notices apart and distribute them liberally around your campus or campuses and student meeting places (dormitories are the best locations of all in which to post your ads).

Spend a few evenings putting your notices up . . . and then

check them periodically, since people sometimes remove them for the phone number rather than copy the information. I've never run an ad in a student newspaper but the rates for such periodicals are quite inexpensive and it's worth a try.

The first assignments are the toughest and, after you've successfully completed a few jobs, the people you've worked for will start sending their friends around . . . and those friends will soon send *their* friends. Word of mouth is still the most effective form of advertising.

CUSTOMERS

A student with a term paper or an application letter to be typed is generally calm and in no hurry. Graduate students, however, are another story. Folks in the latter category are usually [a] looking for a job, [b] negotiating for a job, [c] moving, [d] trying to get some recalcitrant committee member to sign the thesis, or [e] all of these. If a grad student botches his paper he may well lose a job, be fined a large "late fee", or fail to get his degree for another six months. Graduate students, then, are almost always tired, harried, and up against a deadline. I call this complex of symptoms "thesisosis".

A person with thesisosis is half out of his mind. Remember this and treat him accordingly. Remember, too, that his previous experience with secretaries (or anyone connected with a typewriter) may well have led him to expect you to be sullen, lazy, and more than a little stupid. He *hopes* not, of course—when he comes to you, he's praying that you'll be professional, competent, calm, and honest—but he's ready for a dope. So be prepared.

Let your graduate students (and all your other customers as well) know they're in good hands when they bring a job to you. Keep your house or office and yourself tidy. Don't do any silly secretary imitations. Try to appear relaxed and professional. If you have finished work handy, show it to the potential client. Find out when his deadline is and arrange your schedule so that you can complete his assignment with time to spare, *allowing an ample margin for last-minute changes and the correction of errors.*

Take a good look at every manuscript before you accept the job. If you aren't sure you can handle the assignment, turn it down. It's better to say "no" than wind up with a demented grad student freaking out on your hands.

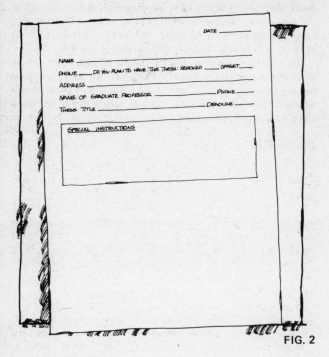

DATE _____

NAME _____

PHONE _____ DO YOU PLAN TO HAVE THIS THESIS: XEROXED _____ OFFSET ____

ADDRESS _____

NAME OF GRADUATE PROFESSOR _____ PHONE ____

THESIS TITLE _____ DEADLINE ____

SPECIAL INSTRUCTIONS

FIG. 2

QUALITY CONTROL

Proofread all your work and make neat corrections before giving finished copy to its owner. He'll probably find other errors and want some final changes made anyway, so—again—allow time for each client to bring manuscripts back for final touching up.

HOW TO CHARGE

I have each new customer list his name, address, phone number, etc., on a simple form that I've devised (see Fig. 2). If the client has any special instructions, I make sure they're entered on the same sheet. The page then becomes my log and billing record as I complete the job ("25 pages text at $.60, $15.00" or "7 tables at $.75, $5.25").

My usual charge is $.60 a page for straight text, $.75 each for pages with equations, a foreign language quote, footnotes, or a table, and $1.00 for every page of bibliography. Ask around to learn the current prices in your area and set your rates accordingly.

When a customer makes a change that requires retyping, I charge for the second work. If I make a mistake that ruins a page, I do not charge for retyping . . . but when there is *both* a mistake of mine *and* a client change on a page, I do recharge for the fresh copy.

Many people have a compulsion to mark boldly through an error with a pen or lead pencil, when just a light pencil notation in the margin would suffice. Since it's almost impossible to make a neat correction over pen or pencil marks in the text, I warn each client against noting errors in that manner . . . and then charge for retyping a page if he does so mark the text. Surprisingly, the need to directly mark typos is so overpowering that many folks quietly pay double for the privilege.

I once had a $120 check bounce and I now accept only cash for my work. If you follow the same rule, be sure to tell your customers ahead of time so they'll have the money ready and with them when they come to pick up their jobs.

Before a new client completes his charge sheet, I give him a page on which are listed my prices, my cash-only rule, and explicit directions for indicating corrections . . . just so he won't feel that I'm trying to outwit him later when I present my itemized bill.

If a customer questions that final bill, I go to the file and pull a copy of his original charge sheet. Some clients will add up the total again, but I've never had anyone argue once they've looked the charge sheet over a second time.

MISCELLANEOUS HELPFULS

Use good quality paper, even though it's more expensive. It takes corrections better and is cheaper in the long run.

If you aren't willing to be meek about commas, don't type for English majors.

When your customer isn't sure where he wants figures and drawings (or doesn't have them done when he brings a manuscript to you), leave off the page numbers and don't type the table of contents. Allow enough time at the end of the job to clean up these details.

If you're not sure what some squiggle means, work on

something else or call the customer and *ask*. If the client can't be reached and you *must* continue, put down exactly what he has in the rough draft . . . it's his mistake, then, and not yours.

If a student makes off with your finished product without paying you . . . a call to the graduate division or his major professor will settle his hash.

Request a typewritten rough draft if you have difficulty reading a person's handwriting. This will cut down on business . . . but it'll also reduce traumas.

Use the backing sheet.

When you make a mistake, admit it and correct it.

Save your waste paper for telephone notes.

Get a dictionary and use it . . . a lot of people can't spell.

Conducting a cash-only business saves troubling with the Infernal Revenue Serpent . . . until they run you to ground. Keep accurate records and avoid trouble.

FINAL WORDS

If my no-nonsense approach in this article gives you the impression that I'm a real hard mama who spends a lot of time jumping on my customers . . . or that this home business is a tough one with too many exacting deadlines . . . I'd like to close by saying "not so".

Typing is an honest and useful skill and I get a craftsman's pleasure from setting up page after page of neat and elegant text.

Ninety-nine percent of my clients have been pleasant and interesting people with worthwhile papers. Many have been so grateful for a professional job that they've returned with both cash to pay their bill *and* a small present. Most have recommended me to friends and some have advised their schools to endorse my work.

You can be your own boss, improve your professional skills, meet interesting folks, and make good, honest money typing college papers. The business will allow you to build your own schedule around a favorite hobby or other interest . . . while you save a nest egg for that homestead or other "big" project.

At least that's the way it works for me. ◓

The above article originally appeared in THE MOTHER EARTH NEWS® NO. 16 . . . along with a great deal of other live-better-for-less and self-sufficiency how-to information. For further information about the magazine—and other books and periodicals devoted to home businesses, self-sufficiency, and related subjects—please see page 367 of this handbook.

GAIL WILLIAMS:
THIS IS, I BELIEVE, THE BEST HOME TYPING BUSINESS OF THEM ALL

MAKE YOUR OWN HOURS. WORK AT YOUR OWN PACE. THAT'S HOW IT SHAPES UP, ACCORDING TO THIS EXPERIENCED INDIVIDUAL, WHEN YOU TURN QUESTIONS AND ANSWERS INTO CASH . . . BY TRANSCRIBING NOTES FOR COURT REPORTERS IN YOUR AREA.

Here, for those who still dream of the Perfect Little Typing

Business, is the one which ideally fills that bill for me. It's an almost unknown home enterprise that I find really interesting, it can be set up on a very modest investment, and the steady income it generates can be adjusted up or down to fit nearly anyone's lifestyle. Perhaps best of all, from a MOTHER-reader's point of view, this particular brand of self-employment—once it's established—can be operated most satisfactorily from the other half of The Dream: The Little Country Homestead.

The secret? Federal, state, and county courts all employ reporters who take down their proceedings in a form of shorthand at speeds in excess of 200 words per minute. Some of these reporters then type up this information themselves. Most, however, prefer to dictate their notes onto tapes and have someone else transcribe them. This is the basis of a home typing business that can net from $300 to $1,000 a month, depending on how fast you work and how much time you want to spend at a typewriter. A few really greedy people make even more than the top figure I've quoted.

Remember as you read the information in this article, that it's based on the situation in Dallas, Texas. Conditions of employment as a court reporter's typist will vary somewhat from one area of the country to another and between small towns and large urban centers. Transcribers in some other localities, for instance, are paid more per page and therefore earn more overall.

The current rate in Dallas is 30¢ a page for an original and two carbon copies. Which means that, to make $1,000 a month you'd have to type 3,334 pages . . . or 111 every single day. A beginner who turns out eight to ten an hour would take 11 to 14 hours to produce that number. An experienced transcriber, however, can do 15 to 20 sheets an hour and could finish that same quota of 111 pages in six to eight hours.

Does that sound like easy money? It's not! To type a large number of pages requires sitting for long periods of time in one position. This often makes the body rebel with stiff, tight back and neck muscles that can be very painful. Before you count on earning a set income, then, you'd better attempt a trial run or two to find out how your anatomy reacts.

My usual schedule is four to five hours of work a day, five days a week. I always bill out at least $500 a month . . . and still have plenty of time to tend the chickens, the goats, the garden, and two super-active little boys.

IT'S NOT FOR EVERYBODY

What are the qualifications for this profitable home business? Obviously, you have to know how to type—and the faster you go, the more pages you'll turn out—but beginning speed isn't as important as you might think. Just sitting there trying to do a few more sheets each hour for a number of months will build your rate more than you'd expect. Regardless of their proficiency at the start, most court reporters' typists hit 85 to 100 words a minute after a few years in the business.

What *does* matter is accuracy and a good vocabulary. If you can't recognize misspelled words you'll never make it in this field, however nimble your fingers. Whenever the reporter dictates an unfamiliar term, look it up to be sure. What sounds like "taret lathe" is actually "turret lathe". You've got to know the difference between "site", "sight", and "cite" . . . or "plural" and "pleural" . . . and be sure which to use where.

Apart from typing and spelling ability, general information—knowing a little bit about a lot of different things—is a great help. In one week you might work on transcripts that contain words like "roentgenogram", "diverticulosis", and "pleural cavity" (medical), "marquise" and "baguette" (a jeweler testifying in a robbery case), and "fracing", "acidizing", and "electric logs" (oil well drilling).

There's also the matter of temperament. You'll suffer through times when you loathe the sight of a typewriter . . . so if you have trouble disciplining yourself and sticking to a schedule, you'd better forget typing at home. Foraging for wild grapes in the fence row may be more fun, but it doesn't bring in necessary cash. Too many days off will cause most businesses to collapse . . . and this one is no exception.

Friends and family can also do you in if they fail to realize that—although you're working at home—you *are* working . . . for money, not love. The greatest asset a domestic typing business can have is an understanding husband or friend who'll stack the dishes and herd the kids outside when you're pushing to finish a job. In some situations, a telephone that unplugs from a wall jack can also be a big help.

Your first and most important step in establishing this business, therefore, is to evaluate your individual circumstances. Can you really work at home without constant interruptions undermining your schedule? Can you say "no" and mean it when friends invite you to join them but there's a big job stacked up by your typewriter? Will your family cooperate? And, while you're sizing up your particular situation, don't omit an honest look at your spelling and vocabulary.

HOW TO LAUNCH YOUR BUSINESS

OK. If you do decide to give this enterprise a try, kick your efforts off by checking out the locality in which you live. Large metropolitan centers have many court reporters, while a rural area may have just one who covers the whole county (and quite likely isn't too busy to do his own typing). Your chances of finding work, then, are obviously better if you live in or close to a good-sized city.

One way to make useful contacts in the field is to ask your friends and neighbors whether they know a court reporter, or someone who types for court reporters. It definitely helps to have an "in", however slight it may seem. Just hanging around the courthouse and making yourself pleasant without being obnoxious can help.

You should also systematically check the phone book's Yellow Pages under "Reporters". Then get a notebook and go to the local library to consult your particular state's *Legal Directory*. The volume should include a listing of all the members of the state Shorthand Reporters Association, arranged alphabetically under cities. Another section of the same book will give the various federal and state courts and the name of the reporter that is assigned to each. Enter all this information in your notebook, with some space for notations beside each name.

Next, type a stack of 3 X 5 index cards—they're inexpensive and harder to misplace in a desk drawer than a printed business card—with your name, address, and phone number (see Fig. 1). Then, armed with the typed slips and your notebook, set out to make personal calls on local court reporters (starting at the nearest county courthouse). Check off the names on your list and keep a record of each person's response.

More often than not, the reporter you call on will already have a regular typist. Still, that typist may be planning—unknown to her employer—to quit next month or to move away . . . so strive to make a good impression and always try to leave one of your cards. (Note, by the way, that I'm refer-

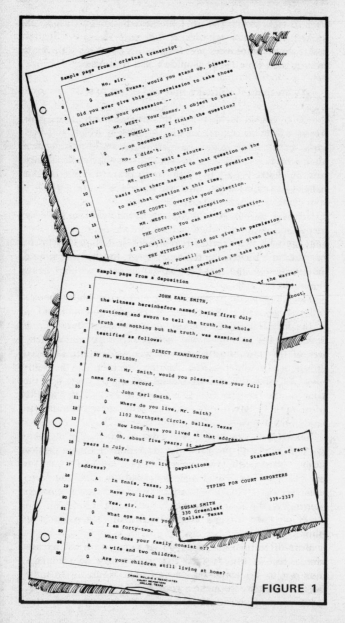

Sample page from a criminal transcript

1   A.   No, sir.

2   Q.   Robert Evans, would you stand up, please.

3   Did you ever give this man permission to take those chairs from your possession --

4   MR. WEST: Your Honor, I object to that.

5   MR. POWELL: May I finish the question?

6   -- on December 10, 1972?

7   A.   No, I didn't.

8   THE COURT: Wait a minute.

9   MR. WEST: I object to that question on the

10   basis that there has been no proper predicate

11   to ask that question at this time.

12   THE COURT: Overrule your objection.

13   MR. WEST: Note my exception.

14   THE COURT: You can answer the question,

15   if you will, please.

16   THE WITNESS: I did not give him permission.

Mr. Powell]   Have you ever given that

person permission to take those

Sample page from a deposition

1   JOHN EARL SMITH,

2   the witness hereinbefore named, being first duly

3   cautioned and sworn to tell the truth, the whole

4   truth and nothing but the truth, was examined and

5   testified as follows:

6   DIRECT EXAMINATION

7   BY MR. WILSON:

8   Q.   Mr. Smith, would you please state your full

9   name for the record.

10   A.   John Earl Smith.

11   Q.   Where do you live, Mr. Smith?

12   A.   1102 Northgate Circle, Dallas, Texas

13   Q.   How long have you lived at that address?

14   A.   Oh, about five years; it

15   years in July.

16   Q.   Where did you liv

17   address?

18   A.   In Ennis, Texas, JO

19   Q.   Have you lived in Te

20   A.   Yes, sir.

21   Q.   What age man are yo

22   A.   I am forty-two.

23   Q.   What does your family consist of?

24   A.   A wife and two children.

25   Q.   Are your children still living at home?

Depositions   Statements of Fact

TYPING FOR COURT REPORTERS

SUSAN SMITH   339-2327
330 Greenleaf
Dallas, Texas

CROSS, MALONE & ASSOCIATES
COURT REPORTERS
DALLAS, TEXAS

FIGURE 1

ring to reporters as "he" and transcribers as "she" simply for convenience. Although this is the most common situation, some court employees *are* female . . . and there's no reason why a good male typist shouldn't also turn his skill to money with my home business idea.)

If you think it will take time and effort to seek out potential employers in person, you're right . . . but this is a much better approach than introducing yourself by phone. Many reporters have had unfortunate experiences with typists, and most get several calls a week from women who want to work at home. A personal visit is more businesslike and is remembered longer. It also gives you the opportunity to find out what kind of dictating apparatus your prospect uses and the type style and pitch (numbers of characters per inch) of his typewriter. All reporters in an area generally use the same sort of equipment, and you'll need this information when you arrange to rent a machine for your first jobs.

Another approach to the business—and probably the best—is through an experienced typist. One of the most skillful transcribers in the Dallas area charges a very reasonable fee for showing aspiring beginners what it's all about and for helping them get their first jobs.

And what if there's no such person in your own locality? Well, if a reporter tells you he has a good transcriber, you might ask for her name and telephone number. Don't be surprised, however, if your request for advice brings a negative response from the typist. If she's really top-notch, she may be too busy to take the time . . . and if she's anything less, she may be too insecure to give prospective competition a helping hand. In the first case you might offer to pay for instructions. It's really worth the cost.

The long-range benefits of working for court reporters outweigh the difficulties you may have in getting started. If you have the perseverance to make a good transcriber, you'll eventually get your first job . . . and if you do reasonably well with it, you'll land a second and a third.

Most reporters are extremely nice people. Keep in mind, though, that your initial assignments may come from the one exception who's so picky and demanding that other typists don't want to work for him or her. Or your employer's dictation may be so sloppy that it's hard for you to do a good job. Just be pleasant, do the best you can, and remind yourself that you're getting your foot in the door.

WHO TO WORK FOR

Basically, there are four types of reporters: federal, criminal, civil, and freelance. As a beginner you'll work for anybody who calls, but—as you gain experience and build a reputation as a good typist—you can be more selective. Here's some background information on your possible employers:

[1] Federal reporters are generally extremely busy and have a heavy workload.

[2] Civil reporters include those in domestic relations, juvenile, county, and district courts. The first two categories handle very few transcripts. County court reporters normally record condemnation hearings . . . which are usually not very long and not the easiest to type because of all the figures they contain. District court transcripts seem to come in spurts so, unless your contact is able to take some depositions on the side, work in this area can be a feast-or-famine proposition.

[3] Freelance reporters are not assigned to a court but take down depositions, conventions, directors' meetings, labor arbitrations, etc. Good ones stay very busy and can be hectic to work for. Still, such a person is a fine source of business if you plan to remain in his area and don't mind the pressure of having to get jobs out by a deadline.

I have continued to work for one freelancer, since we moved to our homestead 65 miles east of Dallas, only because I like him so much and because my husband—who is still employed in the city—is willing to swing through the downtown area on his way home and pick up and deliver for me. When we reach the point where the town job is no longer necessary, I'll either have to give up the contact or go to Dallas myself once a week.

[4] Most typists like to deal with at least one reporter for the criminal courts for several reasons, one of which is the regularity of the work. When all the parties in a civil lawsuit are satisfied with the verdict, there is no appeal and nothing to type. Very few people found guilty of crimes, however, are content with the judgment . . . and most of them are indigent. Still, they have the right to appeal and the state must provide the trial transcripts. This means a steady flow of work to the typist (if the reporter keeps up with his dictation).

Another advantage of criminal transcripts is that they're generally easy to type. The only technical jargon deals with autopsies, ballistics, and laboratory analysis of drugs . . . and the terms can be learned quickly.

If you want to work at some distance from the city, the biggest plus of transcribing criminal proceedings is that there's seldom a push to get out the work. You can just plug along on your own schedule with no rush or pressure. In fact, if you type for criminal reporters, you may have to make only one trip a month to pick up and deliver work. Two such employers would keep the average typist busier than she wants to be (unless she's trying to be the sole support of a large family).

It's a good idea to keep your ear to the grapevine and gradually build a group of contacts that will fit your lifestyle and plans for the future. The last year we lived in Dallas I added one new criminal reporter and gave up three other court reporters to get the workload I wanted when we moved to the country.

WHAT TO EXPECT FROM YOUR CLIENTS

A reporter will furnish transcript paper that is specially treated to erase easily. Usually he also provides carbon paper and, sometimes—if you're working exclusively for him—a typewriter and/or dictating machine.

Your employer's dictation should be clear and distinct (Donald Duck sound effects will drive any typist to desperation). As a beginner you may not have much choice, but as soon as you can, seek out clients who care enough to do a thorough job on their tapes. Good reporters, for instance, dictate "have" as "hayve" to distinguish it from "has" and "had". They emphasize the "-ed" endings on words and spell out unusual names and terms so you don't have to waste your time trying to look them up.

When you start working for a new person, inquire how he prefers to be billed: by the job, by the week, by the month. He won't mind your asking, and thereafter you'll know what to expect.

Usually your contact will choose to pay you when you deliver the completed transcript. In that case be sure to put your bill in the box . . . right on top of the finished job. Some typists order printed invoices that look very proper, but—if you're working for the same two or three people all the time— yellow "second sheets" do as well, are a whole lot cheaper, and show up nicely in a carton of white transcript paper. Reporters, by the way, are extremely good about paying their typists promptly. I don't know of a single transcriber who's ever been ripped off.

WHAT THE REPORTER EXPECTS FROM YOU

Court reporters classify only a few acts as unforgivable sins. Sloppy, inaccurate typing is Number One. Number Two is promising finished work by a certain time and failing to deliver.

Never commit yourself to get a typing job out unless you're positive you can meet your employer's deadline. It's better to overestimate the time required and finish sooner. And don't take on an extra job from a new source without making sure you can still get out the work for your regular bread-and-butter people.

Always take the time and expend the effort necessary to ensure utmost accuracy in your work . . . even if it means repeatedly telephoning a client. Reporters are very patient about phone calls. They'd rather you ring them up twenty times a day than send back inaccurate work.

Do make every effort to learn the personal styles and idiosyncrasies of each of your reporters. I type for a man who dictates "Period straight ahead" to indicate the end of one sentence and the beginning of the next. Once a new typist did a job for him . . . and each time that expression occurred she rendered it as "Pistons in the head". It's hard to imagine anybody not noticing that the phrase didn't seem to fit the context of the deposition. Nevertheless this is a true story, and almost every reporter has some similar tale about a transcriber who didn't use plain old common sense.

HOW TO DEAL WITH IBM

By all means, rent your dictating machine and typewriter the first few months so you can be sure this business suits you before you commit yourself to buying new equipment. The make to ask for is IBM, the only typewriter which can be fitted with a ratchet that will correctly space copy on the transcript paper. Most rental firms are very obliging about putting this device on the machine you hire.

Once you've done several jobs and find you have a steady flow of work coming in, you'll want to get your own typewriter. Most rented machines leave something to be desired, and in any case—when you know you like this line of work—

the money you spend for rental may as well go toward payments on your own (new) equipment.

Your decision to take this step means you'll be dealing with IBM ... and that's an experience in itself. The company's representatives are super-smooth super-salesmen who have to be handled in a positive way. Some of them are not familiar with the kind of work court reporters do and will try to sell you everything in the book except what you really need. Knowing what you want and being very definite about it can eliminate some of the hassle.

One problem in your negotiations with IBM is that the firm can't be sure you're a serious sales prospect when you ask to have a demonstrator machine brought to your house. Many women who make this request are interested only in getting a typewriter to use for a personal project (typing hubby's thesis, for instance) and really have no intention of buying.

About models: The IBM Selectric is smaller, vibrates less, and is more trouble-free than a standard office typewriter. Because it's not as heavy as the standard, it doesn't print as dark and you'll have to change the ribbon about once a week to keep your work looking fresh. The Selectric also has a "quicker" touch which is preferred by fast typists. Contrary to what the salesman will tell you, however, it *is* possible to type faster than the device can operate. Still, in spite of its little quirks, almost all typists prefer and use the IBM Selectric.

The plain vanilla Selectric sells for about $605. For a little extra you can order a court reporter's model that has three special keys (one of which is the question mark in lower case).

This machine can also be ordered in nine-pitch ... which simply means that you get nine letters to the inch rather than ten or twelve. In terms of earning power, it means that for every ten pages you type in ten-pitch, a nine-pitch typewriter will give you eleven. Without actually doing any more work, then, you end up with enough extra pages to cover your monthly payment to IBM. Unless it's forbidden by the court regulations, most reporters prefer the nine-pitch because more sheets mean more money for them, too.

Salesmen take more orders for carbon ribbon than for fabric ribbon Selectrics. Most office secretaries, however, don't type a fraction of the daily linage hammered out by a court reporter's typist and the cost of using carbon ribbons for such work is out of sight. Fabric also gives much better results on erasable paper.

When you're ready to order your typewriter, be very definite that you're doing so on condition that the salesman furnishes you with a machine equipped with the necessary ratchet. Some representatives will conveniently "forget" this detail because they don't want to charge their accounts with the cost of having the service department make the change. Take no chances. Be sure the agent brings the modified typewriter with him when he comes to close the deal. *Insist*: no machine, no down payment.

Orders are not always filled as fast as IBM salesmen promise (especially on a custom article like the court reporter's model) and you'll wind up paying for a rental typewriter while you wait unless you *demand* a loaner machine from IBM. Since placing the order entitles you to this service, make sure you get it.

How you pay for your typewriter will depend on your financial standing. With 15% down and established credit, IBM will carry the account themselves for a reasonable finance charge. The payments run around $25.00 a month for two years.

Your new typewriter is under warranty for 90 days. Thereafter, IBM will encourage you to place it on a service contract. You'll be sorry if you don't . . . one maintenance call without such an arrangement costs almost as much as a whole year of the package deal.

IBM servicemen are angels in business suits who come with remarkable speed and efficiency and are dedicated to keeping the customer (you) happy. They make necessary adjustments and replace worn parts . . . and all this work is covered by the service contract. Incidentally, if you have a good serviceman, drop a note to his department manager. Such commendations will go on your friend's record and help him get raises and promotions.

HOW TO SET UP A WORK AREA

I've tried several different office arrangements and found that the one in Fig. 2 seems best. Of course, you can improvise with TV trays and card tables and a small typing stand, but my present setup is hard to beat for efficiency.

My home office space—which is easily built from 1 X 12's and a scrap of plywood—provides lots of storage for reference books and supplies of transcript sheets. The fresh paper is kept in an open-ended box at the right. I just slip in the proper number of carbons, type the page, and pull out the carbons with my right hand while laying the typed pages in a container to the left.

Keeping the dictating machine on the shelf above the desk cuts down on the use of floor space and gives me a chance to stand up and stretch while I change its tapes. The corkboard behind the typewriter is handy for tacking up word lists and notes.

THE TAX HASSLE

Normally, a home typist is considered a self-employed person . . . which means that—since no one is deducting social security payments for you—you must pay a self-employment tax figured at the rate of .075 when you file your federal return. That's about double the percentage applied to an employee's paycheck.

Under your new tax status you're supposed to file quarterly returns on April 15, July 15, October 15, and January 15. If you're accustomed to having withholding taxes and social security painlessly extracted by an employer, these occasions can sour your outlook for weeks. The best way to make sure you'll have the money is to deduct 20% from each check you receive and put it into a special account. (The percentage is easy and quick to compute and the extra that isn't used for taxes will go to pay other business expenses.) This method helps you avoid a lot of rebellious feelings about a system you've got to live with.

It's only sensible, of course, to pay no more tax than you have to. Read up on the deductions the IRS permits for a business operated at home. Keep accurate records of all supplies you purchase as well as of the number of miles you drive to pick up and deliver work. When you buy a new or used typewriter or dictating machine, be sure to file Form 3468 and claim the investment credit deduction for the year in which you purchase the equipment.

IN OTHER WORDS . . .

It takes time and effort to get started in any enterprise, and this one is no exception. Although every transcriber I know began in a different way, most agree that getting the first job

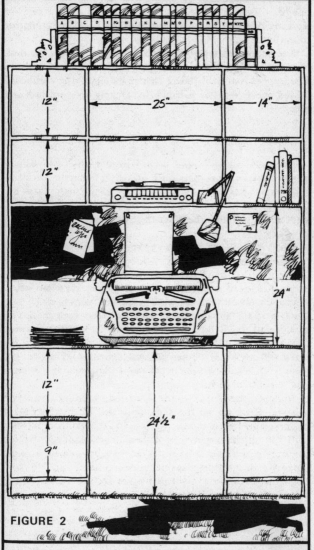

FIGURE 2

A well-organized work space is a must for the home typist. The above diagram shows the arrangement of Gail's office.

was their biggest hurdle. Accurate typing, common sense, and reliability seem to be in short supply, however, and there's a constant demand for competent typists . . . so you'll find no lack of work once you're established.

Few home businesses offer the steadiness and flexibility of typing for court reporters . . . and few can be launched for such a small investment. (Down payments on a typewriter and dictating machine shouldn't be more than $150 and the monthly installments are reasonable. The only overhead is for ribbons and erasers.) And finally, how many paying propositions can be conducted so easily from a peaceful country hillside 65 miles from the nearest city? ◐

WHAT YOU'LL NEED

DICTATING MACHINE: Whatever the local reporters use.

TYPEWRITER: IBM Selectric, 11-inch carriage, fabric ribbon, Courier 72 type, Keyboard 48 with 24-tooth ratchet.

POSTURE CHAIR: Your seating can be almost as important as your typewriter. Find a good adjustable posture chair that fits your particular anatomy (one with a high back is usually preferable). Experiment with different adjustments until you find what works best for you.

The height of the typewriter shelf and the height of the chair may determine how many hours of work you can do a day. I eliminated a catch in my back by lowering my working surface, raising my seat several inches, and putting a block of wood under the back edge of my typewriter.

BACK BRACE: Camp Model 351 can help a lot if you have a tendency to slump. The support will tend to eliminate those tight, sore muscles between the shoulder blades.

TYPEWRITER RIBBONS: Webster T-16, No. 2 Inking, Code No. 052225 seems to work better than IBM. Even if you don't do a lot of typing, ribbons dry out from exposure to the air and have to be changed once a week.

SOFT ERASERS: A.W. Farber-Castell Magic-Rub, Peel-off, Paper-Wrapped, Vinyl Eraser No. 1960. Although these have to be specially ordered by an office supply store, most art and drafting goods dealers carry them in stock. A regular, hard, typing eraser scratches the surface of transcript paper.

CARBON PAPER: Almost any major company's top-grade "solvent" product will give good results. If you have to furnish your own, try IBM's. Many times the salesmen from various manufacturers will send you small quantities free as samples.

To save carbon, type 20 pages, trim 1/4 inch off the top of the sheet, and do another 20 pages before you throw the battered remains away. (First try just turning the piece upside down . . . sometimes the lines of typing will fall in the unused spaces between the worn spots from the first 20 pages, and you won't have to do any trimming.)

Always keep solvent paper stored in its box or it will dry out and give very poor copies.

DR. SCAT!: A good, cheap product with which to clean your machine's type.

PAPER CLIPS: To attach to the sides of typed pages as markers when you have questions.

CLEAR-PLASTIC PROTECTORS: Get several, and a metal ring to hold them together. Slip in the forms you use for typing title pages and agreements, as well as the index from a state map showing counties and cities. Hang the whole bunch from a hook near your work area.

DICTIONARY: *Webster's New World Dictionary* is a good choice, but the people you work for may prefer another.

50,000 WORDS: Small, indispensable word speller and divider published by Follett Vest-Pocket.

SECRETARY'S HANDBOOK: *Standard Handbook for Secretaries* by Lois Hutchinson (McGraw-Hill, $7.95) will help you keep the rules of capitalization and punctuation straight and sort out confusions over "affect" and "effect", "awhile" and "a while", etc.

ALMANAC: Handy for verifying spellings of names. An outdated edition works fine.

TELEPHONE DIRECTORIES: The local phone company will provide you with free copies of the directories to other cities. Get them for major centers in a hundred-mile radius.

ZIP CODE DIRECTORY: This guide is available from the Superintendent of Documents, U.S. Government Printing Office, Washington, D.C. 20402 (Stock No. 3900—00248, $15.65).

MAPS: These should include the state in which you live, neighboring states, and the major cities of the area in which you work. Get them free from service stations. The index from an old U.S. atlas is especially helpful because it lists all the counties and cities in every state.

NAME BOOK: *Name Your Baby* by Lareina Rule (Bantam No. P3283, $1.25) is good because it gives common nicknames of famous people. You'll be glad to have it late some night when you want to be sure how to spell "Barbara Stanwyck".

MEDICAL DICTIONARY: The really fine ones are expensive and good reporters will spell the words out for you anyway, but *The New American Medical Dictionary and Health Manual* by Robert E. Rothenberg (Signet Q3451, $1.75) can be helpful.

PHYSICIAN'S DESK REFERENCE BOOK: A useful guide to the spelling of drug names. Since these manuals are provided annually to the medical profession, you may be able to persuade your family doctor to part with his old copy when the new one comes out.

DRUG TOPICS REDBOOK: This trade publication alphabetically lists everything carried by drugstores, and can be even more help than the PDR book ... so get friendly with a pharmacist and have him save you his old copy. Where else could you find out, quickly, the correct way to type "Alka-Seltzer" if there wasn't any in the house? ☉

The above article originally appeared in THE MOTHER EARTH NEWS® NO. 25 ... along with a great deal of other live-better-for-less and self-sufficiency how-to information. For further information about the magazine—and other books and periodicals devoted to home businesses, self-sufficiency, and related subjects—please see page 367 of this handbook.

BOBBI MC COLLUM:
MORE ABOUT HOME TYPING

Several months ago, I launched a home typing business based on Gail Williams' article in MOTHER NO. 25 . . . and when I wrote MOTHER (NO. 31, pg. 128) with an offer to help others get started in the field, I received such an onslaught of letters that I've put together the following notes in self-defense. My remarks are a composite of Gail's tips, my own experience, observations by other typists, and the answers to some questions posed by my respondents. (Many of those who contacted me were relatively new subscribers and hadn't seen the Williams piece . . . which I strongly recommend that anyone interested in this work-at-home business should read.)

SKILLS

You'll be paid for home typing by the page or by the line . . . and the faster you work, of course, the higher your "hourly" earnings will be. Most experienced transcribers hit 80 to 100 words per minute. If you're now plugging along at 40, though, don't despair. A few months of six to eight hours per day at the keyboard will bring your speed up. Just be sure your accuracy keeps step! Flying fingers mean nothing if you constantly drop out small words or need to make corrections every few pages.

Much home typing is done from dictation . . . and if you've never tackled transcription, it's not difficult to learn. This skill, like any other, is built by practice. Simply rent a typewriter, sit down with your back to the television, and pound away as your favorite newscaster talks. If you're unfamiliar with dictating equipment, libraries contain books on the use of business machines.

EQUIPMENT

Before you make a heavy investment in equipment, it's a good idea to rent the basics while you determine whether or not you like typing at home enough to make a business of it. If you do buy a typewriter later on, don't let anyone talk you into "economizing" with a portable or a manual . . . they just won't turn out work that measures up to professional standards. What you want is a full-size, electric, *office* typewriter. I started with an Adler "C" model (which I still have), but prefer the IBM Selectric most of all because of its lack of vibration and its interchangeable type styles.

A service contract on whatever typewriter you finally buy will cost slightly more than repair calls initially but will save you a lot of money in the long run. And, whenever your machine will be down for service, notify your clients of the fact and don't take on any jobs in the meantime . . . unless you can get a loaner that's identical to your own model. If you have to make modifications in the work later on, you can't very well borrow the temporary replacement just for that purpose!

In my experience, all legal typing must be done on a machine with standard pica type, 10 digits to the inch. Gail Williams, who works for court reporters in the Dallas area, suggests a nine-pitch modification (nine characters to the horizontal inch) in localities where this is permitted, since fewer words per page mean a better rate for the typist. None of the deposition services around Los Angeles, however, use anything but a 10-pitch machine.

Standard pica type is also necessary for most thesis and dissertation work. However, certain universities (Brigham Young in Utah, for one) now find that the increased numbers of such documents, and the space needed to store them, are making the smaller "elite" type increasingly desirable. If you do use elite type, adjust your fees accordingly to compensate for the additional words per page.

Ms. Williams' article in MOTHER NO. 25 also mentions the need for a "five-line ratchet" . . . and when I threw that term at my business machine serviceman, he just looked blank. Gail is right, though: There is such a thing, and it's a necessity for legal and scholarly work. What the gadget does is enable you to half-space for the placement of such figures as degree marks and coefficients. My machine—like many others—came equipped with this extra, but if yours lacks the capability it's an easy modification to make.

Another special feature you'll need for thesis typing is square brackets . . . but if your typewriter doesn't have such characters, most schools will accept the marks when they're carefully hand-drawn in black India ink. The same goes for certain mathematical symbols, such as the square-root sign.

The only dictating machine I've encountered—and it seems pretty universal—is the Stenorette. Although an older, used unit can be purchased for anywhere from $25.00 to $150, I preferred to buy a new one (which is the only model with a variable speed control). This slows the rate of playback and is more than worth the additional investment every time you run into a client with an unfamiliar accent, lousy speaking technique, or poor manners. A couple of persons I've typed for, for instance, do their dictating during lunch or dinner . . . and a phrase like "multiple abrasions, lacerations, and contusions" comes across badly at best when mixed with a mouthful of mashed potatoes. If you can't slow the playback speed, such material is hopeless to transcribe.

WORK AREA

I started out working on two TV trays and the arm of the couch, and I have just one word for that routine: DON'T! Find yourself a quiet, out-of-the-way corner, establish it as *yours*, and guard it fiercely. Typewriters are sturdy pieces of equipment, but constantly moving one from place to place is bound to cause problems.

I spent $100 on a sort of stand-up bookcase (new) with a fold-out table for my typewriter and two shelves behind closable doors that keep stationery both out of sight and clean. Various small organizers—which you can make by, for instance, inserting dividers into boxes—will add to the neatness of your work space. Use them for convenient storage of a good supply of typewriter ribbons, erasers, paper clips, rubber bands, manila folders, type cleaner, etc. And don't let tax forms, important papers, bills, coffee cups, catalogs, and the like clutter your typing area!

Remember, too, that you won't be able to type for very long with a sore back and aching shoulder blades. You'll need a decent chair, but it doesn't have to be an expensive one. I bought mine used, from a junk store, for $5.00.

REFERENCE WORKS

Reference books are time and work savers, and their cost is tax deductible. Keep a dependable almanac, dictionary, telephone directory, area map, and zip code book on hand.

If you're working for physicians or court reporters, you'll also need some help with medical terms. *Syllabus for the Surgeon's Secretary* by J.A. Szulec (Medical Arts Publishing, Detroit, Michigan, 1969) is a good all-around reference, and I can recommend either *Taber's Cyclopedic Medical Dictionary* (12th edition edited by Clayton L. Thomas, F.A. Davis Co., Philadelphia, Pa., 1973, $9.50) or *Dorland's Illustrated Medical Dictionary* by William A. Dorland (W.B. Saunders Co., Philadelphia, Pa., 1965, regular edition $13.50, deluxe edition $17.00). Another useful guide—*Physician's Desk Reference* (PDR)—is a manual provided annually to the medical profession which lists drugs under various classifications. Ask your doctor for his last year's copy.

PUBLICITY

Advertising will help you build your business . . . but there's no need to go overboard. A well-placed business card (as Gail has suggested, you can type up your own on 3" X 5" file cards . . . which are both less expensive than "regular" printed business cards and don't get lost so easily) will attract as many clients as an ad in the middle of a large newspaper's classified section. Letters and phone calls to likely prospects also give good results.

LEGAL TYPING

If you want to zero in on Ms. Williams' specialty—legal typing—you'll find court reporters and deposition services listed under "Reporters" in the Yellow Pages of the telephone directory (or the clerk of your local court can tell you how to get in touch with them).

A word of caution regarding the legal field: Some court reporters and deposition services have an annoying habit of not paying their typists until their clients pay them. If both attorneys involved in a case want a copy of the record, your payment for the second carbon isn't always guaranteed . . . nor is the fee for the work you do on a cross-examination, if any. The problem is that the firm which originally hired the reporter isn't always willing to pay for the transcription of the adversary's questions. When you do collect your money, however, you can expect—around here—to average 50¢ a page (considerably better than the 30¢ paid in Gail's parts).

SECRETARIAL SERVICES

Another possibility for the home typist is to work for a secretarial service (also listed in the Yellow Pages). Such firms usually offer around-the-clock transcription to law firms, physicians, psychiatrists, and large businesses. Normally they'll deliver and pick up your jobs . . . and some also provide typewriters, Stenorettes, ribbons, erasers, stationery, and typing paper. They don't pay quite as well as court reporters but are easier to work for, get their checks out bi-weekly, and deal with material which is less boring than depositions.

Incidentally, if your clients don't pick up and deliver and they're located some distance from where you live, try UPS. For $2.00 a week a messenger will come by your house daily Monday through Friday, the service takes only 24 hours door to door, nothing ever gets lost, and the cost is tax deductible. Just contact the nearest United Parcel Service office . . . it's listed in the phone directory. (There's nothing like working through the post office to make you appreciate UPS. I once made the mistake of *mailing* a finished job and it took three weeks to go 50 miles.)

MEDICAL TRANSCRIPTION

If you're experienced in medical terminology—and this isn't something you can fake—typing for psychiatrists and law firms that handle personal injury cases can be very profitable. Since

most typists can't or won't handle such work, the specialty is well paid.

Being a nurse, I sort of fell into my favorite job: typing for a psychiatrist who dealt with personal injury cases going into litigation. He turned out to be a model employer, who both asked for my preferences regarding dictation technique and then conformed to those guidelines. What a sweetheart! He spelled all names twice (once on the tape and once on a written form accompanying each job), made most of his own corrections or paid me extra to do them, rarely sent rush jobs, didn't care if the copy was verbatim (depositions, in contrast, must be totally accurate to dictation, down to a's, and's, and the's) . . . and handled very interesting cases. He also furnished me with a typewriter, ribbons, stationery, erasers, and paper clips, and all work was delivered and picked up by his service. The money was good, the typing was easy, and I really enjoyed the whole experience.

I should mention that few dictators are as nearly perfect as that doctor. If you come across something incomprehensible—either on a tape or in written copy—don't hesitate to call your client and ask questions. I've never been snapped at for doing so . . . and even if you are, it's better than guessing wrong and having to retype a page.

THESIS AND DISSERTATION TYPING

If you live near a university, registration with the graduate student office will net you thesis and dissertation work . . . which can be very profitable. A highly experienced thesis typist I know gets 75¢ per page for straight copy and $1.30 each for tables. To qualify for that kind of money, however, you must be a grammatical expert and know *all* the various forms for theses, bibliographies, and the like. (In any case, you should familiarize yourself with some of the more popular styles: Campbell's, Turabian's, and the American Psychiatric Association's, for instance.)

Every college and university has a list of specific requirements for a proposed study: style of type, table and appendix format, enumeration procedures, margins, bibliographical conventions, and overall arrangement. Ask the students you type for to furnish you with a copy of these directions for your reference.

Another requirement for such scholastic works is that they must be done on special paper, usually of 20-pound weight and 50 percent rag content. The larger universities carry the necessary stock. (Since the paper is frequently imprinted with the institution's watermark, however, be sure you're furnished with enough for all corrections and the final draft.)

Thesis copy (which may be handwritten) is generally not too difficult to handle. Unless you're a well-organized person, however, the work can be a pain in the neck. You should know before you begin that a supervisory committee will read each draft, make critiques, and demand corrections . . . and you'll have to type and retype all the successive versions. It's important to make a note of margin settings, table style, and any peculiarities of a given job, *and keep all this information together* until the student notifies you that he's really and truly finished. I had no idea what I was getting into on my first attempt, and spent a lot of time redoing tables that didn't maintain the required continuity of the study.

Yet an additional hangup with theses is the fact that the candidate for an advanced degree may be working against time. I remember one occasion when I promised to complete a "small section"—originally supposed to be less than 80 pages—in 48 hours. No sweat, right? Wrong! The job turned out to be closer to 180 pages, including a totally unstructured bibliography, and I typed for 36 hours straight. The $10.00 bonus I collected was small payment for four days' recuperation in bed while a backlog of other clients' work built up. Moral: See the manuscript before you commit yourself, and don't promise what isn't feasible. Your two biggest responsibilities as a typist are accuracy and meeting deadlines. If you can't finish the work, don't take on the job.

There's one more point you should know about academic typing: A graduate student who is doing his Ph.D. for an out-of-town university will have to travel there to take his orals (a requirement for the completion of the doctorate). Because he may have to make last-minute corrections in his dissertation during that period, he'll be provided with the names and addresses of secretaries near the school . . . along with a note of what typewriter and type style each one uses. Be sure to go over the list with your client and point out which typists have machines identical to yours, so that any late changes will match the work you've already done.

TAXES AND THINGS

Clients vary somewhat in their handling of deductions and suchlike. Both the deposition services I worked for withheld FICA (social security) from my checks, for instance, while the secretarial service and the doctor didn't. All, however, sent me W-2 forms at the end of the year. (See Gail's article, reprinted in this book, from MOTHER NO. 25 for some notes on how to be a self-employed taxpayer.)

It's essential to keep careful financial records and to hang on to the receipts for all supplies. Note that—while you can't deduct the total purchase price of things like typewriters in one year—you *can* allow for depreciation over a number of years.

Above all, don't be too proud to get help with this matter. I was a bookkeeper for five years, but I still don't do my own taxes. It's worth the $20.00 fee to collaborate with a professional.

AND FINALLY . . .

Good luck to all of you who enter the growing field of home typing . . . and never forget that you're offering a valuable service. Your clients are getting a real break every time you deliver a neatly typed job without any accompanying worry about upkeep of office equipment, sick leave, paid holidays or vacations, personality differences (I've met face to face only one of the people I've typed for), unions, coffee and lunch break scheduling, and all the other headaches that walk in the door with an office staff. Your service—if done well—is worth every penny you charge.●

The above article originally appeared in THE MOTHER EARTH NEWS® NO. 34 . . . along with a great deal of other live-better-for-less and self-sufficiency how-to information. For further information about the magazine—and other books and periodicals devoted to home businesses, self-sufficiency, and related subjects—please see page 367 of this handbook.

RECYCLED PROFITS

This section of our guide is designed to squeeze just a little of the built-in waste *out* of modern life. To getting one more use out of "used up" items. To helping shutins, little old ladies living on social security, and economizers of all ages and persuasions thwart at least a small portion of the flimflammery of our current "consume, consume, consume" society.

June Fingulin's explanation of how she cleared over $250 from a garage sale can be of value to anyone who's ever wished that he or she could trade some of his or her family's accumulation of *things* . . . for a fast infusion of solid, green cash. If you've tried unsuccessfully to work such a transaction in the past (don't despair, June's initial attempt to hold a garage sale was a flop too), you're sure to appreciate the subtle marketing and pricing tips that Ms. Fingulin has discovered.

And then it's on to Clark Hinkle and Robert Williams . . . who—between them—cover almost every possible aspect of cashing in the thousands of coupons that some manufacturers and food processors deviously use to promote their wares.

No, you'll probably never get rich from reading this one section of the book alone. But it's nice to know that you—or your children or that retired couple down the street—can always pick up a little extra spending money "with your left hand" by recycling items and scraps of paper that most of today's citizens look upon as worthless. ◓

JUNE FINGULIN:
GARAGE SALES CAN BE VERY GOOD

Since the term was coined shortly after World War II, "Garage Sale" has come to mean many things to many people. Originally, I believe, it meant cleaning out your garage and inviting the neighbors in to see if they would like to buy the things you were going to throw out anyhow. This was found to be so lucrative that the idea (as good ideas will) has spread and garage sales have become a part of our culture.

Knowing that such a sale can be successful and having one pay off for *you* can be two different things, however . . . and a lot of folks continue to pass up some easy "recycled" money just because they mistakenly believe that "nobody would be interested in *my* junk". We felt the same way . . . until a recent long distance move forced us into holding our first garage sale. Wonder of wonders! It was so successful that we plan to have many more and we'd like to tell you all the "trade secrets" we learned from that first experience.

As we prepared for our cross-country move we quickly

realized that—with today's high cost of shipping—we couldn't afford to take one bit of dead weight with us. Unfortunately we literally had a garage full of the commodity: the beat-up end table I had planned to refinish for over five years, an old utility cabinet that should have been thrown out long before my mother-in-law gave it to us, the record stand with a cracked top, a toy tractor and red wagon our youngster no longer played with, assorted fruit jars, a lamp retrieved in the dim past from some dismantled office . . . and this was only a partial list.

My economical soul wouldn't tolerate paying someone to haul our mountain of memories to the dump so my first thought was to sell the whole mess at once to a secondhand furniture dealer. Several phone calls, however, soon taught me that the dealers were interested in only a few of our pieces . . . and willing to pay precious little for those.

One trader was finally honest enough to tell me, "The only way you can make any money on that stuff is by selling it yourself." Well, I at least had an idea of what the secondhand market for various items both was and wasn't.

Armed with that new knowledge, my husband and I decided to sell the accumulated "treasures and trash" ourselves . . . and we ran a garage sale ad in the local paper. This bit of experience was rather costly since we paid about $5.00 for the ad . . . and it brought practically no response at all.

Well! Getting rid of that stuff was becoming a real challenge but I wasn't beaten yet! I dusted off the typewriter, invested in some light green paper and a felt-tip marker, and "artistically" created some note-sized posters which I placed on every neighborhood grocery and laundromat bulletin board in the immediate vicinity. At least this advertising was virtually free!

The bulletin board notices aroused the interest of our six-year-old so I made up some "handbills" for him to distribute to the houses of his neighborhood friends. We even thumbtacked a few to telephone poles . . . I'm not sure it's legal to do this but we didn't get any repercussions. I did the handbills mostly to give our little boy a chance to participate . . . but we later found that those little slips of paper brought quite a few people to the sale.

Next I put up a huge cardboard sign in our yard (lettered darkly with my trusty marking pen). The information on a yard sign should be brief and easily read from a passing automobile.

Just *when* to hold a garage sale depends on your personal schedule. Since I was home all day we "never closed" from one weekend to the next. Maybe you'll be able to do that, maybe not. The important thing is to be sure your notices, handbills, and yard sign are out for several days *before* the event begins. And use all three methods of attracting customers: in talking to people who phoned and came in, I found that the three ways of advertising were just about equally effective and I consider them all worthwhile.

We did little else to prepare for the sale other than put everything together in one area. We did no fixing, repairing, or painting although I did make sure that everything was clean.

To the assorted junk from the garage I added all the household items I'd been wanting to get rid of for a long time: a cabinetful of dishware odds and ends, a couple of old shag rugs, and a bedspread I just hated. The sale, in other words, gave me an excuse to get rid of a lot of things I'd always disliked . . . but never felt I could afford to throw away.

A word about prices: don't set them too high. Remember that you've already gotten good use from your sale items and the folks interested in buying the articles are looking for a bargain. Give them one.

I found it wise *not* to put a fixed price on anything. I always had a good idea of what I felt was fair for some of the larger items (keeping in mind what I'd have to pay someone to haul it off if I didn't sell it), but my customers didn't know this. When anyone showed even the slightest interest in an article I would try to get him to make an offer (being careful not to quote a specific price myself). I found in most cases that the offer was more than I had expected to get and I would then "reluctantly" accept it anyhow.

This psychology seemed to work almost every time. If people think they're getting a bargain they'll buy almost anything. Of course, if I wasn't willing to sell an article for the amount bid, I would simply say so.

Then there's the "free gift" technique. If I couldn't get a prospective customer to make an offer I would sometimes quote a price myself rather than risk losing his interest. If he seemed to feel my quoted price was too high I generously threw in something else I was having trouble getting rid of anyhow. It often worked.

The articles that sold easiest were furniture (especially chests of drawers and bookcases), garden implements, barbecue equipment, outdoor furniture, and children's toys. Many folks seemed to need tools and garbage cans. There was little interest in clothing, costume jewelry, purses, shoes, and other personal items.

By the end of the second weekend we had sold almost everything we intended to sell . . . and a few things we hadn't! Things like a beat-up bed frame with mismatched springs and discolored mattress. I was actually ashamed to show the old bed to anyone and I hid it . . . until a young couple with a "bouncing" three-year-old offered me $8.00 on the spot for the "trampoline".

All in all, we realized over $250 from the sale of that junk and I haven't missed a bit of it since! ●

The above article originally appeared in THE MOTHER EARTH NEWS® NO. 9 . . . along with a great deal of other live-better-for-less and self-sufficiency how-to information. For further information about the magazine—and other books and periodicals devoted to home businesses, self-sufficiency, and related subjects—please see page 367 of this handbook.

CLARK HINKLE:
RECYCLED REFUNDS

"People who don't refund often say, 'What's the use of spending that time . . . you only get back fifty cents.'

"Right, only fifty cents. But ask any child. Most of them will stand and trade dimes for half dollars any day. If you send in four refunds and get $2.00 back, you've spent 40¢ postage and realized $1.60 for your time. Eight half dollars back will net you $3.20. Invest $4.00 in postage and net $16.00 out of your $20.00 return.

"Refunds are also for dollars—even $2.50 and $3.00—and the postage remains the same. So you can easily 'invest' some labels and $1.00 in postage to get back $12.00 . . . and clear $11.00. Few investments will give that return in, say, a month . . . from 'trash' you'd throw away anyway."—*Money Tree*, Box 686, Manchester, Missouri 63011 . . . the finest and most complete refunding publication we've seen. Sample copy, $1.25.

The interesting thing about recycling is the number of variations on the game. I mean, there's nothing wrong with combing trash piles for good, usable items from our throwaway system: It conserves both the planet's resources and your hard-earned dollars. But, as long as you're digging in the dump for usable *things*, you might as well *make* some dollars by picking up the cold, hard cash that's buried there too.

$3   *and Save $3.00*   WD-10

To receive your $3.00 Refund from Sunlight Corporation, buy a Sunlight Self-Cleaning Oven Toaster-Broiler, Cat. No. 343 (COW) or 242 (SDSW) only from your local retailer. Complete this form and mail it, together with the carton end panel showing model number and product features, as proof of purchase, to Sunlight Self-Cleaning Oven Refund, P.O. Box 00000, Chicago, Illinois 60650.

To qualify for refund, purchase must be made between September 1 and November 30, 1974. Claim for refund must be postmarked on or before December 10, 1974. Limit of one refund per family. Offer good only in U.S.A. Void where prohibited, taxed or restricted by law. Allow 30 days for payment.

NAME _____
                                    (please print)
ADDRESS _____
$3 CITY _____ STATE _____ ZIP _____ $3

If you know what to look for, there's a surprising number of "checks" and "vouchers" with your name on them just waiting to be picked up, anytime, anywhere. NO investment necessary. It's the closest to "something for nothing" I know. All you need is a mailing address and access to a high-class set of trash piles.

The lady that turned me on to this idea told me she was making from $70.00 to $90.00 a month for about an hour's work each day. Another showed me a score sheet indicating she had netted $50.00 for a month. Anyone can do it and make money and—like everything else—the more you have going for you, the more you'll make. You are the key and you can make as little as you like or . . . try a little harder.

What we are discussing is the cash refund bag as it is handled today by manufacturers in an effort to get you to try their products. To quote some of the recent offers: Maxim Freeze-Dried Coffee will pay you $1.00 for the inner seal from one of their jars of coffee plus the label from any breakfast product. H.J. Heinz offers a refund of 25¢ for six soup labels. You can get a $1.00 refund from Salada for the tops of three packages of tea. Ultra Brite offers $1.00 for the panels from two tubes of toothpaste.

At any one time, approximately 50 companies are paying cash refunds to promote their products. The average consumer sees only a tiny portion of these offers because store managers just do not display information on all possible refund offers. Some promotions are published only in newspapers or certain magazines.

Fortunately, for those who want to dig deeper into this source of cash, there is a small bulletin published monthly that covers the field. The bulletin is *Quick Silver* published by

Eggleston Enterprise in Milford, N.Y. 13807. This periodical is about three typewritten (both sides) pages, lists almost all available refund offers, and sells for 50¢ a copy, $2.75 for six months, or $5.00 per year. And you can earn back the subscription price by sending the editors information on refund offers in your area. They'll give you 37¢ for each tip they use. They also guide you as to which offers require an official refund certificate and which do not. Approximately 90% of the listings are valid without certificates.

Many of the promotions specify one to a family and the big refund operators that I talked with were using up to ten different addresses in order to milk an offer for that many dollars instead of a single buck.

The refunds are made on dog food, soap, coffee, frozen foods . . . almost everything sold in the leading chain stores across the nation. The newspapers are full of offers for 5¢ to 50¢. These are certificates that are presented at the register for a discount. In many cases you buy an item for 50¢ and give them a coupon worth 10¢. You then send in the label of the item and get a cash refund of 50¢ and another coupon to buy something else. There have been several offers where, after the initial purchase, a product is free for the next few weeks while the offer lasts.

The back of supermarkets, restaurants, and other trash piles offer wonderful picking for labels and box tops worth cash refunds. When Sunbeam was once offering $5.00 for the front panel from the purchase of an electric razor, a rubbish pile in the rear of a store provided me with two panels. Through the use of two addresses, $10.00 was soon on the way home to me.

I questioned one lady about her trash pile picking and tried to find out if it bothered her to be seen foraging through the empty boxes in back of a supermarket. "What would you do if you saw a dollar bill lying in the trash?" she asked.

The price was right, I decided. You don't really get something for nothing . . . but then you don't lose anything either. If you work at it, scout out a source of labels and box tops, and set up a couple of friends to receive mail, you can soon be getting quarters, half dollars, and dollars in exchange for the debris from our Great Consumer Economy.◒

The above article originally appeared in THE MOTHER EARTH NEWS® NO. 6 . . . along with a great deal of other live-better-for-less and self-sufficiency how-to information. For further information about the magazine—and other books and periodicals devoted to home businesses, self-sufficiency, and related subjects—please see page 367 of this handbook.

ROBERT WILLIAMS:
MORE ON RECYCLED REFUNDS

Taking advantage of refund offers—even if you don't buy the products—is just a matter of careful planning and a few minutes' work each week. I save all the national brand food and detergent labels and packages I can get my hands on (because some sponsors purposely make offers in which unusual parts of a package must be returned, it's necessary to save entire boxes). I file all these packages (you can knock them flat to save space) alphabetically according to brand name in large boxes in the basement and I can find any given package in seconds.

How do I learn about all those refund offers? I spot some (and the more plentiful cash-off offers) while scouring through the magazines and newspapers I collect from relatives and neighbors. By the way, I save the papers and sell them to a scrap paper dealer for 60¢ per hundred pounds. It's no fortune but it makes good ecological sense and brings in stamp money. I also recycle the magazines by giving them to a local nursing home.

Although I do get many blanks from this reading matter,

such coupons add up to only a small percentage of all current offers. This is where a subscription to one of the many refund bulletins now published comes in handy. I tried several before I found a bulletin that really paid for itself in convenience and service. It's called *Friendly Neighbors* and it's published by a very nice lady who makes it her business to find out and tell her readers about all current offers.

Neighbors is divided into two sections. The first is a list of refunds in the order in which they expire, with all the information you need to use the offer. The second part is about five pages of advertisements from many people who want to trade, buy, or sell spare coupons, box tops, trading stamps, and other unusual items.

Since I can receive only one refund (all blanks tell the customer that more than one refund to an individual constitutes fraud) from each offer that interests me and no refund from the offers I don't care for, I use the ads mentioned above to sell or trade extra refund blanks, cash-off coupons, or box tops and, so, benefit from some offers several times. Recently

Friendly Neighbors, formerly published by Carol Bionda, is now edited by Jeanette Turniansky. Jeanette tells us she will continue the newsletter's refund coverage and add other features on living better for less. Sample copy, 60¢. Send self-addressed, stamped envelope with inquiries. New name and address for the publication is:

The Treasure Chest
P.O. Box 1132
New Brunswick, New Jersey 08903

Another refund publication, *Silver Linings Refund Bulletin*, is edited by Karen Quigley. Sample copy, 60¢. Karen tells us she'll send a copy of "How to Refund" free to anyone who sends a self-addressed, stamped envelope.

Silver Linings Refund Bulletin
1612 Ferry
Waukegan, Illinois 60085

I traded 200 or so cash-off coupons for the same number of refund blanks. Although I already had most of the blanks, I received several I could use and I'll save the others to trade later.

When I first started refunding I spent too much time looking through piles of blanks for offers. So I devised a system using two files. In one file I put one of each refund offer and all of the cash-off coupons I think I will use. These are filed alphabetically according to brand name. I even keep the coupons in an envelope so I can take them to the supermarket with my shopping list.

The other file is inactive. In it, I put "spare" coupons and blanks that I intend to trade. It's important that this file also be carefully kept in alphabetic order. Sometimes I see advertisements in *Friendly Neighbors* wanting 30 or 40 all-different refund coupons in exchange for an excellent trade. With my extras filed by brand name I can pick out my end of the swap in seconds.

There are other time and money savers that I use while refunding or doing any business through the mail. I buy No.

10 and the smaller, personal size envelopes in quantities of 500 or 1,000. This saves much money and many trips to the store.

I also buy stamps in rolls and sheets. Rolls of regular stamps and sheets of current commemorative stamps. When I have to make out a stamped, self-addressed envelope, I use a commemorative stamp and keep it when the envelope comes back. When the commemorative issue is no longer sold at the post office—usually within just a few months—I take mine to a dealer and sell them.

When making out those self-addressed envelopes, and for all return addresses, a rubber stamp comes in handy and saves much time. It costs little and can be used for years.

All the little angles on refunding that we use to save and make money become increasingly important as we learn to get by on less and less. ⬥

"Refunding is 'penny ante' to some people and they can't be bothered . . . but there's an old adage, 'A penny saved is a penny earned,' and the refund trail is many pennies. I know a woman near here who made the money for a down payment on a cottage on Lake Taneycomo and she has since earned enough refunding to make the monthly payments. I know others who finance their vacations this way, buy luxuries, supply lunch money for the kids or just put an extra treat on the daily table.

"I'm in the middle years and I'll tell you, if I knew when I was a bride what I know today I could have had my house paid for with what I've thrown away in the trash.

"Many refund offers expire December 31 each year and you try to get everything you've accumulated during the holiday rush into the mail between Christmas and New Year's Day . . . and it takes a while for the companies to get them all back to you. Last March I had a single 'pay day' of $100 in cash, free food, and merchandise when the 1969 refunds caught up."—Lois Choate, former Editor-Publisher, *Money Tree*, November 1970.

The above article originally appeared in THE MOTHER EARTH NEWS® NO. 6 . . . along with a great deal of other live-better-for-less and self-sufficiency how-to information. For further information about the magazine—and other books and periodicals devoted to home businesses, self-sufficiency, and related subjects—please see page 367 of this handbook.

ULTRA LOW COST

It isn't too hard to set up some kind of self-employment enterprise if you already have several thousand dollars to work with . . . but how do you start any kind of business when you have less than $100 to invest?

"That's easy," says Andrew Safer. "I founded my window-washing service on $25."

"It doesn't cost much more than that to put yourself in the business of painting houses," says Joel Ellis, "and the payoff can be a lot more substantial." (Arthur C. Berard, Donald W. Geary, and Ray Miller flesh out Joel's experiences in the house painting field for you.)

"For a *real* low-cost service enterprise of your own," adds Henry C. Horstig, "you might try my cement repair idea. It'll only cost you $5.00 to give it a whirl."

"To heck with those brute labor ventures," says Chuck Crouse. "My shoestring service—supplying news reports to radio stations on a freelance basis—is clean, interesting, and gives me prestige wherever I go!"

Well, no matter. Each of the experts who contributed to this portion of the book has firsthand experience with his own specialty. If you're really smart, you'll pick everything you can from what each one has to say . . . and then apply the best of *all* their ideas to a brand-new "super-low-cost" business of your own! ◒

ANDREW SAFER: HOW TO CLEAN UP WITH A WINDOW-WASHING BUSINESS

It was about the time when I was getting fed up with college, fed up with taking money every month from my father (who really couldn't afford it), and fed up with the whole dependency bag . . . that a friend jokingly suggested I set myself up as a professional window washer.

Well, why not? Regular jobs were hard to find and I didn't want to fill out W-2 forms or gear my life to an alarm clock anyway. I decided to investigate the idea.

Mind you, I didn't know anything about washing windows aside from what we all learn as kids . . . Windex, paper towels, and smears. So I thumbed through the Yellow Pages of the phone book to "Janitorial Supplies", zeroed in on a local supply house, and went on down to look over the tools of the trade.

I immediately leveled with the guy in the store, told him I didn't know a dang thing about the business, and asked him to clue me in on the equipment I'd need. He did and here's the gear I settled on:

SQUEEGEES. For starters, two (one with a blade 6 inches wide and another 18 inches across) are enough. It's important to get squeegees with flexible rubber edges that are responsive to the touch. My favorite model is the *Master*, made by Steccone Products Co. of Oakland, California.

POLE. Any old wooden pole to which your squeegees can be securely fastened will do . . . but I went pro right from the beginning and bought a fancy aluminum model that extends out to 18 feet in length.

BRUSH. One is probably about as good as another, as long as you can attach it to your pole and use it to slop on the cleaning solution.

BUCKET. If you already have a standard pail of some kind you may well want to use it . . . although I bought a watertight canvas bucket that is perfect for traveling. I can collapse the flexible container, stick it in my backpack with the retracted pole and my other equipment . . . and carry the entire business wherever I go.

CLEANING SOLUTION. I've tried several window cleaners and like Amway L.O.C. best (mainly because it's biodegradable and I can sprinkle the waste water on the surrounding shrubbery when I'm done with a job). Basic H is also acceptable and vinegar works fine. Ammonia stinks.

ODDS AND ENDS. You'll need a sponge, rags, and scouring pad ("Tuffy" brand plastic scouring pads—available in any supermarket—are the only ones I've found that don't scratch glass). And don't forget your bookkeeping department . . . a 15-cent spiral-bound notebook for business records.

All this gear ran me about $25.00 (approximately $10.00 of which went into the fancy pole), so we're not talking about a helluvan investment. Remember that your tools are just as important as you are . . . so buy good stuff, treat it with respect, and make it last. I still have all my original equipment after six months of heavy use.

Your next step—after properly assembling a set of tools—will be to take the stuff home and practice on your own filthy windows. I start by putting the L.O.C.—only five to ten drops for each gallon—into my wash water. (Soap suds are a hindrance and I scoop most of them out.)

You'll probably have to experiment a bit to determine the angle at which your squeegee should meet the glass for fastest and cleanest work. Hold the blade in your hand until you've mastered this basic window-washing skill and then try it the hard way . . . with the rubber wiper mounted on its pole.

The secret is *wetness to wetness*. Douse the glass thoroughly, dampen the squeegee's edge with a sponge and *then* run the blade down the smooth surface. Some of the rubber wipers seem to have streaks built into them, so if you have difficulty controlling yours, try another.

When you can really make those windows sparkle, start ringing doorbells in your neighborhood and try to drum up some business.

After a short time—providing no major catastrophes (like putting your fist through a $400 picture window) have occurred—you'll start feeling pretty confident. Go down to a printer at that point and order yourself 500 business cards with a catchy slogan (you'll be surprised how much effect that slogan will have). My cards read:

"I'll bring clarity into your life"

Andrew Safer

PROFESSIONAL WINDOW WASHER

ADDRESS   PHONE NUMBER

With business cards in hand, start contacting the shopkeepers and store owners in your town. Act like a professional: Present your card and always try to establish monthly or bi-monthly accounts. Just being confident of the value of your service should get you through the sales pitch and land you some regular jobs.

I've tried advertising in local newspapers and found that I still obtain most of my work by stomping around town, ringing doorbells, and presenting my card. Actually, although you may not relish this part of the business . . . it's a great way to gain a fresh perspective on the ole home town, or to become acquainted in a new area. You do have to learn to take the good with the bad, however. On days when people are gruff and you can't find a single job, it's best to take the

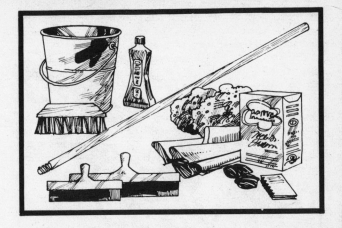

situation in stride, go on home, bake some bread or otherwise cool off . . . and try again when the stars are more fortuitous.

Remember, whenever you're bidding for work, that streak-free window washing is a valuable service and you should charge what your time is worth (I figure mine at $3.00 to $3.50 an hour). Calculate how long a particular job should take and give your prospective customer an estimate. Bear in mind, too—when presenting a quotation—that haggling is often the name of the game: be willing to bend a little to get some of those choice assignments.

Will it work? It has for me! I moved to Missoula, Montana last fall . . . just in time to put up and clean people's storm windows before winter set in (putting up and taking down storm windows—where the climate warrants such activity—can be a nice supplement to your window-washing enterprise). I've since parlayed that running start into steady residential work and ten regular business accounts.

Being a professional window washer is—to me, at least—a fun, honorable, and profitable business. What's more, every average-sized town can support one or two freelancers in the field . . . so, if the enterprise appeals to you, check out the possibilities in your area. With a little hustle, you too can clean up washing windows! ●

The above article originally appeared in LIFESTYLE! NO. 4 . . . along with a great deal of other live-better-for-less and self-sufficiency how-to information. For further information about the magazine—and other books and periodicals devoted to home businesses, self-sufficiency, and related subjects—please see page 367 of this handbook.

JOEL ELLIS:
THE HOUSE PAINTING BUSINESS

If you really want to help "Keep America Beautiful" . . . learn the house-painting business! You'll find, as I did, that the venture can bring you a good income and many fringe benefits: outdoor work, varied location, a choice of hours, and plenty of chances to meet new and interesting people. You'll also have the satisfaction of performing a valuable service. A home, after all, is a lifetime investment which its owner wants to protect.

HOW TO GET PAINTING JOBS

Of all the good, inexpensive ways to hustle painting jobs, the best is word of mouth: One satisfied customer tells another . . . and the system goes to work for you as soon as you've got a first assignment in a given neighborhood. A nearby homeowner sees you in action, approaches casually, asks a few questions . . . and just minutes later you may be across the street at his place, looking over a potential job. One paint crew will often get two or three homes to do, all in the same block.

First, though, you've got to get that original contact. Use as many free sources of publicity as possible . . . for instance, the community bulletin boards in supermarkets and laundromats.

Your hand-printed bulletin board notices should be worded to appeal to a particular neighborhood. "Student seeks house-painting jobs" is often a good approach (people seem to think that student labor comes cheap). An offer of "free estimates" is also attractive, since it assures the potential customer that he won't be ripped off. On the bottom of the note write the phrase "House Painter" and your phone number, vertically, eight or ten times and cut between the slips. Tear off a few to make business look good.

If your local radio station or newspaper has a swap service, get yourself listed (or take a three-line ad in the classified section of the paper for $3.00 to $5.00).

Another good source of jobs and information is a local paint store . . . one that carries a good, reliable line and does a high volume of business. A friendly management can help you get started by giving you a lead in return for using their products. In many cases, the firm that supplies your materials will also open an account for you so you can paint now and pay later.

ESTIMATES

A good paint store can also be of assistance with your first estimate. Some of the larger firms have special representatives who advise customers about their problems during the summer home-improvement season. If you can, get one of these troubleshooters to help you size up your first job . . . and ask him how he does it.

Once you've painted a few houses you'll have a feel for the most important part of preparing an estimate: figuring how long the work will take. Remember to allow for the following hassles:

Unboxed eaves (these will slow up even the most experienced painter).

Dormers that have eaves and siding.

French windows, with their many panes.

Patios.

Awnings which must be removed.

Necessary minor repairs.

Small leaks. If you spot one of these, recommend caulking over the defective seam. The suggestion can save the customer more expensive mending in the future, and shows that you're concerned.

Bad surface. If the house's old paint is peeling off, check with the owner and plan time and materials for scraping and spot priming (or a complete primer coat).

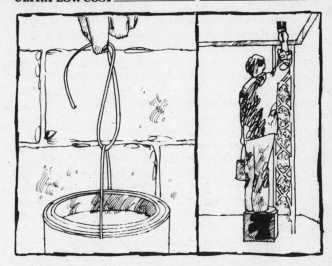

I estimate a job one side at a time: two man-hours for the eaves, two and a half for the peak, two for the windows, four for the space above, below, and between the windows.

An estimate without a firm price is satisfactory to some homeowners. If you're asked for a set figure, be wise, reckon in all the problem areas, and leave yourself enough time to cover any hang-ups.

Some customers want a contract price, a requirement which brings you into competition with other painters. Only you can set your rate because only you know how valuable your time is and how well you estimate. The time/dollar ratio you arrive at will determine your dollar-per-hour figure. If you feel insecure about such a formula, however, call a painter for an estimate and ask for his hourly charge.

MATERIALS

You should come to an agreement with your potential customer about what is included in the job and who is going to supply the materials. You can obtain the paint and either have it charged directly to the homeowner or added to your estimated bill. Either way, always buy first-grade, high-quality products. Good paint can make you look good, so don't cut corners here. Sometimes, though, the customer has his own ideas about what brands are best. Even though it's *you* that has to use the stuff, be tolerant.

Here's a checklist of other items you'll need, and some comments on choice of materials:

[1] Brushes ... perhaps second in importance only to the paint itself. The best tool gives the best results (and lasts an extra painting season, too). I like a 2-1/2-inch-wide nylon brush with a round handle. This size can cover narrow siding and—due to its length—spread to reach a wide swath. Larger widths get heavy as the day goes on.

Nylon holds its shape and cleans up well ... but to keep any good brush in top condition requires care. Some painters prefer to suspend—not stand—their brushes in thinner and linseed oil overnight and shake them out in the morning. Others wash them in oleum immediately after use. In either case, make sure the tool's bristles are well cleansed to prevent hardening.

[2] Spirits of oleum (for cleaning and thinning).

[3] Ladders. I suggest a 6- to 8-foot stepladder and a 12- to 14-foot extension type (or you may need a 24-footer). My preference is wood, for good reason: In windy weather your support can sometimes get away from you and do some undesirable moving. If the ladder is aluminum—and comes in contact with a powerline—you have a good chance of being on the evening news.

[4] Dropcloths. At one time the professional house painter's only option was expensive light canvas. Now there's also plastic, which is cheap and repels paint effectively but does have disadvantages (it tears and doesn't drape as nicely over bushes). You can use old sheets if you prefer.

[5] Scrapers. A one-and-a-half or two-inch Red Devil scraper, kept sharp with a file, can save you time and make the tedious job of surface preparation a breeze. Putty knives and razor-blade scrapers are also handy to have around.

[6] Rags.

[7] Used nylon stockings, a good supply. When paint gets scummy and kind of skaggy-looking, hold a piece of nylon over an empty bucket and pour the lumpy liquid through the fabric. Voilà, a free strainer and a use for a discarded item. (A little splash of oleum on top of the contents before the can is closed for the night will help prevent the problem.)

[8] Simple tools: hammer, nails, adjustable wrench, pliers, wire cutter, screwdriver, file (for sharpening the scraper).

[9] Wire (a few coat hangers will probably do) ... handy

for hanging paint buckets on the ladder.

[10] Old newspapers.

[11] Small box (wooden case or milk container) for carrying supplies in and standing on.

[12] Safety glasses.

[13] Painting clothes: hat, shirt, and pants or overalls. The traditional dress of the painter is white, for the very good reason that it helps keep you cool in the sun. A loose white shirt from the Red Shield or Goodwill store should last a painting season. If you really get into the business and want to look professional, white painting overalls are a fine investment. They're roomy, with plenty of stowage for tools and cloths.

[14] Shoes. Your footwear should have steel shanks so your feet won't wrap around the ladder as if you were trying to hold on with them.

ON THE JOB

Before you start operations, it's best to establish a safe, undisturbed place as a storage area for paint and brushes. Spread the spot with newspapers first.

Then you can get on with the job of preparing the building's surface in the manner you previously agreed on with the homeowner. In some cases, you'll have to do a vigorous allover scraping with the help of all hands on the paint crew. Remember, at such times, that chips of the old coating can be a nuisance in rose bushes and your eye. Plan ahead and protect.

Try to avoid using a torch or a power sander to remove oil paint. That's a long, hard job and will probably take more time than you expect.

Minor repairs are best made at this point. If you come on bad siding or loose or weak eave troughs that weren't spotted in your original inspection, report the problem to the owner and hope to solve it without changing your estimate.

With the preliminaries out of the way, the painting can begin. Always start with the under-eaves at the topmost point and work downward.

How do you reach the upper siding on a house of two or more stories? One way is to use two extension ladders and ladder jacks with an extension plank. This arrangement takes teamwork to set up, is somewhat cumbersome to move, and may consume more time than it saves. The alternative is to give each painter his own ladder and let him move as needed. With a little practice, a person can cover a large area in this manner.

Now a few miscellaneous hints to make the job easier and the results more professional:

If you have any question about whether some area should be painted, your best motto is, "If in doubt, leave it out." You can always go back and do the section later.

As the work proceeds, be careful of lap marks . . . the visual buildups that sometimes result when an ending and a beginning section meet. In particular, avoid painting in the sun (which can dry the coat too quickly and cause this problem). If you do find yourself in a sunny spot, feather out the ends of your strokes: that is, draw the paint out to a thin disappearing streak on uncovered wood. This will help prevent the unsightly lap.

Then there's the business of keeping the paint where you want it. Nothing ruins a job like spots on shingles, driveway, mailbox, and porch lights. A little effort and a discreet use of dropcloths will keep the surrounding vegetation and other uncoated areas in their original condition. If a spill should occur—and it will—clean up at once. (Moral: Never carry more paint than you care to mop up.)

When you're working on a dormer, you need a dropcloth on the roof plus a few rags to catch any chance drips. Some nails driven into a convenient place to hold the paint container should help to prevent major spills.

A window-trimming brush and a little practice will enable

you to keep paint off glass and screening. If a drop does splat on a screen, dip a short, stiff-bristled brush into a small can of oleum, dab the spot, and clean up with a cloth.

When in confrontation with flying, stinging creatures (hornets, wasps, etc.), retreat. It's handy to know that such beasties are in a better mood—and fly slower—in the morning. If your presence enrages them even at that hour, take along a knotted rag for self-defense. A quick flick will deflect a marauder, knocking it to the ground and dazing it for a few precious minutes.

Finally, rest periods should be taken in an orderly manner so as not to look like a demonstration in progress on the customer's lawn.

Before you know it, you'll be a veteran painter who looks at houses in terms of jobs: "That's a $250 place . . . that one would go $400." How much you can make in a season depends on a lot of variables, but one thing is certain: A summer of house painting can supply a good chunk of winter survival money. And, once you've got your hand in, you can always fall back on this useful skill when you need cash. ●

The above article originally appeared in THE MOTHER EARTH NEWS® NO. 28 . . . along with a great deal of other live-better-for-less and self-sufficiency how-to information. For further information about the magazine—and other books and periodicals devoted to home businesses, self-sufficiency, and related subjects—please see page 367 of this handbook.

ARTHUR C. BERARD:

"HOW MUCH PAINT WILL YOU NEED?"

Some paint estimating suggestions:

[1] Compute the number of square feet of surface to be covered: First determine the distance around the house, in feet. Then find the average height to the eaves and add two feet to that figure. (This automatically takes care of the paint you'll need for the gables.) Finally, multiply the former result by the latter.

[2] Ascertain from your paint dealer approximately how many square feet each gallon of undercoat covers. Then divide the total area by this figure.

[3] Similarly, learn the coverage of a gallon of topcoat house paint and divide as in [2].

Example: Let's say the house is 20 by 40 feet with an average height to the eaves of 13 feet. Multiplying 120 (the perimeter) by 15 (average height to eaves plus two feet), we find that the surface area is about 1,800 square feet. A good grade of undercoat or primer covers about 450 square feet per gallon, and a top-quality house paint covers 500 square feet per gallon. A little simple arithmetic reveals that four gallons of undercoat and three and a half of house paint are needed.

Before you place your order, however, there's another factor to be considered: the condition of the surface. If it's unusually rough, heavily textured, dry, or porous, it may require 20% more paint for the first coat. Remember also that corrugated metal requires one-third more paint than usual because there's more area to cover per square foot. For the same reason, narrow-lap siding uses up to 10% more paint than wide.

No matter what kind of surface you're painting, allow 48 hours' drying time between coats. ◆

The above article originally appeared in THE MOTHER EARTH NEWS® NO. 28 . . . along with a great deal of other live-better-for-less and self-sufficiency how-to information. For further information about the magazine—and other books and periodicals devoted to home businesses, self-sufficiency, and related subjects—please see page 367 of this handbook.

DONALD W. GEARY:
HOUSE PAINTING HINTS

House painting is such a monumental task that most people don't know where to begin . . . or, if they do know, they don't want to hassle with getting paint all over themselves or spend their weekends or vacations perched on top of a ladder. And that's where I come in.

Last spring I placed an advertisement in a suburban newspaper: "House Painting—reasonable and efficient, free estimate—call _____." The notice cost me $1.60 a week and brought in about five weekly inquires from prospective customers. This was the start of a profitable business.

When I receive a call I make an appointment to visit the prospective client as soon as possible. My rule is to explain to the homeowner at our first meeting that I'm not a professional painter, but have experience and believe I can do a good job. It's always best to be up front with people . . . they appreciate knowing that they'll have satisfactory work done at a price below the going rate.

My next move is to walk around the house and get a clear picture of what's needed. This survey includes some basic questions: Will there be a significant color change? Are there any areas in need of repair (broken leaders and gutter, rotten wood, etc.)? Will the owner take care of these problems, or will I? (I always state whether or not I'm qualified to do so.) Does the customer want one coat of paint, or two? (The first goes on slowly, the second more easily because the covered surface is smoother and less absorbent.)

I also ask at this point whether the homeowner can supply an extension ladder (either his own or one borrowed from a neighbor). Most often he can, but if not I arrange to borrow or rent one. A good ladder costs about $185, which is why I don't have my own even though I've painted over 25 houses.

When I'm making an estimate I carry a clipboard and pad with me and make notes about the job: approximate hours and cost, date to begin, and any special instructions (remove storm windows, put up screens, paint both, clean gutters, etc.).

My estimate is based on a window count (because the frames are the most time-consuming areas to paint, what with the detail and the care that's needed to avoid smearing the glass). Each window—and every door—goes down on my sheet as one hour . . . and if extensive putty replacement is needed I allot extra time. Then I figure about three hours for the long side of a house, one to three for railings and porches (depending on length and type), and variable periods for trim according to its nature. Individual homes vary so much that rigid scheduling isn't possible, but my rough guides work out pretty accurately in practice.

These calculations give me an overall time estimate—one to three days—which I multiply by my hourly rate. When I employ a helper, I add his hourly pay to mine and then multiply.

The amount you charge should be fair to both the homeowner and to you. If you have some experience I'd recommend asking a minimum of $4.00 per hour. Raise your charge as you improve, but never compromise yourself by demanding the exorbitant rip-off rates of commercial painters.

I don't buy paint unless the customer insists, since I prefer to have him or her select the grade and colors . . . but I do urge the individual to go for the best he can afford. If I must supply the materials, I stick with a good brand such as Benjamin Moore, Dutch Boy, Sherwin-Williams, or Sears. I'm particular because I know that the quality of the paint will directly affect the quality of my work . . . not that sloppy workmanship with good materials equals a professional job, of course, but cheap products won't look good or last long no matter how they're used.

Two basic types of paint are available: oil-based and water-based (latex). Modern methods of production have improved the durability of latex to the point that it actually surpasses the oil type. I prefer a water-based formula myself, for several reasons: It dries in about one hour so that two coats can be applied the same day, it's easier to handle and stroke on, and the brushes clean up with soap and water.

If you're going into the painting business, it's a good idea to visit a few dealers to get paint charts and find out about the available products, their prices, methods of application, and expected life (which can vary from three to ten years).

Most house-painting jobs consist of four major tasks. The first is surface preparation, which can entail anything up to removing all the old paint or replacing parts of the structure. In most cases, though, what's involved is some scraping, sanding, and caulking with maybe a bit of priming here and there. The whole business should take about half a day for the average home and—if done well—will give you a good base for the work which is to follow. Remember, paint won't adhere properly unless the underlying area is free of dirt and loose coatings.

I usually begin by hosing down the outside of a house to remove most of the soil. Then I scrape any peeling, cracked, or chipped spots. Areas which have been taken down to the bare wood get a splash of primer (or two coats of regular paint will suffice if the patch is small). Finally, I replace any loose or missing putty around windows and recaulk window frames, doors, and chimneys where needed.

The second major task is to paint the trim and windows. The trim is usually simple unless the house is an old one with overhanging eaves. In that case you'll be reaching overhead (wear a hat) and using muscles that will be sore for a while. Care with the windows saves time in the long run because you won't have to go back later and scrape the panes.

Then comes the main body of the house ... the easiest part because you can use a wide brush and make long strokes. (Just don't overextend your reach when you're standing on a ladder!) For large, smooth areas I often use an industrial roller, a bushy affair that holds a lot of paint and in most cases will cover as well as a brush ... with the added benefit of almost supersonic speed. I've finished an entire home—excluding windows—in one day using a roller and extension rod. I'd suggest, though, that you stick with a brush until you get really good.

The last task is to clean up the area around the house, by gathering up any stray paint chips, old caulking, and putty and throwing them away. At the same time I survey the completed work and touch up any spots I missed or didn't cover well. I know that if I'm satisfied the homeowner will be happy too, and that's good advertising.

What I've told you is basically all there is to house painting (except that it's nice to have a good companion at home to massage your tired muscles). This skill is helping me earn money to get back to the land and—even after I'm there—should bring me some bucks for things I might otherwise have to do without. If you're planning a break—or have already made one—and you're short of cash ... think about financing part of your new life with a paintbrush! ●

The above article originally appeared in THE MOTHER EARTH NEWS® NO. 28 ... along with a great deal of other live-better-for-less and self-sufficiency how-to information. For further information about the magazine—and other books and periodicals devoted to home businesses, self-sufficiency, and related subjects—please see page 367 of this handbook.

RAY MILLER:
FEEDBACK ON HOUSE PAINTING

I've just finished reading "House Painting" by Joel Ellis and "Painting Hints" by Donald W. Geary in MOTHER NO. 28 and found that they made a lot of sense. Both authors, though, failed to stress some points I think are essential.

I worked for ten years as a carpenter and have been in business myself for five years as a general contractor and builder . . . and, although I don't like to insist on signed contracts, pay exorbitant insurance rates, etc., that's the way it has to be or I'd find myself on the short end of the stick. Here are some suggestions that MOTHER's readers might think about before grabbing a brush and going to work.

[1] Get the customer to sign an agreement, and be very specific in that contract about what you are and aren't to do. Otherwise, you may find yourself stuck with jobs you never

expected because the homeowner *thought* you were supposed to do them. After all, until you've got all the money in your hand (in cash), the other fellow has you by the seat of the pants . . . and he knows it. Believe me, I've been there.

[2] Don't fall for the "extras" deal . . . the one where the owner says, "As long as you're on the spot you might as well do so-and-so, and I'll pay you extra." It's fine to pick up odd jobs—in fact, they'll help you break even if you find you've underestimated the original work—but make out an "additional work order" and have the customer sign it. If he's not out to screw you, he'll understand that this protects him as well as you.

[3] When you write up an agreement, specify how and when you are to be paid for your work. Get at least a third of the money—preferably half—down before you paint or, at any rate, on the day you start the job. This advance will cover the cost of materials and some wages. If you hire an assistant it's an absolute must, for he has to be paid whether you are or not.

Remember, no matter what kind of nice guy you think your customer is, the down payment will sometimes be all you'll ever get. You may even be surprised to find out that people you thought of as friends will stick it to you for a couple of bucks . . . so at least make an effort to protect yourself.

[4] Try to deal with the person who pays the bill. Otherwise you may find yourself in the middle of a domestic quarrel *and* not getting any money for a job the head of the household didn't OK.

If the lady of the house asks you to do something extra and it's her husband who handles the checkbook, bring the request to his attention in a casual way. For instance, next time you see him you might mention the day when you'll be able to do that additional work. If he doesn't know what you're talking about, watch out!

[5] Now we come to the matter of insurance. If you're of age, work by yourself, and own nothing but the shirt on your back, don't carry any. The homeowner will have to cover whatever damage you do, and he can't sue. (Be careful, though . . . he *can* get a judgment against you.)

On the other hand, if you've busted hump to get a homestead or some acreage, you can lose it darn quick if you don't have coverage. I know! I don't like paying the fat-cat insurance companies either, but it sure beats seeing my home taken or having a judgment granted against me.

Think about it. What if you employ a helper and he or she gets hurt (or killed)? Even if the injured party doesn't want to sue, there may be a wife, parents, or relatives who feel differently. Also, if you're not covered, the homeowner is responsible for the accident on his property . . . and you can bet *he'll* sue you.

(Most states, incidentally, require that you carry compensation insurance for your employees whether you hire them for one day or a year. This also gets you into withholding taxes, social security, etc. . . . and Uncle will have no mercy if he catches up with you and finds that you're not doing what he thinks you should.)

Or suppose you're up on an extension ladder slapping on paint and the wind is blowing the wrong way. You just may be painting someone's home or car half a block down the street . . . and you're going to have to pay for the damage. Some people may allow you to compound the auto and wax it or paint the speckled side of the house. I don't have to tell you, though, that most owners will be seeing dollar signs. They can and will live with the spots, but they want money to help them forget.

What all this boils down to is liability insurance. You'll wish you had it in any of the cases I've mentioned . . . or if you happen to drop something on a kid's head from a good way up . . . or if your ladder tips and you get paint on a driveway outside or a rug inside.

These are some of the reasons why painting contractors, and general contractors like me, have to charge the "rip-off prices" mentioned in Mr. Geary's article. I'd be glad to work for $4.00 an hour if I didn't have to pay Uncle and the insurance companies half of it.

I don't like to be the one to dampen someone's fire, but what I've said is true: Some customers just seem to be waiting for a sucker to come along. Fortunately, they aren't an everyday occurrence—for the most part, working for people is interesting and enjoyable—but the painter must always keep up his guard. That's what makes me want to find a homestead and get out of this hassle. ●

The above article originally appeared in THE MOTHER EARTH NEWS® NO. 31 . . . along with a great deal of other live-better-for-less and self-sufficiency how-to information. For further information about the magazine—and other books and periodicals devoted to home businesses, self-sufficiency, and related subjects—please see page 367 of this handbook.

HENRY C. HORSTIG:
A NICE LITTLE CEMENT BUSINESS

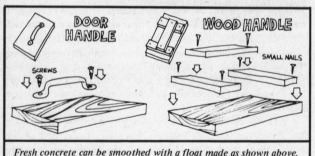

Fresh concrete can be smoothed with a float made as shown above.

There are many alternative ways of earning some bread without getting into the 9-to-5 rat race. The contracting of small-scale concrete repairs is one that any able-bodied man can start with less than a $5.00 investment and—with a little sense and a fair amount of hard work—parlay into an operation as large as he wants to make it.

You'll need a bag of cement (a sack of light cement costs less than $2.00), a hammer, chisel, small broom, some sand, gravel, a five-gallon can of water, some old boards, and a small float. (The small float is a piece of smooth 1" X 4" board about nine inches long with a handle on top, used for finishing off the concrete. Once your business is rolling, you may want to invest in a good trowel . . . but, chances are, you'll still keep that old float handy and use it often.)

Put all these supplies in the back of your jalopy and drive to a suburban area of any big city (one-family houses, five to ten years old, in the middle income section are the best prospects). Cruise along slowly until you see a crack or broken section in the sidewalk, someone's drive, or the foundation of a house. As soon as you see anything that needs cement repair, stop and speak to the owner.

Point out the liabilities involved if someone falls on a broken sidewalk and emphasize that expensive repairs later can be completely headed off now with the proper low-cost preventive maintenance. When you quote a price of only $2.00 to $5.00 for most little jobs, they're usually yours and you can begin immediately.

If the crack is small, enlarge it to a width of about two inches with your hammer and chisel. Mix some cement, sand, and gravel (usually one part cement, two of sand, and three of gravel is a good mix) directly on the sidewalk or a piece of your scrap lumber. Add water until the patching material is the consistency of soft dough, wet the crack well so the new concrete will adhere to the old, and trowel the new filler into the old crack. Tamp the new concrete firmly, level and smooth its surface with the float, sweep the surrounding area with your broom, cover the new work with an old board, and collect your money.

Operate this little business only on good days, as a rainstorm can ruin your work, and—once you find a prime neighborhood—go back day after day until you've covered it completely.

Try to take only the smaller jobs, at least in the beginning, and you'll earn the most for the least effort. Later, as you plow some of your cash into better equipment, you can tackle the larger projects. A friend of mine started patching sidewalks in just this way when he was laid off from his regular job in the 1940's. Soon, he was earning over $200 a week for three days' work. He later expanded, hired help . . . and now owns a full-scale contracting business of his own. ◒

The above article originally appeared in THE MOTHER EARTH NEWS® NO. 14 . . . along with a great deal of other live-better-for-less and self-sufficiency how-to information. For further information about the magazine—and other books and periodicals devoted to home businesses, self-sufficiency, and related subjects—please see page 367 of this handbook.

CHUCK CROUSE:
HOW TO BE A ONE-MAN OR ONE-WOMAN RADIO NETWORK

I have recently discovered, to my delight, that a broadcast journalist can make it on his own as a freelancer. In fact, I'm now making my living this way and I'm going to tell you how I do it. I want to emphasize right in front, however, that this article is written for folks who already have some grounding in news reporting. If your experience in communications is limited to a few months of tearing copy off a teletype or to working as a copy boy or advertising salesman, you may not have the preparation needed for this freelance journalism.

All right, news reporters. Now that we've sorted ourselves out, I'll lay down two ground rules: [1] The following instructions are not meant to tell you how to rake in so much money in three months that you can take it easy the rest of the year. Rather, I'm going to show you a way to get out from under a boss . . . or to survive when you're without a job. [2] Remember that I work in *radio* news. Your field might be TV or newspapers. In either of the latter cases, you'll want to think "photographs" when I say "audio tape". All right . . . here we go.

I became a radio "stringer" quite suddenly when I found myself without a job just one week before the legislature of my state convened. I didn't want to leave the area and I didn't like the idea of collecting unemployment compensation . . . so I got on the phone to a number of radio stations.

I did not confine myself to stations located in my state. I also contacted broadcast studios just over the border . . . studios which might logically want to use coverage of major events within my state. I was fortunate in that there are three all-news stations in just such ideal positions. I called each of the three and offered to serve as their stringer at the capitol . . . with telephoned reports of the action there.

The stations I called were [A] located in cities large enough to give them competition from other broadcasters, thus forcing them to offer "exclusives", and [B] known for having fairly active news departments.

Two key points: I guaranteed market exclusivity (I would take on only one station per city) and I would charge a station only for the stories it accepted. In fact, no one was committed to take any of my reports at all. Generally, the larger stations thought my quoted price of $2.00 per accepted story was dirt cheap . . . and the smaller broadcasters thought it was reasonable enough. The only exception was an all-news station owned by a major network: It had an established practice of paying ten dollars per report.

In three days of calling, I "signed up" five stations. No written contract was drawn. I simply sent each accepting radio station a letter that put in writing what I had offered on the phone. The letters also included my home address, home phone, and capitol phone.

Most state capitol buildings have press rooms. In my case, there were two: a crowded, noisy one housing newspaper reporters and a quiet room for broadcasters tucked away on the fifth floor. The executive director of the Legislative Management Committee (ask around to learn whom you must see) set me up with a desk in the broadcasters' room and I ordered a phone.

Since I had been paying my home telephone bill on time, I did not have to make the $75.00 deposit usually required on new business phones. I already owned a cassette tape recorder and I bought several new blank cassettes and a set of batteries for it. I also wound an induction coil with which to feed taped audio into the phone (instructions later). A ream of cheap paper and some file folders, and I was set to go.

In my state, the Governor has a brief, informal news conference at 9:30 each morning. I make it a point to scan the morning paper before I go in and I always get to the conference just before it begins. Usually, the Governor doesn't have much to announce at these gatherings and the sessions are taken up with questions from the dozen or so reporters who attend regularly. I'm quite fortunate in that the Governor permits cassette recorders to operate during the meetings: His predecessor did not.

After the morning conference I stop by the main press room to pick up any mail (mostly releases from political parties and various state agencies) and then go on up to my desk on the fifth floor.

There is usually material for one or two stories in each news conference. I write them up, select appropriate cuts of 10 to 30 seconds from the tape, and start calling my stations.

Rarely does every station buy any given story. Some want local angles and two all-news stations have union contracts which prevent me from feeding them tape. For these two outlets I prepare special straight-voice reports that run a little longer than the stories I give the other studios.

All these reporting calls are made collect and the receptionists, who recognize my name, accept promptly. I quickly outline the content and length of the story or stories I have and each station's newsroom people decide on the spot whether or not they want my offering. If they do, they roll their tape and I feed.

With the morning submissions out of the way, the rest of my day consists of attending legislative committee hearings, catching legislators in the halls or in their offices for short interviews, and running back to write up and feed any stories that result.

Naturally, this arrangement works best when the legislature is in session and the volume of news is highest. Still—even when the legislature is in recess or on vacation—there's a functioning government to report on and—based in a capital city—you should have little trouble finding enough news to keep you busy and well fed. There are potential pitfalls in this business. however, as you can easily deduce from the following list of pointers:

[1] Don't be tempted to goof off just because no one's there to keep track of your hours. Stay on the move, talk to people, stop in at various offices, and get to know all the legislators and state officials.

[2] Honestly represent your stories to the stations. Your service is valuable to them only so long as you give them fast service on substantial stories that are well written and well read.

[3] Don't take sides in either political matters or personality disputes. You need to be well thought of by everyone . . . and that includes competing reporters.

[4] Be prepared to be treated as a second-class newsman for a while. As word gets around that you really *are* on a half-dozen stations, you'll be taken seriously. One day the publicity man for a party organization suddenly started giving me the red carpet treatment. I later learned that he had heard one of my reports on a network-owned news station the night before.

[5] Don't act self-important. Humility and a willingness to admit you don't know some things will open more doors to you than strutting around spouting call letters.

[6] Do look relatively straight. My hair is somewhat long and I have a beard . . . but I keep both trimmed and I wear a sport coat and tie.

[7] Don't grind personal axes. Spend a little extra time at hearings of the Environment Committee if you like . . . but don't become known as "the guy who's a nut on (fill in the blank)".

[8] Do keep records. The larger stations with well-established stringer systems will keep track of your feeds and pay you promptly . . . but smaller stations will need a weekly statement. Some will pay you by the week and others by the month but none will take out withholding tax; set aside money for Uncle Sam yourself.

As for technical goodies, you should have a good cassette recorder . . . not one of those $39.95 jobbies. Built-in radio is unnecessary and you would be wise to replace the dainty little mike which usually comes with a tape recorder with a quality $20.00 low-impedance model. A weighted desk stand for your mike is useful for both news conferences and office interviews. Keep the recorder's heads clean and replace its batteries often. If your machine slows down in the middle of the Governor's budget message . . . .

You can spend $12.00 for an induction coil to feed audio into the phone or, for $2.00, you can make your own. Wind about 80 turns of No. 22 enameled wire onto something slightly larger in diameter than the earpiece of a telephone. I found that the plastic top from a can of roach spray did very nicely! Wrap the finished coil tightly with plastic electrical tape. Solder the leads to about three feet of "coax" (single conductor with shield) and solder the other end of the coax to a male plug which will fit the output jack of your recorder. With that done, you're well equipped to enter the field of freelance radio reporting.

The advantages of my job are numerous and obvious. I work for no boss, I deal with interesting people, I cover news which is interesting and—usually—of greater importance than that which I covered from a station newsroom, and I get the ego satisfaction of being heard on several radio stations.

I get paid too! My list of clients has now grown to eight and I've taken on a partner who works half time. I pay him with checks from the three most recent stations for which I string, and the two of us bill from $180 to $240 per week.

Some final thoughts: Much of what I've said here can be adapted to other situations. You may work for a small studio in a largish city . . . and be able to report local news of statewide interest to stations in other parts of the state. If you happen to live in a quiet area which suddenly becomes the locale for a major news story, you can use these same techniques to sell your coverage of the event.

And remember: Six months of feeding news to a list of stations is the best possible preparation should you decide to go back on a payroll. The stations you've been stringing for will be particularly good prospective employers . . . they'll know you, and their listeners will be familiar with your voice and style. You'll be selling in a one-man seller's market! ⬦

The above article originally appeared in THE MOTHER EARTH NEWS® NO. 9 . . . along with a great deal of other live-better-for-less and self-sufficiency how-to information. For further information about the magazine—and other books and periodicals devoted to home businesses, self-sufficiency, and related subjects—please see page 367 of this handbook.

KITCHEN DOLLARS

Check out the "old" money in any big city or small town on this continent and you'll find that many are the family businesses (and, sometimes, fortunes!) based on grandma's walnut cake, Uncle Joe's barbecue sauce, or some other such "secret" food formulation.

Perhaps that's why so many would-be entrepreneurs dream about building a going enterprise [1] around something that he or she—or other members of the family—can produce right in a house or apartment kitchen but [2] which becomes so popular that the production of its specialty must soon be moved to a "real" bakery or professional food factory.

And this age-old longing for "a little food business of my own" is *not* dying. If anything, it has enjoyed a renewed life during the past few years as more and more people have turned to "natural" and "organic" diets . . . thereby creating an expanding demand for such foods.

In this section you'll learn how one young couple in British Columbia cashed in on this trend on a very small scale and how two dynamic California partners have tapped the market in a much bigger way. You'll also find that both of the described operations have been conceived, set up, and run with far more than mere monetary profits in mind. Which is exactly as it should be with any self-employment venture. If all you intend to work for is money, there's plenty of "regular" jobs (even in this time of high unemployment) already waiting downtown. ◖

MICHELE SEVIN:
HOW TO START
YOUR OWN
NATURAL
CANDY
FACTORY

Did you ever dream, as a child, of living in your own candy factory? Well, Michael and I did it! And then we made that childhood fairy tale become a grown-up moneymaker when we invented a health candy—Almond Date Balls—and distributed our product successfully to natural food stores throughout British Columbia.

It all started one rainy, dreary evening when I timidly brought home a small box of coconut-covered date rolls which had caught my fancy at the local supermarket. ("Timidly" because we were out of work and Michael had said, "We can't afford treats.") My thrifty husband tasted the candies anyhow, and grudgingly admitted that they were good. "But man, it's really a gyp!" he added. "You can get a whole *pound* of dates for 31¢ and this smidgen in fancy wrapping costs 75¢." He stalked off moodily.

Next evening, when I attempted to enter the kitchen, Michael shouted, "No, no, don't come in here. This is to be a surprise." Reluctantly I acquiesced and waited—full of suspense—in the living room. Finally he appeared, eyes gleaming triumphantly, with two steaming bowls of creamy dates the consistency of pudding. It was fantastic, and with the addition of some sunflower seeds (my insight) the date surprise tasted even better.

The following evening I took a hand in the fixings. This time we tried shaping the soft, creamy dates into balls and rolling them in coconut . . . simple and delicious. So delighted were we with our sortie into the world of candymaking that each night from then on found us deep in further confectionary explorations. Soon we were happily (and inexpensively) making date candy balls—adding and mixing new toppings each time—for special occasions and friends' birthday presents.

Later—when we were expecting a visit from my parents, whom we hadn't seen for a year—our preparations again included the making of date candy balls . . . with two notable refinements: mixing cinnamon in with the dates and adding an almond on top. Here's how we did it:

THE BASIC ALMOND DATE BALL RECIPE

4 pounds pitted dates (loose or broken up)
1 cup water (1/4 cup per pound of dates)
1 teaspoon ground cinnamon
Almonds (unblanched)
Sunflower Seeds (hulled, unroasted, unsalted)
Poppy Seeds
Sesame Seeds
Granola (preferably homemade)
Coconut (medium ground)

Bring the water to a boil and add the cinnamon. Drop in the dates and cover the pan with a heavy lid. After a minute or two, turn off the heat and let the pot sit for about five minutes or until the fruit inside is soft. Then purée the dates with a potato masher (or cream them in a blender) until they're smooth.

When the date mixture is cool enough to handle—the cooler it is, the less sticky—scoop out a small amount, shape it into a ball, and place an almond on top. Then roll the morsel in a bowl filled with sunflower, poppy or sesame seeds, and granola or coconut. (Other toppings to try are ground peanuts, wheat bran, or wheat germ . . . or, for an extra-special treat, mix peanut butter or tahini with the dates before coating them.)

We've found that the candies stay fresh for a month at room temperature, or much longer if refrigerated.

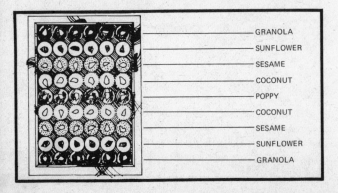

GRANOLA
SUNFLOWER
SESAME
COCONUT
POPPY
COCONUT
SESAME
SUNFLOWER
GRANOLA

My parents were thrilled with our inventiveness and throughout their stay they never stopped telling us how good the candies were. When they left, they asked to take a box with them (for the family back home).

In the days that followed the folks' visit, we thought a lot about how we could find work that would harmonize with our free-spirited lifestyle. Then one morning Michael went off early . . . and returned a while later laden with 20 packages of dates and bagfuls of almonds, coconut, granola, and assorted goodies. "Are you nuts? What's all this for?" I exclaimed, flabbergasted.

Michael, however, had an idea and got right to work on it. For a few days we lived with dates and bowls of coconut, sesame seed, poppy seed, and whatever all over the place. Finally it was finished: ten pounds of Almond Date Balls, neatly boxed. When we took this first "production run" to a friend who ran a natural foods restaurant, he said he'd be happy to sell them for us. So we arranged the balls on an oval plate near the cash register . . . and, to our delight, almost every customer left the restaurant with one in his hand (or mouth!).

Then we went into business! We found that we could buy 70 pounds of pitted Iranian dates from a wholesale bakery supplier at a very low price ($14.00) . . . and could also get coconut, almonds, poppy seeds, and cinnamon from the same source. At first Michael made his own boxes but soon found that 54 balls fit very nicely in the bottom of a Continental Yogurt carton (cut down with a razor knife).

To pack our candies, we covered the bottom of a box with paper toweling and arranged nine rows of different flavors, six pieces to a row. After some trial and error, we finally came upon a very attractive display: We placed granola-coated balls at both ends of a box, followed by sunflower, then sesame, then coconut, and finally poppy in the center. The single dark row stood out well against the white of the coconut. We then taped a piece of clear plastic wrap over the top of the package to keep the candies clean and fresh . . . and voilà, the box was finished.

Finally, we inserted a homemade sign, supported on colored toothpicks, into the side of each box, and set off with our product to the various health food stores all around Vancouver. When we entered a shop we simply held out the candies. Invariably the salesperson oohed and aahed: "Oh!

Doesn't that look *good*!"

Almond Date Balls, in fact, sold themselves. Our market soon expanded to include the university, an avant-garde cinema, an herb shop, and some local groceries . . . and before long Michael and I couldn't make enough to meet the demand.

Success, however, brought one minor hang-up: sheer bulk. Each box of 54 balls weighed about three and a half pounds. That gets heavy in large numbers, and the soft candies crush and damage easily . . . so we soon purchased a used Volkswagen bus to make our deliveries.

Here's how the finances worked out: Almond Date Balls retailed at 15¢ apiece, the stores bought them from us at 10¢, and each ball cost us a little less than 3¢ to make (not including labor, or distribution expenses such as gasoline). In other words, every box sold, wholesale, for $5.40 and brought us $4.00 gross profit on our material cost. The average shop took two batches at a time, although some would buy as many as five or more.

We generally used up a whole 70-pound carton of dates in one week and turned out about 25 boxes of Almond Date Balls. The same amount of candy also required around seven pounds of almonds, three of coconut, three of sesame seeds, four of sunflower seeds, and one and a half of poppy seeds.

The following is an approximate breakdown of costs of ingredients per pound *(. . . as of winter 1973 and you know what's been happening to food prices between then and now.—MOTHER.):*

dates	$ .21	per lb.
almonds (single most expensive ingredient) . .	1.25	"	"
cinnamon (goes a long way)	1.50	"	"
coconut	.35	"	"
sunflower seeds	.60	"	"
sesame seeds	.65	"	"
poppy seeds	.70	"	"

We also spent 70¢ for a box of clear plastic wrap, and the same amount for two rolls of designed paper toweling, about every three weeks.

Counting the time required for setting up and cleaning up, you can figure about one hour's work per box (that's approximately $4.00 gross profit per hour) . . . or five work hours per day for five days per 70 pounds of dates. Then, on the sixth day, all 25 boxes are piled in the van for delivery, and the seventh day is one of rest. So, for five hours' daily work (at one's own convenience) at home or on the back lawn—and one day of toting boxes—the candymaker has earned $100. That's minus the cost of transportation . . . which we never considered, for delivery time was always shopping time with us. While we sold our candies at the natural food stores, we did our marketing there too!

Another advantage of the candy business is that it needn't confine you to one location. When summer came around, we prepared a large batch of the balls, packed it in three big plastic buckets with tight lids (recycled bakery supply containers), and took the containers along on an extended holiday camping trip to the Okanagan . . . B.C.'s fruit-growing region. All the other ingredients proved equally adaptable to travel: Large plastic bags held the coatings, and the boxes, plastic rolling bowls, wooden spoons, and wrapping materials packed neatly into the back of the van.

Whenever we found a nice public campsite—preferably with water nearby—and the weather was warm and sunny, we'd stop and make our candies on the grass or at a picnic table. Michael would scoop out some dates from a bucket and place an almond on top, and I would roll the ball in a bowl of poppy seed, coconut, or whatnot and place it neatly in the already cut and prepared box.

We had no trouble selling Almond Date Balls on the way. In fact, that's how we paid for our trip and the wonderful fruit on which we feasted all summer. Once we came upon an outdoor crafts and pleasure fair and set up a little table of our own. People were delighted to watch and sample . . . and, since we didn't have to pay any commission to a store, all the profit was ours. By the end of just one day our pockets were jingling merrily.

This is the first time we've told the Almond Date Ball story in its entirety. You see, we're not in the candy business anymore, but have suddenly and unexpectedly become freelance writers. With luck, maybe we'll be back to give you news of that scene . . . and by then we may, just as suddenly and unexpectedly, be doing something else again. ●

The above article originally appeared in THE MOTHER EARTH NEWS® NO. 29 . . . along with a great deal of other live-better-for-less and self-sufficiency how-to information. For further information about the magazine—and other books and periodicals devoted to home businesses, self-sufficiency, and related subjects—please see page 367 of this handbook.

CAROL STAUDACHER:
MAKING IT IN
A NATURAL
FOODS
BAKERY

"It's like we created something good, and it's *such* a good thing we can't let it go," says Gary Bascou.

The good thing that Gary and his partner, Rich Josephson, have created is a fine natural foods bakery, Staff of Life, in Santa Cruz, California.

"To be able to do a business trip and something of social value at the same time is rewarding," Rich states. "The bakery was an ongoing business when we bought it, although it had already changed hands three times because of disorganization. We paid $1,500 for the entire operation which included a retail store, storage space, and a bakery that covered only 750 square feet altogether."

Neither Rich nor Gary, who both have degrees in anthropology, had any previous experience in the baking field. Armed with their strong belief that people should eat only nutritious fare instead of chemical-laden non-foods such as white bread, they began their business.

"We tasted foods that were supposed to be healthful, but they were dry and bland," Gary explains. "So we slanted our whole business toward making an honest product that not only was totally nourishing but *tasted* good too."

Staff of Life now produces over sixteen different kinds of bread. Some of the most intriguing are sourdough buckwheat rye, mixed sprouted bean, sesame whole wheat challah (egg bread), and vegetable herb. The basic flour for all the blends is freshly stone ground from organic whole wheat and no sugar, no white flour, no hydrogenated fats, no preservatives, and no artificial food coloring is used.

Gary and Rich's apple bread, for instance, contains the following ingredients: freshly stone ground, organic whole wheat flour; organic apple juice, pulp, and pieces; filtered water; pure honey; expeller pressed crude safflower oil; organic date pieces; sunflower seeds; yeast; naturally dried sea salt; and cinnamon. With all these makin's it's not surprising that a loaf of apple bread weighs one and a half pounds!

In the beginning, none of the people at Staff of Life had any knowledge of large-quantity baking techniques. "A number of the pastry girls were excellent home cooks . . . and they picked up the mass skills as they went along," Rich explains. "Mostly they just scaled up small tasty recipes to larger proportions. First they tried the ingredients at ten times the original recipe, then twenty times, and so on. The final product was tested at each level to see if it tasted right. With bread, for instance, the thing that's most important is that the texture be the same whether you're making one loaf or a hundred."

The pastries which developed from this technique were many: carob brownies, dream bars, mock pecan pie, maple butter cookies, eggless sunflower cookies, seven kinds of macaroons, and a variety of fruit cobblers.

Rich Josephson always checks the weight of Staff of Life's loaves.

The bakery's popular orange walnut cookies wholesale for 12 cents each and have the following ingredients: organic whole wheat flour, honey, malt syrup, date syrup, fertile eggs, organic oranges, walnuts, pure vanilla extract, Royal Baking Powder, and naturally dried sea salt.

"It's impossible," Rich explains, "to buy *all* organic ingredients. When we started out, for instance, natural oil was unobtainable. Now, finally, we're able to get natural safflower oil. We filter all our water to take out the impurities. In place of sugar we use date syrup and raisin syrup (which we get from Henrietta Ranch in Fresno, California), Red Star Maple Syrup, unsulfured Grandma's Molasses, and honey from a private supplier. The molasses is the most nutritional of all the sugar substitutes."

"When we can't find what we need in an organic form we at least use unrefined ingredients," Gary explains. "On the other hand, sometimes an organic ingredient is available but at a prohibitive price, which means we have to go with something of lesser quality so as not to pass the high cost on to the consumer."

Rich and Gary try to aim their products toward the new-type, funky, natural food stores. But how do they get into these stores to begin with, and *how* do they sell $5,000 worth of Staff of Life products each week? The two partners simply visit the stores themselves with a sample box containing three kinds of bread, some granola, and some pastry. "Everything we make is tasty," says Rich. "We take a loaf of bread, the store owner opens it, samples it . . . and the product sells itself."

Gary points out that bread is most easily used for comparison. That is, there is a tremendous difference between a good loaf and a bad one. "We get a lot of older folks who come in to buy our bakery products and say, 'I haven't had bread like this since I came from Europe.'"

Fifteen percent of Staff of Life's business is done in retail sales right from the bakery, and 85% of the operation's turnover is wholesale. Other than being listed in the Yellow Pages of the telephone book, Gary and Rich have never used any advertising. However, Staff of Life products do make it up and down the highways from Marin County to Carmel, California. San Francisco is the biggest sales area of all, with Berkeley and Carmel running second and third.

Rich tells of a friend who recently "developed two

excellent routes for the bakery. He gets twenty percent off and does his own trucking. The guy now services about thirty stores along with some colleges and universities that've begun carrying our products in cafeterias and snack bars."

Each delivery route is serviced once a week. Bread will keep a minimum of seven days on the shelf, and some types will last up to two weeks. "But we cannot live by bread alone," Rich points out. "If that was all we tried to sell, we'd go out of business in a hurry. Bread is a foot in the door to get you inside, but you can't survive on it. Pastry makes more of a profit because the unit you sell it _in_ is so much smaller in proportion to what you sell it _for_. It's more of a luxury item," explains Rich. "Prices for pastry and breads vary according to the ingredients. Most pastries wholesale for from 12 to 17 cents each while our breads usually wholesale for from 50 to 65 cents."

"In the baking trade you should get three times the cost of the products in your wholesale price." That, explains Gary, is the baker's rule of thumb. One-third of the cost should be for ingredients, one-third for payroll, and one-third for distribution and profit or loss (because of spoilage of products).

Gary and Rich like to sell to the consumer in bulk since individual packaging is often just as expensive (or more so) than the ingredients for their products. The two bakers distribute their pastries in cake boxes but, of course, do individually label and cellophane wrap their bread. The Food and Drug Administration closely inspects those labels to make sure they're accurate and meet FDA requirements.

Regular inspections come also from the County Health Department, although Josephson is quick to point out that the officials involved have never hassled the bakery. "Health inspectors haven't come down on us for _who_ we are," states Rich. "And they've never asked us to do anything that was unreasonable. They give us enough time to take care of things."

Before opening the doors, a bakery must first pass sanitary requirements . . . then a business license may be issued. The cost of this varies according to area . . . Staff of Life paid $30.00 for theirs.

Another necessary business-type need that had to be filled was insurance . . . product liability, accident, workmen's compensation, and fire and auto coverage.

Gary takes care of the bookkeeping, but he and Rich use a

Satisfied patrons heartily agree that natural foods can be delicious.

Certified Public Accountant for the taxes and accounting. "I would advise a CPA for any new business," Rich says. "It's worth it. In the beginning we were selling cookies for 13 cents apiece, and they were costing us more than that to make. We were into creative baking and weren't doing much with the business aspect of it. Our CPA made us realize that we had a problem. He took a look at the books and told me, 'Hey man, your ratios are off. You'll be in the red in about two months.' We were. We realized then that we had to analyze our costs and adjust our prices."

None of the employees are union workers, and the bakery uses alternative trucking as opposed to union carriers. Rich defines that aspect of the operation as, "Hip people who have trucks and use them to supply natural food stores with merchandise."

After two and a half years of owning Staff of Life, Rich and Gary are able to meet all their bills and pay themselves each a salary of $75.00 a week. "We're not into making a lot of money," says Gary, "but we *do* want to make a living." They pay their twenty-four employees anywhere from $1.85 to $3.00 an hour. The top wage goes to an engineer who keeps everything running: electricity, gas, refrigeration. "If he doesn't know how to fix it, he reads a book and learns how," Rich says.

"Four or five people walk into the bakery every day and ask for work," according to Gary, "and we hire only those who have good energy and good vibrations. If you employ a dud, it drags you down. When hiring, we'll talk to a person for half an hour and try to pick up vibrations. We want someone who has a feeling of what we're trying to do. He must want more than just a job."

Every few months the folks at Staff of Life have a general meeting . . . basically a potluck dinner with wine and a rap session. "The people can get out any bad feelings, criticisms, or comments they need to make. We get everything out in the open and cleared up that way," says Rich.

Rich and Gary are both so enthusiastic about their successful effort to create "just good food" that they intend to stay with it awhile. "We're so totally involved in the undertaking that it's impossible to put a time limit on our activities. I might want to do this for the next twenty years," says Rich. Consumers who have tasted Staff of Life products think that's a good idea! ●

A RECIPE

For your very own down-home cooking enjoyment you can try this "just good food" Staff of Life recipe.

EGGLESS SUNFLOWER SEED COOKIES

1/2 cup safflower oil
1/4 cup honey
1 teaspoon vanilla
Dash salt
1 cup sunflower seeds
1 cup whole wheat flour

Mix first five ingredients well. Add 1 cup whole wheat flour and mix until *just* blended. Dip out by teaspoon onto waxed baking sheet and flatten into rounds. Wet hands with water as necessary. Bake at 350° F for 8 to 10 minutes, or until golden brown.

The above article originally appeared in LIFESTYLE! NO. 2 . . . along with a great deal of other live-better-for-less and self-sufficiency how-to information. For further information about the magazine—and other books and periodicals devoted to home businesses, self-sufficiency, and related subjects—please see page 367 of this handbook.

SPARE ROOM CASH

"We've got a spare room (or basement or garage) we don't use. Can you tell me of any little businesses that my family could operate out of that space? We're not really looking for a fortune . . . but we do need to pick up a few extra dollars every week to help us with today's high cost of living."

If I've received one letter like the above since founding THE MOTHER EARTH NEWS®, I've received a thousand. It sometimes seems that half the families in North America are looking for a way to wring some welcome bucks out of an otherwise unused back room.

Well, the very nature of that spare room usually rules out woodworking, welding, and dozens of other "dirty" but profitable moneymaking ventures. And such "artsy" crafts as ceramics and the manufacture of "gift" items— while clean enough to set up anywhere—are a glut on the market.

Henry L. Farr, however, has come up with a very acceptable craft—the repair of tents, tarps, sleeping bags, and other sewed outdoor equipment—that is both neat and profitable and which makes an ideal "back room business". And Mary Anne Underwood and Virginia Schmitz are anxiously waiting to give you a crash course in the establishment and operation of a home upholstery enterprise.

Either undertaking is easier to master than you probably think, can be satisfyingly profitable, and allows you to schedule your time as you see fit. ●

HENRY L. FARR:

THERE'S GOLD IN THEM THAR TWILLS

In the cloudy May chill of the greenhouse shed, my neighbor Don Harris pushed a finger at the big rust blob on the frame of his cultivator—new last year—and aimed a kick at the corroded engine.

"One season," the young gardener growled. "Just one season. And now . . . $600 shot." He snatched up the cover—blown from the farm machine by winter gusts—and balled it in his fists. "If only I'd had some tiedown cords!"

As Don poured out this calamity to me over our property fence, I thought of the many damaged tarps and the bags and covers with torn straps or missing grommets I'd seen around farms and homes. Why, in my own attic I had a gashed brown leather satchel awaiting repairs. And then the idea came to me: Why not salvage some of these objects and make myself a dollar doing it?

Days later, I was in New York City selecting a rebuilt industrial-type sewing machine . . . a Singer, Model 31-15, with a new motor and work board and a price tag of $135 cash or $15.00 per month rental. (I ended up trying it a month, then paying off the balance.)

"This machine will take most any canvas and all the new fabrics," the dealer boasted, "and you can use bulge-eye, diamond, or ball-point needles. We'll teach you to run it in half an hour." He beckoned a woman from the inner stacks. With her guidance, I pushed lightweight fabric under the presser foot and learned to change threads, stitch roll piping, and make curved seams. I practiced changing needles, too, because I broke two of them during the instruction.

After this lesson I bought a starting supply of findings . . . small essentials such as threads, pipings, laces, and remnants. A collection of rayons, twills, leathers, and vinyls—plus canvas which I had to buy at a specialty store—finished my shopping, apart from some tools and fittings which I ordered later by mail. (See my note on "Supplies and Information".)

Back home in our big old house, I started my mending business in a spare bedroom by setting up my Singer on a half sheet of plywood. The slab was supported by two carpenter's horses that I built myself, and I solved the weight and vibration problems by anchoring the sewing machine right through the tabletop and into one of the sawhorses. After a couple of evening sessions and some direction from my wife, I was ready to take orders.

My first jobs came simply from talking with friends. Soon, however, I found more ways to make my services known: I took out a weekly one-inch display ad in the local paper and formed the habit of leaving two business cards wherever I stopped. Later—in the fall and again in spring—I had boys deliver and spread around bunches of big, splashy handbills that urged potential customers to bring in their work before the rush. And these days, now that I've got my hand in, I have several sets of before-and-after photos of difficult jobs I've done which I use to great advantage to prove the quality of my work.

Back there at the start, of course, some of the orders that turned up in response to my advertising were trickier than I'd bargained for or called for supplies I hadn't foreseen.

I was a bit alarmed, for instance, when—very early in my venture—a friend drove into the yard and unloaded armfuls of damaged and worn summer-camp equipment: [1] a torn green canvas partition about three feet wide in need of hanger hooks . . . which I didn't have on hand, [2] a beat-up yellow boat cover fitted with No. 5 grommets . . . which I also didn't have, [3] two tent flies, one too far gone for salvage, and [4] a ripped hammock that could be mended but not by a beginner. And—as if those repairs weren't demanding enough—the camper then ordered a cover for a government-surplus telescope on a stand and two long, blue nylon duffels with zippers and hand straps.

When items like that hammock first came in I was glad that I had set up a "farm jobber" . . . an established firm that had agreed to do jobs for me on a 50% commission basis when the work was too big for my equipment or beyond my skill. If you want to go into the mending business yourself, I'd strongly recommend such an arrangement.

Even though some of the initial orders were too tall for me, I soon found that plenty of work came my way . . . mostly, I believe, because inflation and high prices have made people think "repair and save" instead of "discard and buy new". The result is that many folks like my camper friend bring in damaged items which have long lain stashed away for want of grommets, straps, and repairs.

Organizations, too, are watching their budgets these days, and churches and clubs quickly became good customers. In fact, my first rug repair was done for the local Elks: I stitched a heavy maroon binding around a nine-foot circular piece from the club's reception hall and finished two long runners with green trim. Then, later—when I pointed to rust in the oven of a range in the Baptist church and explained that a boot would stop most of it—the pastor's wife was sold and ordered "a good big drape to keep out the wet".

I've landed repair jobs with businesses, too, by showing the owners how I can help them do their work easier, faster, and cheaper. (Of course, I study the situation ahead of time, check the materials I'll need, and think out what questions and excuses the proprietor may have so I'll be ready with good answers.)

In my experience, people not only want to repair or prevent damage but are willing to pay well for work that increases their comfort and convenience. For instance, a lot of covers, straps, boots, bags, and holders are made so skimpily that they're too tight or short. Many lack handholds and tie cords, also, or have too few grommets set too far apart. The owners are often pleased to have these faults corrected.

Along with normal repairs of this kind, I've had some pretty unlikely orders . . . like the time an official car pulled up in my driveway. "Got a monkey out here," called a policeman friend. "The carnival people needed a special job, and I thought of you." A showman climbed out of the car with a cinnamon-striped animal on his shoulder and carried it into the basement, where—after some measuring and cutting— we soon had a harness basket made up for the little performer.

Another unusual request—and one I remember a little sadly—came from an elderly pastor who brought in an old white felt banner. "Here's a gold and silver flag I used to carry in Sunday school parades," he explained. "Can you repair it?"

Unfortunately, I couldn't. The long streamer, from a forgotten temperance society, was too fragile to hold even the softest threads of smooth yarn. The retired minister folded the banner under his arm and left.

Such "missions impossible" aren't common, though, and most of the skills I needed to repair normal equipment came with practice. The dealer had already shown me all I needed to know about the sewing machine, and my other materials came with full directions. Also, the tools I ordered arrived with diagrams and explanations which I tore off the cartons and tacked up near my work table.

Even so, I made mistakes. For example, one of my early jobs was to punch grommets into the hems of a Boy Scout kitchen fly. That seemed easy enough, but the first wind tore down the cover . . . because, instead of punching directly into

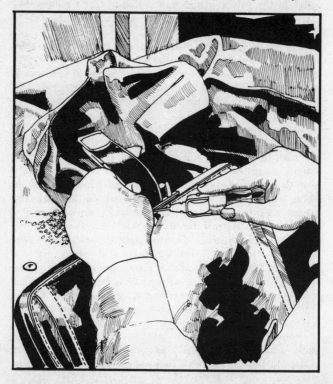

the edges, I should have stitched a 4" X 4" fabric reinforcement above and below each grommet piece. That's the sort of thing one finds out only by experience, so—if you go into the repair business yourself—don't let your early errors get you down.

What I learned from the Boy Scout incident was especially important because—apart from patching—most fabric repairs are concerned with eyelets and grommets. The former are those metal "holes" (as my grandson calls them) which are pressed into cloth to take laces and cords. To install one, I simply pierce or punch the material in the right place. Then I fit an eyelet into the inexpensive tool that's made for this purpose, shove the gadget into the hole, and press down.

Grommets—the heavier eyelets that protect perforations in tough materials—are set in rather the same way. First I puncture the cloth with a hammer and a little tool that comes

with the metal parts . . . or I sometimes use a leatherworker's "wheel" punch. Then I place the toothed half of the grommet, teeth up, on the small anvil (also part of the kit) and press the fabric down on top. Finally I add the grommet's smooth ring

SUPPLIES AND INFORMATION FOR THE FABRIC REPAIR BUSINESS

If you decide to start your own repair shop, an excellent Government publication—*Starting and Managing a Small Business* by Ralph Metcalf—is available for $1.35 from the U.S. Government Printing Office, Washington, D.C. 20402. You might also order SBA Bulletin No. 115-A, *Free Management Publications*, from the Small Business Administration, 1441 L Street, Washington, D.C. 20416.

You can ask Sun Chemical Corp., 185 Sixth Ave., Paterson, N.J. 07524 for sample swatches and materials . . . or for questions about leather, write *Make It With Leather* magazine, P.O. Box 1386, Fort Worth, Texas 76101 and request the address of the nearest branch of Tandy Leather Company.

I buy my tools and large metals from the Barco Co., P.O. Box 25459, Los Angeles, Calif. 90025.

From MOTHER'S General Store, P.O. Box 506, Flat Rock, N.C. 28731, I bought a $2.25 sewing awl with detachable needles . . . the only tool for reaching hard places in golf bags and suitcases. The same company can provide a Tapex riveter for $15.50 and a package of various sized rivets.

After a nasty fire in a canvas bag factory I picked up a salvaged sewing machine . . . but I still hold on to my 31-15.

and give it a bang with the punch . . . and there it is, a finished-looking permanent job.

Grommets come in various sizes, and normally a separate punch is needed for each. Therefore, when I noticed that business was getting good, I invested $50.00-plus in a Barco Model 9307, which takes several sizes of grommets and snap fasteners. The tool rapidly paid for itself.

Where holes for lacing can't be fitted in, gripper snaps are used to close fabric. I started out with a $2.00 Clinton Gripper set which has special seven-inch-long pliers, a supply of fifty No. 104 eyelets in several colors, six pairs of fasteners, and a small die that is placed in the pliers' jaws for this work.

Other fastenings—like D's and large hooks and eyes—are attached by turning over a corner of the material and cross-stitching it with sail cord . . . or, if the item isn't to be placed near a corner or the edge, I use a strip of the fabric to hold the piece of hardware on.

As you can see from what I've told you, this sort of operation isn't very difficult, and such work used to be a popular home business. As recently as 10 or 12 years ago several people in my community were handling leather, canvas, briefcase, porch cover, sling, and sail repair. Today, though, there's not a single person besides me who'll take that kind of mending.

"People are too fussy," says my own shoe repairman. "And these new fabrics . . . well, I just can't keep up with 'em." He'll do an occasional job on his machines for me, but not for the public. Of course, this lack of competition is one reason why I find that the work comes in quite handily. In fact, business is so good these days that I've discontinued my newspaper ad!

As for the money, I average between $2.00 and $3.00 per hour and usually get in about two hours when I spend an evening on repair work. A neighbor boy helps me with grommeting and makes deliveries.

My spare bedroom enterprise has now spilled over into the basement, my customers seem to be satisfied (no complaints so far), and the future looks pretty good up our way. So, if you're like me—hate waste and don't mind a bit of extra money—why not give the fabric repair business a whirl?●

The above article originally appeared in LIFESTYLE! NO. 4 . . . along with a great deal of other live-better-for-less and self-sufficiency how-to information. For further information about the magazine—and other books and periodicals devoted to home businesses, self-sufficiency, and related subjects—please see page 367 of this handbook.

MARY ANNE UNDERWOOD: OUR FAMILY UPHOLSTERY BUSINESS

Although we didn't know it back then, our family's home business really began several years ago when Billy (my husband) and I upholstered some of our own furniture to save money. Friends and relations saw the results and were soon asking us to do pieces for them. We felt we weren't skilled enough, but they insisted that we try . . . so, to supplement our income, I started re-covering a couch or chair now and then in my spare time.

My first tools—a claw hammer, screwdriver, scissors, and sewing machine—made for very slow progress. The living room doubled as my workshop and was always a mess. Then friends told friends about my sideline, and before long our porch was full of ragged furniture. At that point my family complained about the clutter and insisted that if I *must* do such work I was going to have to move it out of the house.

At the time, my husband owned and operated a service station . . . not very profitably, what with the nine others in town. "Well," we thought, "if there's all this furniture around just begging to be refurbished, why not sell the business and open an upholstery shop?" We purchased an old one-room house for $120 to serve as quarters for the new enterprise, and set out to get the information that would make our idea pay.

Our first step was to write the State Comptroller at Austin, Texas, requesting an application for a store license and a sales tax number. (These cost us $10.00 a year and entitled us to sell material.) Then we stopped in at a shop in Brownwood and asked the owner where he bought his fabric. A phone call to the company he named—Durotex Supply in Dallas—brought us a visit from a salesman who turned out to be most helpful and encouraging. There was a great opportunity in the upholstering business, he told us, if we would work at it. He gave us some material, vinyl sample books, and a supply list, told us which tools and findings we'd need to start with, and quoted the going rates for furniture renovation in Dallas. These seemed high to us and we adjusted the prices to a realistic level for our small town.

Our first purchase was a good secondhand commercial sewing machine and accessories ($80.00). We've since found that one essential for upholstery work is a narrow left- or right-hinged cording foot ($1.85) to form those decorative ribs you've noticed around the edges of stuffed furniture.

Actually—as we learned later—you can sew heavy fabric on any machine if you spray the seam line with a silicone friction reducer. The product (which also has many other uses) now costs $2.35 per 20-ounce can and is an economy considering the price of a new commercial sewing machine. Nevertheless, our older model has turned out to be a very good investment.

Furniture padding is often formed into tufts which are held in place by metal buttons covered with upholstery fabric. Accordingly, we bought a Handy Jr. button press and a die and cutter, with five gross of molds, at a cost of $41.15. (The same outfit would run $62.70 today.) The price of the molds and die and cutter varies with size. We chose Number 30 buttons because they're the most common and can stand in for any others that may originally have been used on a chair or couch.

Fabric can be attached to the frame of a piece with tacks or staples. We bought a used Markwell hand stapler for $7.00 (the electric and air models are too expensive for us). Later, when the price of Markwell staples rose to $5.00 per thousand, we inquired at the local lumberyard and found we could buy

Arrow staples at $2.25 per thousand in the 5/16-inch size we use. To cut expenses, we turned in 4-3/4 books of our Green Stamps for a heavy-duty Arrow staple gun kit. The staples are now running $4.10 per box, but we're still ahead of the game.

We found a tack lifter—one of our most used tools—at the hardware store for $1.40 . . . $1.79 these days. Then we ordered a good No. 160 tack hammer ($2.85 then, $4.35 now) and a wooden webbing stretcher (up from $1.20 to $2.85) from Durotex Supply. We also bought a pair of eight-inch shears, although most shops use the more expensive ten-inch length.

Our first supply order consisted of the following: 1 roll of cotton padding, 1 roll 5/32" welting cord, 1 pound No. 8 tacks, 1 pound No. 14 webbing tacks, 1 roll supertwist nylon button twine, 1 spool No. 18 nylon handstitch thread, 1 roll 1/2" tack strip, 1 roll BFM webbing, and 20 yards of black cambric. (A glance at the box with this article will give you an idea of former and current prices.) Burlap comes from the feed store in the form of sheep wool bags ($2.25 each). Unraveled and opened, they measure 40" X 128". We use King Co. spray glue ($3.50 a can) to stick pieces of foam together.

Upholstering is a trade that anyone can learn by trial and error, but I'll try to give you some idea of how the work is done.

The first step in re-covering a piece—a chair, for instance—is to take off the old fabric, beginning with the part that was applied last. This is usually the dustcover under the bottom. If there is none, start with the ruffle or the back and remove it with your tack lifter.

You'll normally find that the back section was put on at the top with a tack strip and then turned down and tacked or stapled under the bottom of the frame . . . and that's just what you'll do later when you replace it. Some chairs also have a metal tack strip down each side of the back, but this is expensive and we prefer to blindstitch the edges by hand.

After the back, the outsides of the arms come off . . . then the insides of the arms, the front of the backrest, and the seat. If you think you won't be able to remember where all the pieces go, label the parts as you remove them. Note the order of removal, too, and reverse it when you put on the new material.

As a chair is stripped of its cover, we take the cotton padding off the seat and back, retie the springs, and fit new burlap over them. This is the foundation of our upholstery job, and a sudden collapse of the underpinnings a few weeks later would be very bad for business. If the wooden parts of a piece of furniture need refinishing, we do so before we put on new material.

As a rule, a chair or couch or whatever is reassembled the same way it came apart, with new covering cut to the old pattern ... but if we come up against something we can't figure out, we call a shop in the next town and ask what to do. Our aim is to restore the article to its original condition. It gives us great satisfaction when a customer tells us that a piece of furniture looks just the way it did when he bought it new.

One of our greatest accomplishments was the restoration of an 18th-century early Victorian couch. The antique had escaped a fire with bad burns to the cover and wood. The damage was so bad that the first thing we did was tear off the old fabric and throw it away.

When we tackled the woodwork, we found that all our scraping and sanding couldn't take off the black discoloration. We tried mopping with a hot, strong lye solution (one cup lye to one gallon of water), followed by a rinse with clean water and a vinegar wash to stop the caustic from eating the wood. Traces of blackness still lingered even after that treatment, and we escalated to swabbing with full-strength bleach. Five bleach treatments later, the surface finally looked the way we wanted it to.

The customer had asked us to refinish his couch to match two early Victorian chairs we were also covering for him. We studied the color and tried to duplicate it by mixing clear varnish with a little maple stain, a little fruitwood, and a very small amount of mahogany. Then we sanded the piece again, treated it with wood filler, and applied our varnish mixture.

TWINE, TACKS, DOLLARS AND CENTS

Just like everyone else, we're feeling the rise in prices . . . especially in the cost of running our small business. Our materials and vinyls are already up 30¢ to $3.00 a yard, and on September 1, 1974 we received our new supply price list with a warning: "All prices subject to change without notice."

Here are the current costs of our most-used supplies, with the going rates back when we started our shop:

ITEM	WAS	NOW
Silicone	$1.75	$ 2.35
King Co. spray glue	2.25	3.50
5/32" vinyl welt cord	3.95	6.25
No. 18 nylon handstitch thread	1.10	1.50
Ruby spring twine, 5 pounds	5.25	11.75
24/4 sewing thread, 1-pound cone	4.10	6.00
Cotton, grade C, per pound	.20	.30
Black cambric (for dustcover), per yard	.18	.30
Arrow staples, per thousand	2.25	4.10
1/2" tack strip, per pound	.75	1.00
No. 4 tacks, per pound	.75	1.50
No. 6 and No. 8 tacks, per pound	.65	1.35
No. 10 and No. 12 tacks, per pound	.60	1.35
Burlap wool bags	1.40	2.25

The dried coating matched the chairs perfectly.

Next we installed webbing, tied the springs, added burlap and padding . . . and turned our minds to the problem of how to recreate the cover without a pattern. Our strategy was to find a picture of a similar couch in an antique book and count the tufts and channels in the elaborately upholstered backrest. Then we measured the piece we were salvaging and figured out how wide each section of its design would have to be to create the same effect. It took us one whole day just to make our calculations and draw a pattern to fit, but at last we were able to finish off our masterpiece with a cover of green antique velvet.

We made $100 on that job on top of the cost of materials . . . and our salesman told us later that in Dallas the charge for labor in restoring such an antique would have been twice as much. It's true that the prices we ask are less than we could get in a large city, but we enjoy life in a small community and prefer to raise our children away from crime and violence.

Here are some examples of our current rates for labor on various types of furniture:

Early American chair (with ruffle) $45.00
Early American couch (with ruffle). 75.00
Large overstuffed chair (without ruffle) 40.00

These figures include a recent increase to cope with the growing cost of our supplies. We used to ask $50.00 for a sofa bed, $30.00 for a studio couch with wooden arms, and $20.00 for a matching chair, but now charge $5.00 to $20.00 more depending on the findings we use.

The cost of material is figured separately. We have a selection of fabrics available through our shop and must pay a 5 percent sales tax on all we sell. If the customer doesn't buy cloth from us, we charge $2.00 extra for each yard it takes to cover his furniture (some firms levy a much higher surcharge). This payment covers necessities other than yard goods: welt cord, staples, tack strip, cotton, burlap, thread, dustcover, and cutting time. Some days we net $50.00 on labor and material.

We've come a long way in the three years since we started our business, and have learned many timesavers and shortcuts (examples are the silicone, the cording foot, and the King Co. spray glue). We've also expanded recently from just renovating furniture to making fancy seat covers for autos and watercraft, boat canopies, and snap-on protectors for the beds of pickup trucks. Another sideline is sewing gun cases, caps, and purses for customers out of the leftover scraps of their material.

People seem pleased with the quality of our service . . . so much so that customers' out-of-town friends and families now bring us pieces of furniture from as far as 200 miles away. The business has grown so that we run about a month behind (we don't want to hire extra help because it would add to our overhead and tie us down too much). Our clients say they don't mind waiting because they like our work. We had planned to expand our building, but—what with rising costs

The Underwoods run their business from this $120 cottage.

and the uncertain economic situation—have decided to wait
and see how things turn out.

Special thanks go to our salesman from Durotex Supply,
who has been more help to us than anyone else. Each time he
comes by he gives us useful pointers, and we're indebted to
him for much of our success in this business.

One thing we like about our new trade is that we can run
the shop from our home. That means no rent, utility bills, or
other overhead expenses . . . and, more importantly, we can be
with our children during the day. Billy and I enjoy our work
together. If it's a perfect day for fishing, though, we'll close
our doors and go . . . knowing that no one will complain, for
we're our own bosses. In short, we're satisfied with the
upholstery business and recommend it to anyone who wants
nearly complete control over his or her working conditions.●

*The above article originally appeared in THE MOTHER EARTH NEWS® NO. 30 . . . along
with a great deal of other live-better-for-less and self-sufficiency how-to information. For
further information about the magazine—and other books and periodicals devoted to home
businesses, self-sufficiency, and related subjects—please see page 367 of this handbook.*

VIRGINIA SCHMITZ:
HOW TO REUPHOLSTER FURNITURE

Don't let the title scare you off! Upholstery is just one more activity that's wrapped in mystery for no good reason whatsoever. Once you get past your mental block, you'll find that every piece of stuffed furniture is *made* so that the fabric can be replaced when it wears out ... and anyone with basic sewing skills and simple tools (hammer, screwdriver, pliers, staple gun) can do it. There's no need to take an expensive course, or any course at all. Your own sofa or whatever will give you all the instructions you need as you go along.

My "teacher" was an easy chair that my husband, Jim, and I bought when we were first married. It was sturdy, attractive, and very comfortable. Three children later, though, its covering had become badly soiled and worn. Professional reupholstering (we checked) would have cost more than the original price of the entire article ... fabric, frame, and all. Although we talked about doing the job at home, the chair's curved arms and deeply tufted backrest made the undertaking seem so complicated that we were afraid to try. Then the poor thing got to looking so sad that we had to choose between discarding it or tackling its renovation ourselves. So our adventures in reupholstery began.

My first move was to purchase some inexpensive dress-weight cotton material. I knew it wouldn't hold up as upholstery, but figured that if the job turned out well we could duplicate our success later in better-grade fabric. As another precaution, I bought several yards more than I estimated we needed ... with an eye to all the mistakes we were going to make.

Somewhere in the back of my mind, you see, lurked the notion that upholstery was made like a slipcover; that all the pieces were first sewed together, then pulled over the furniture, and only by some magic of professional skill did the covering fit like a glove. As we removed the old fabric from our chair, though, we were pleasantly amazed to find that it wasn't done that way at all. Instead, each section was stapled individually to the frame. This simplified matters immensely, since the only sewing necessary was the making of several darts and miters and the case for the seat cushion.

Despite our inexperience, the completed chair looked brand-new and professionally done. We had exercised care and patience to get the details right, yet the work hadn't been at all difficult. We were so proud of our masterpiece that we showed it to whomever stopped by, and soon friends and relatives were asking us to reupholster articles for them. Although we didn't earn any money by doing so, we did gain a great deal of experience with various fabrics and styles of furniture . . . enough that I feel ready to supply loose guidelines for anyone who's interested.

My first pointer is that you don't *need* guidelines, loose or otherwise . . . not really. The furniture itself, as you dismantle it, will tell you how it was made. There are no mysterious inner goings-on to confound you. Still—for those who want them—here are some suggestions:

Let's say you have a chair you want to overhaul. Start out by examining it closely. Note all details: skirt, welting, trim, buttons, etc. Poke into the seams. Are they really sewn—as they appear to be—or are they stapled or tacked? Commit the construction to memory.

Next look over the item to find the piece of fabric that should obviously come off first: usually the back or bottom. Carefully remove it by prying it loose. (Don't *rip* the cover free . . . you'll be using it later as a pattern.) If your memory isn't completely trustworthy, pin a paper on the segment of cloth to identify it as "Number One" and to remind you of its location on the chair. Then note which section ought to come off next and treat it in the same way, marking it as "Number Two, outer right side" or whatever.

Keep making notes—mental or written—on how and where the fabric is attached to the frame . . . and don't disturb the batting or stuffing beneath. Carefully smooth out any lumpy padding (this is very important if you want the finished product to look even). It's best not to remove the cushion casing unless you feel it's absolutely necessary, since the innards usually fall apart and lose their shape. Just cover right over the shabby material.

After all the ratty covering has been removed, step back and say, "Lord, what have I done?" This isn't really a necessary part of the procedure, but everyone does it on first seeing a favorite piece of furniture stripped down.

When you've recovered from the shock, you'll need new fabric to attach to your hypothetical chair. A few words about cloth at this point: Jim and I have worked with various grades, from medium-weight cottons to very heavy tapestry materials. The tapestry was beautiful, cost $14.00 a yard, and will undoubtedly last many years . . . but as far as I'm concerned, the birds can have it. Apart from the expense, the luxury textile's thickness and stiffness made it so difficult to work with that the value of increased wearability was negated.

Medium-weight, softer fabrics are far less trouble to handle than heavy ones, and wear better than one might expect. Even the cheap dress cotton I used on that first chair surprised us by lasting four years. Still, it isn't easy to find a suitable pattern in ordinary yard goods, and I've settled on the more inexpensive drapery and upholstery materials as my usual first choice. Lately, though, I've thought that some of the new printed sheets would look wild on furniture. They're high-priced as bedding but would be a bargain as chair covers. Anyhow, use your own imagination.

One caution: Before you buy fabric, notice whether any parts of the old covering were cut on the bias to stretch around curves. If they were, some stripes or plaids won't look very attractive if used as replacement material.

Some people make a big point of measuring yardage so closely that not an extra inch of fabric will be left. I don't. I take loose measurements, figure on the high side, and order more cloth than I think I'll need. There's always excess material, and it never goes to waste . . . in fact, it's one of the bonuses of doing my own upholstery. For example, I had enough fabric left from my first job to make matching curtains and throw pillows: a touch that suggests interior decorators and lots of money, when in reality I spent far less than I would have for blah store-bought ready-mades.

Smaller amounts of leftover material can be used to make valances, footstools, covered wastebaskets, or what have you.

OK, back to our naked chair. Take all the pieces of old covering and flatten them out (clip open any darts or seams). Arrange the shapes on the new fabric so as to waste as little as possible, *and remember to leave an extra inch around each segment.* (If your earlier research turned up any parts that must be cut on the bias, be sure to lay them out that way.) Place the cushion itself on the yard goods and trace around it twice for top and bottom. Measure its sides for length and width and mark out a strip to fit . . . again with an inch over for a seam allowance. Cut out all the parts, and keep each old piece together with its replacement for identification purposes. Use the scraps to make welting, trim, buttons, and such.

When you apply the new material, you'll simply reverse the order in which you stripped off the sections of old covering: The last worn piece you removed from the chair will be the first new one to go back on, and so forth.

Use your heavy-duty staple gun to attach one side of the first piece of material to the chair in the same manner in which the old covering was fastened. Gently but firmly pull and stretch the cloth from the opposite direction and staple down the far border. Then secure the third side, pull gently from the free edge, and fasten it down too. This is much easier done than said . . . fortunately, because the manner in which the material is stapled and stretched across the frame is the secret of professional-looking upholstery. The covering should be taut, without sags and wrinkles, but not so tight that there's no "give" and the fabric tears. If you're not satisfied with the way things are going, remove the section and start over. Mistakes are easily corrected as they happen but impossible to fix later.

Sometimes a section of the original fabric is attached by means of a metal strip of tacks. When these are removed they usually become bent and are impossible to reuse. I'm sure they could be purchased, but we don't bother. Instead, Jim cuts a piece of cardboard the length and width of the metal strip and staples it in place (again, much more easily seen on your own article of furniture than described). If the last side of the last piece was originally fastened with such a strip, I just secure it with blindstitching.

When I cover the cushion I baste the casing first to be sure the fit is good. Then I sew it on the machine, leaving an opening in the back large enough to insert the contents, and blindstitch the slit.

After all the fabric has been replaced there may be some tiny imperfections. A few blindstitches taken here and there will eliminate these ... or you can just live with them, since you'll soon begin to notice that even brand-new furniture has minor flaws which the average person never spots.

If you want to keep such imperfections to a minimum, though, beware of shortcuts. Jim and I re-covered a chair for a friend ... who then decided to do his own sofa, but felt that our way was too much trouble. Instead, he left the original fabric in place, traced newspaper patterns from the couch itself, and stapled the new material right over the old. The result didn't reach the standard we've come to expect of our own work. Every piece of furniture is different and you must remove the covering to find out how your particular article was done ... or so, at least, it seems to me.

Another reason why Jim and I have had good results with home upholstery is that we've always worked with pieces which were basically sound and only needed fabric replaced. There's so much good furniture floating around that it isn't usually necessary to bother with something that's popping its springs. On more than one occasion we've raided the dump for perfectly usable articles which someone has discarded only because the material was soiled. (Of course, one has to get there before rains mildew the stuffing.) At garage sales, faded and worn pieces often go for a few dollars. Folks just aren't aware that they could renew the covering so easily and inexpensively.

And there you have the only course in upholstery you'll ever need. Jim and I have worked together because we like to ... but one person could go it alone. It just takes a bit longer. Love and peace! ◓

The above article originally appeared in THE MOTHER EARTH NEWS® NO. 30 ... along with a great deal of other live-better-for-less and self-sufficiency how-to information. For further information about the magazine—and other books and periodicals devoted to home businesses, self-sufficiency, and related subjects—please see page 367 of this handbook.

YOUR OWN STORE

Although a great many people tell me they'd like to have a "little home business", it's quite apparent that their *real* dream is the establishment of an actual store of some kind . . . so that the mess and hustle of the enterprise can be conveniently kept separate from where they actually live.

And, believe me, that makes a lot of sense. Although my wife and I started THE MOTHER EARTH NEWS® in our living room, we were ecstatic when—one year later—we were finally able to move the magazine's operation out of our house and into quarters almost a mile away.

For that reason, and since every business described in this portion *can* be run out of a residence if you prefer, this section is the largest one in the book. And it's packed with the "trade secrets" of quite a variety of interesting little enterprises: a rock shop, secondhand store, bicycle shop, coffeehouse, craft store, silver shop, paperback book exchange, and used-book store.

Of this selection of business possibilities, only the bicycle shop requires a "real" investment of several thousand dollars. All the others can be launched on little more than loose change, some time, a smattering of entrepreneurial sense . . . and sheer, raw guts.

The payoff? In most cases as many or as few dollars as you're willing to work for . . . plus a great deal of satisfaction, as the following authors frequently point out. ◗

GARNET

RUTILE

SMOKY QUARTZ

SO YOU WANT TO START A ROCK SHOP...OR DO YOU? MAYBE YOU'RE DREAMING INSTEAD OF A LITTLE CANDLE BUSINESS YOU CAN OPERATE OUT OF YOUR HOME...OR A LEATHER SHOP...OR YOU'VE DECIDED TO PUT YOUR PAINTING ON A PAYING BASIS...OR YOU'RE EXPECTING AN OUT-OF-PRINT BOOK SERVICE TO FINANCE YOUR BREAK FROM THE 9-TO-5 DRAG. NO MATTER. BE IT A HOME MAIL-ORDER OPERATION OR STOREFRONT EMPLOYMENT SERVICE: THE BOOKKEEPING, MANAGEMENT, BUYING, MARKUP, DISCOUNT, ZONING, CREDIT, INSURANCE, TAX, AD-VERTISING, AND OTHER PROBLEMS OF A FAMILY BUSINESS ARE MUCH THE SAME. THE METHODS THAT WORK FOR A ROCK SHOP WILL ALSO WORK FOR THE SANDAL MAKER, PET SHOP, AND HEALTH FOOD STORE...AND THE PLACE TO GET THOSE METHODS IS FROM A SUCCESSFUL SMALL SHOP PROPRIETOR.

ARTHUR E. VICTOR, ASSISTED BY HIS WIFE, LILA MAE VICTOR, IS THAT SUCCESSFUL PROPRIETOR. THE VICTORS, UNTIL THEIR RECENT SEMI-RETIREMENT, OPERATED ONE OF THE WORLD'S BETTER KNOWN "ROCK HOUND" EMPORIUMS. THEIR TWO BOOKS, *GEM TUMBLING AND BAROQUE JEWELRY MAKING*, ($2.00 AND NOW IN ITS 18TH PRINTING) AND *SO YOU WANT TO START A ROCK SHOP* ($2.00 AND IN THE 5TH PRINTING) HAVE HELPED HUNDREDS OF OTHER EN-THUSIASTS ESTABLISH THEIR OWN FLOURISHING ROCK SHOPS.

THE FOLLOWING EXCERPTS OF THE MORE GEN-ERAL INFORMATION FROM *SO YOU WANT TO START A ROCK SHOP* SHOULD HELP ANYONE START ALMOST ANY SMALL BUSINESS ON A SOUND BASIS. FOR MORE DETAILS ON THE SPECIFICS OF ESTABLISHING A ROCK SHOP, GET BOTH THE VICTORS' BOOKS FROM: THE VICTORS, 1709 SOUTH CEDAR, SPOKANE, WASH-INGTON 99203.

ARTHUR & LILA MAE VICTOR:
SO YOU THINK YOU WANT TO START A ROCK SHOP

Hundreds of thumbnail-sized rock shops start each year and hundreds of others quit or fail, but so do the "failure" rates of all businesses make dismal reading. Statistics are against success and the saddest statistical facts are that most failures could have been prevented. Poor planning, no market analysis, insufficient capital, and lack of technical knowledge are all contributing factors, but the amazing thing is that most small businessmen are not aware of their lack of "know-how". This lack of knowledge is not a sin (who among us can assert he knows *everything* about anything?). But he who knows not and knows not that he knows not is headed for serious trouble and in a hurry.

Rather than belabor the reasons for failure, let us take the positive approach. Many rock shops prosper and their proprietors are happy, contented people; some have grown to a national prominence. And to the best of our knowledge every one started in their backyard or glassed-in front porch, even as you and I.

If this little book can help you plan your enterprise or at least give you some indication of the type and kind of knowledge needed for success, it will have served its purpose.

REQUIREMENTS OF A ROCK SHOP PROPRIETOR

First is capital—money to start the enterprise, buy the stock, and carry the overhead costs—until sales develop to a point where income is greater than output. Certainly this amount will vary depending upon your particular circumstances, but there must be *some* money. Probably, five years will pass before you can take money from the business. During that time every dollar of profit will be reinvested in building up the stock and improving the shop.

Then, there is your knowledge of the lapidary field or a specific field if you intend to specialize. You should know the "jargon of the trade"—the descriptive terms needed to order supplies—and you must know what services and supplies your prospective customers will expect you to carry in stock. You must know something about business methods, bookkeeping, stock control, and profit and loss statement. This bookkeeping knowledge is readily available to you and can be easily acquired, but the technical "know-how" is not standardized and is not available except by long and patient digging, and we mean literally and figuratively.

Let us "personalize" this technical knowledge point by applying it to your own activities. Suppose you are a first-class machinist (or an accountant or printer or almost any occupation) and you have your own little shop. Your friend drops in and says something like this: "I have sold insurance for thirty years but I have always wanted a nice little shop like this. I have saved a few bucks. What do you think about me starting a little shop like yours?"

Hobby shops and rock shops in particular are unlike any

other long-established retail stores. Rock hounds are not in a class with the person who tries every shoe in the shop for an hour or so and suddenly says, "It has quit raining, I can get out on the street now." The infinite variety and the creative artistry of our rock hobby results in what we might call "slow selling". The absorbing interest often results in much delightful conversation with low dollar volume of sales.

So check your own personal characteristics . . . your temperament. Do you like to visit? Do you enjoy meeting new people? When you meet a stranger can you think of something to say that will put him at ease and start him talking? Can you be genuinely interested while Joe Blow tells you for an hour how he found that big geode up on Red Top, and all the while there are a stack of orders to fill, letters to be answered, a dozen rings to set, etc., etc., and dear Joe, thrilled at his find, rambles on and on?

How about the other members of the family? Most little shops are a husband-and-wife operation. Is the "other half" interested and willing to work, and will you both be content to be "tied down" with a shop?

You must establish regular and consistent open hours for the store. If you "live in the back of the shop" these open hours will not deter your rock hound friends from dropping in at all hours of the day or night.

LOCATION AND SIZE

The ideal situation would be to select an area containing a multitude of potential customers and set your little shop in the most accessible spot. For most of us that will not be possible or practical. The shop location is already established. Maybe we are starting in the family home; perhaps only one building is available in our end of town. As a result of this fixed location we must depend upon customers available to that location. Your original investment may seem small and because of this you may think that failure will not hurt very much. Once you are committed the "returning will be as tedious as the going over". The general tendency in small inexperienced businesses is to attempt to bolster an unprofitable venture with more and more resources until the drain becomes a catastrophic financial loss and the resulting failure a terrible blow to the pride.

There is nothing standardized about this rock business. If

you wanted to start a drugstore, pages of statistics are available. Experience has shown that a given number of people in a trade area spend so many dollars per year at a drugstore. Divide that figure by the number of drugstores and one has a rough idea of what to expect in gross sales. There will be figures available concerning density of traffic, car traffic, and buying habits. Nothing approaching this type of information is available for a rock shop. You are on your own when making a market analysis for your shop. If you were contemplating starting a shop you must, of necessity, have planned to sell

something to somebody. All right, who are they—is it the
100-200-300-500 rock hounds in the trade area, and how big is
this trade area? Will your customers be tourists or a circle of
friends? Will your customers come from immediate areas or
from all over town or even perhaps from the surrounding
countryside? Is your place of business easily accessible to these
customers? Can they find it easily? Maybe you plan to make
up and sell finished jewelry. What and where are these
potential customers now buying? Or are you going to fill a
need not now supplied by anyone? Are there competing shops
in your trade area? Suppose you are able to compete
successfully and divide the customers with your competition . . . is there enough business for all shops or will your
opening develop a session of cutthroat competition and, as a
result, no one making a profit? Or do you anticipate a growing
market with room for all to expand?

ZONING ORDINANCE

Find out about zoning ordinances. If starting in your
residence, you may discover restrictive regulations as to type,
size, and character of business permitted. There will be
limitation on signs and outdoor displays.

MANAGEMENT

Many books have been written about business management.
Entire college courses are designed as business administration.
We can only hope to stimulate your interest and outline a few
basic principles. Your success will be based upon a combination of knowledge and skills plus a little luck and much
common sense. One important bit of knowledge is an
awareness of your limitations and the will to seek help and
accept guidance.

Do not be reluctant or afraid to seek competent advice. The
Small Business Administration has a Service Corps of Retired
Executives. As the name implies, these are successful businessmen who have retired, but who wish to help others. They
volunteer their services at no cost to help other small
businessmen with management problems. A call or letter to
your nearby Small Business Administration office might
provide you with a local experienced businessman to discuss
your plans for starting or problems that may disturb you after
you are in business.

STOCKING

Your first managerial decisions have dealt with the establishment of the shop, probable growth, your own ability, and capital available. Now use the market analysis to determine the kind and size of stock you will need. This will be modified by what you have on hand as an accumulation of years of hobby activity and will certainly be controlled by the amount of money you want to invest (or risk) in this new venture. Set up an account and list all the shelves, showcases, office machines, tools, signs . . . everything in the shop that is not "merchandise for sale". Add to this the cash you intend to invest . . . this will be your capital account.

Make another inventory of all merchandise for sale. Figure this on cost or market value, whichever is the lower. To this inventory add everything you buy for sale and subtract everything you sell. Note that you have two inventories, one for items not for sale and another for those items that are for sale. Keep these separate because at income tax time they will have entirely different effects on profits and depreciation figures.

The amount of goods you buy will be governed by the amount of money you have to invest, the stock on hand when you started, and the estimate of sales volume as determined from your market analysis. No one but you can make the decisions. No two situations will be identical, but here is a good point to determine if you have something in which you can excel in offering to the public. Try to find some "specialty" that you can advertise as unique to your shop. Henry Kaiser said of his success: "Find a need and fill it." Gauge your stock both as to quality and variety to fill a need of your expected customers.

From your market analysis you have estimated gross sales and decided upon the kind of variety of merchandise needed. You also have an estimate of the overhead operating expense . . . and don't forget you must maintain your living expenses too. (One rock shop proprietor advised us to say, "For the first three years there must be two incomes . . . one to live on and one to support the shop.")

BUYING

All your life you have been buying as a consumer or an investor. Now you are buying for immediate resale at a profit (you hope) and an entirely new type of consideration is required. As a merchandiser you must sell your stock and buy more stock and sell that and buy more, each time taking your markup as gross profit. Thus the more times you "turn your stock", the more profit on the original investment.

Let us illustrate how important this idea of turnover becomes, especially if you have only limited capital. Suppose you use $75.00 of capital money and buy $75.00 worth of merchandise to be sold for $100. It arrives and you sell it. $75.00 is used to replace the merchandise and $25.00 is considered gross profit. If you do that four times in a year you will have a gross profit of $100 on a capital investment of $75.00.

Some shops may approximate the operation of a small community hardware store. These stores have a record of perhaps a three-time turnover of stock. Thus their stock value would be one-third the annual sales. The markup on most hardware items is about the same as lapidary equipment and supplies and a three-time turnover seems to be reasonable in determining profit from the operation. If turnover runs to four times per year, perhaps larger stock purchases would be indicated with subsequent reduction in unit costs. If the

turnover drops to one and one-half . . . perhaps profit would be improved by smaller purchases and a reduction of stock.

As a very rough estimate and guide you might consider that your stock value should about equal the first year's gross sales.

Business management is much more than purchasing stock and watching the inventory. It includes pricing, checking costs of operation, alertness to change, and constant attention to a multitude of details. We have enlarged upon stock control because it will be one of your first considerations and seems to be a source of trouble to most small inexperienced shops.

MARKUP AND DISCOUNT

"Markup" is a percentage of purchase price and "discount" is a percentage of selling price. On any one item the actual dollar figure will be identical but the percentages will be different. As an example, an item costing $75.00 is to retail at $100. The gross profit will be $25.00. Figured as markup this $25.00 is 33-1/3% of the cost of $75.00, so we say the "markup" is 33-1/3%. This $25.00 gross profit is 25% of the selling price of $100, so we say you purchased at a 25% discount.

The terms "retail price" and "list price" as used by a wholesale firm have the identical function—that is, a figure to use when determining discount—but the term "list price" may or may not represent an accurate or reliable retail price.

As an example, a $10.00 retail price item (list price) may be quoted at wholesale something like this: retail (or list) $10.00, 1 to 6 items, 15% discount; 7 to 11 at 20%; 12 to 24 at 25%; over 24 at 30%.

There is good reason for this change in discounts as you will soon discover. Let us take an extreme example. Your customer wants a cap and jump ring to fit a special stone. For one-half hour he tries every cap in the place on the stone and finally makes a great decision. You charge him ten cents for the cap and five cents for the ring. You put them in an envelope, which cost money, and write up the sale on a sales slip, and that cost money. The customer may say something about the high price of findings or may wonder why you don't get a horse and gun. You sold those items at over 1000% markup but you lost money on the transaction. The next customer wants a gross of caps and an ounce of jump rings. You charge him $5.00. The sale is made in ten minutes. Your markup probably was 35% but you made $1.50 gross profit.

Markup must be adjusted item by item and also by volume or size of individual sale. The varying markup must average out 25% to 30% of gross sales or you will be in serious trouble.

Such standard items as picks, saws, machinery, grinding wheels and grits, and sanding cloth have a suggested retail price established by the supplier. Don't cut these prices. His experience, much broader than yours, has shown that these suggested retail prices are the minimum that must be charged to produce a reasonable profit. He is just as interested in meeting competitive prices as you are, but he also wants you to make a profit so you can grow in size and become a permanent outlet for his merchandise. We keep repeating that gross profit is not net profit. It takes net profit to buy groceries. Gross profit is up near the middle of the balance sheet; that little figure called net profit down in the lower right-hand corner is the important one.

PURCHASE ORDERS

Do not write out your orders in the form of letters and intersperse your requests for merchandise with comments about the weather or your latest attack of arthritis. Use a separate letter and use a printed purchase order form for ordering. Number these purchase orders and keep a copy. You may specify method of shipment and delivery date.

When opening an account with a supply house don't just scribble a note on any old piece of paper and say, "Send me so many of such and such. My state tax number is so and so." Write a nice letter on good printed stationery. Tell him who you are and something of your volume or how much you anticipate purchasing from him. Give a reference such as your bank. Be sure to include a state or city tax or license number if required in your community. You will be surprised at the friendly, helpful letter you will receive in return. You may know very little about him but he knows nothing about you . . . so introduce yourself. Along this same line, a word of praise or appreciation for a favor or good service will prove to be most helpful.

ROCKS AND SLABS

Word travels fast by grapevine and the new, inexperienced rock shop will soon be visited by all the local traders, all the truck sellers, and tailgaters within reach. They will offer you the "last of this available" or a special hand-picked something or other. Purely and solely to help you, they will even be willing to trade some of their stone for *their selection* of your stone. Unless you know what you are doing, don't do it!

First-class agate is continually rising in price as the demand increases. You may be shocked to discover agate you purchased five years ago at fifty cents per pound retail, now quoted at $1.35 per pound wholesale in 100-pound lots. Suppose you buy a hundred pounds of this $1.35 stone. How do you price it to your customers who buy one-half pound to five pounds at a time?

Let us follow that stone and see what happened to it before you got it. First, it was mined or picked up and sold to your supplier as "mine run" or "field run" at perhaps thirty cents per pound.

Suppose this supply house bought a thousand pounds for $300. To make a reasonable profit it should be sold somewhere near $750, which would be $75.00 per hundred pounds not $135. But this was "mine run" so it must be graded ... perhaps it grades out something like this: 250 pounds high grade, 300 pounds medium grade, 300 pounds poorer grade, and 150 pounds worthless country rock stuff. Depending upon many factors, the supplier might elect to reach his $750 selling price by pricing the grades as follows: 250 pounds high grade, $1.35; 300 pounds medium grade, $1.00; 300 pounds poor grade, 50¢. This would bring in just a little over the $750.

Now you have that hundred pounds of stone. It cost you $135 plus freight and you (as your supplier did) decide that you must sell it for $275 (in the little sales) to make a reasonable profit. A few kinds of stone may be of such uniformity that you could throw the entire hundred pounds in the bin for customer selection at $2.75 per pound. Many, many kinds of stone, even well-graded stones, will vary in desirability by color, markings, or shape, stone by stone. Such a stone, if uniformly priced for customer selection, would probably result in a fourth of bin remaining of unwanted stones. To lower the price on this residue is to lose money and no customer is happy to return to your shop and find the price reduced after he made his purchase.

Two things can be done to alleviate the problem of residue stone. First and least desirable, simply raise the price and finally dispose of the rejects at a bulk price or cut or tumble it yourself. The second and more desirable method would be to price the stone piece by piece . . . to a total of that $275.

This way the customer has the choice of selecting two stones of equal size . . . one a perfect stone for $1.50, the other imperfect at $1.00. He may elect to take the poorer stone but he feels good about it. You have been fair with him and all the subsequent customers who will pick over the pile.

Don't ever, ever put a per pound price on a pile of stone, or, when a customer picks out a particularly beautiful stone, tell him, "That is too good a stone to sell at the regular price, I will have to have $3.00 per pound for that one". If he doesn't do you bodily harm on the spot, you can be sure he will never return.

Now another thing to watch, particularly as you start, is this pile of stone in the backyard. Collected over many years, the supply of jewelry bragging rocks, mineral specimens, crystals, and whatever else you may have accumulated is now called merchandise for sale. You may consider a sale at any price virtually clear profit because it cost very little in money. Watch it! That stock will have to be replaced at current wholesale prices and unless you know your prices and recognize value you may find you have sold it much below wholesale replacement cost.

Somewhere we said something about the desirability of having a display of finished material or specimens or bragging rocks as examples of the lapidary art or to stimulate interest in the hobby. If you have such a display and it is not for sale, mark it plainly so the customer will know it is only for display. Don't let him unknowingly pick out a piece and ask the price only to be told, "That is not for sale."

Everybody starting a shop wants to know where to buy. This information comes with experience and trial and error plus, perhaps, considerable expense. Look through the advertisements in the rock magazines *(listed at the end of this article)*. Transportation will be one of your costs of goods, so select a wholesale house near you and perhaps one in another part of the country. Send for their catalogues and tell them, as has been suggested previously, who you are and what you expect to do . . . and always send your sales tax account number and local license number. In comparing prices be sure you know the quality involved and don't send for catalogues from everybody expecting that someone will be way down low on price. Competition being what it is, you will find merchandise of similar quality somewhere near the same price wherever you buy it.

As a beginning shop your purchase will, of necessity, be in small quantity and limited variety. Don't scatter these little purchases throughout a dozen supply sources. Give your orders to two or three reliable firms. As you grow in volume and experience, as you learn the "jargon of the trade" and understand the quality and descriptive terms, and as you learn what merchandise your customers want, then begin to explore the possibility of finding specialized sources of supply. Buy what your customers want. Don't be governed by your personal likes or dislikes but don't compromise on quality, and don't handle merchandise that you know will not stand up in use (even if there is customer request for it). Findings that tarnish quickly and machinery with poor bearings, too light a construction, or poor design (even if low priced) will not build confidence in the reliability of your shop. You may lose a few sales but not a customer.

There are many items desirable as stock, such as gold pans and tools, that must be purchased from sources basically outside the lapidary field. Consult the wholesale houses via the telephone book because these items may not be advertised or available from lapidary supply houses and can probably be purchased locally with no transportation charges involved.

One final word about buying. Pay your bills when due, conform to the wholesalers sales policy, and take all cash discounts.

TAX NUMBERS AND LICENSES

A license is a permit or an authorization and may carry with it requirements of public health, safety, sanitation, fire protection, and, in some instances, technical and financial qualifications. The fee is usually small and paid each year upon renewal. A license may be cancelled for cause.

Tax numbers or, as they may be called, "registration certificates" are usually issued for the duration of the business and are not renewed each year. Sales taxes vary by locality and may include the state, the county, and the city. Call the various taxing agencies listed in the phone book or call your local Better Business Bureau or the Small Business Administration. Some states and cities levy a tax upon all business and occupations, usually upon total volume regardless of profit. All these taxes will have rules and records you must keep that are subject to audit by the taxing unit. Be sure to tell the taxing unit the details about your proposed shop . . . what you will be selling—wholesale and retail—and some indication of your expected volume. The volume and nature of your business may determine the reporting period which may be by the month or the quarter or, in some small shops, by the year.

Sales taxes are not designed to become a tax upon a tax. The consumer pays an excise tax only once when he buys from the retailer for his own use and ultimate consumption. Goods purchased for resale pay no excise tax.

Your wholesaler is not a policeman. He will not follow an item of merchandise into your shop and check on whether or not you use it or sell it or whether you collect the correct tax, but (and this is *most* important) he must be assured that you understand the terms of the sale: that *you know of your obligation to collect the tax* according to the law and that this obligation is a *part of the condition under which he sells the goods*. Furthermore, he wants that "certified" in writing.

Regardless of whether or not he requires you to sign a lengthy statement or only asks for your excise tax account number or if you only state on an order "for resale, tax number so and so" you have obligated yourself to collect the excise tax. Ignorance of this law is no excuse and you may be subjected to a lot of embarrassment, delinquent penalties, heavy fine, and even imprisonment. You might discover yourself "breaking rocks", not polishing them!

CREDIT

You'll find it to your advantage to establish a credit standing from the very start. Check the telephone book and call your nearest Dun & Bradstreet office. A credit reporter will stop by and ask questions about your business experience, assets (cash and property, insurance), and your liabilities (debts, mortgage obligations). Tell him all the facts. When you identify yourself to a new supplier to obtain credit, you can refer him to Dun & Bradstreet.

Credit is essential to business growth; few businesses can afford to operate on a strictly cash basis. You'll find a credit rating valuable in establishing new sources of supply and in keeping open the flow of goods to your business.

How much credit should you grant to customers? The answer is none . . . do a cash business.

INSURANCE

One of the hidden costs of doing business is a little matter of insurance. Probably you now carry fire, theft, and personal liability. You may find these policies (in fine print) exclude and do not cover any type of retail business activity. So if you're in your own home or separate business building now open to the public, you will need storekeepers liability, fire, and theft on goods for sale as well as personal liability. This broad coverage may cost you from $1.50 to $2.00 per day for your home and stock, but you can't afford to take the chance of defending a one-hundred-thousand-dollar lawsuit for damages to a customer who fell on the icy sidewalk or through a glass showcase.

BOOKKEEPING

In the days before sales tax, business and occupation tax, and income tax, if we came to the end of a year with a few bucks in the bank, the shelves stocked, and the bills paid, we felt pretty good and it was no concern to anyone else.

Now, every penny of expense must be recorded in its proper place . . . goods purchased for sale, repairs, supplies, advertising, labor, transportation, office supplies, taxes, rent, power, light, telephone, interest, travel, and more. Every penny taken in by sale, trade, or labor, interest or rent must be classified as to source and then reclassified as to wholesale or retail and is subject to local or state (or both) sales tax. It may have to be classified again to meet a varying business and occupation (B & O) tax on different types of services or goods.

Sound complicated? Well, it is, and unless you are thoroughly familiar with the accounts needed, consult a good accountant or tax consultant. He will set up a comparatively simple system by which these records can be maintained. We cannot emphasize too much the necessity of doing this *when you start*. Don't wait six months or until the end of the year. You will find you can't remember when you acquired that big saw or whether you had 500 or 1,000 pounds of a certain rock when you started. Another bookkeeping item is a ledger book for accounts receivable. You may try as hard as you can to do a full cash business but there will be people who owe you money . . . maybe only for a few days or until they receive an invoice. Record these in the ledger and keep it accurate.

All this bookkeeping is really a blessing in disguise because from these records you can tell how your business is progressing. Trouble spots will show very soon and corrections can be made. Accounting has been called the voice of a business . . . listen to it.

Bookkeeping services are available for hire and the fees are not excessive. These services are flexible and can be adjusted to suit your source documents (sales slips, bills, invoices, cash receipts, etc.), using them as the record of original entries to a complicated and sophisticated system which would involve all of the multitude of books, ledgers, and account classifications needed. Or arrangements (and training) might be provided for the average person to maintain the records himself, with an occasional audit and annual summary by the expert accountant.

Don't go overboard. All you will need is a comparatively simple, single entry system. Until you grow into a $100,000 business you will not need the complicated accounting systems used by large corporations.

Start this by identifying the sale in the left-hand column, either by name or sales number. The next entry would be the total cash received including all taxes. The next column heading might be "State Sales Tax Collected", and the next "City Sales Tax".

At the end of a tax paying period the column totals will give the information needed. On a separate sheet under these same column heads, the monthly totals can be entered consecutively to make a convenient month-to-month and year-by-year record for managerial use.

These sales records must be accurate and balanced at the monthly or quarterly tax paying period and you will be so much interested in "how the business is doing" that you will have an incentive to take the time each day to keep them up to date.

No monthly or quarterly reports are required of expenditures. Once each year, at income tax time, you will be required by law to determine these figures. There is a great tendency to neglect this most important part of your records. Expenditures paid by check are not much of a problem. You have the check stub and always the cancelled check. Questions might arise as

to the purpose of expenditure, but the expenditure is on record.

The cash expenditures are the neglected and forgotten items that can cost you real money come income tax time. Be sure to keep the invoices or make a memoranda slip for every out-of-pocket purchase; list stamps, light bulbs, fuses, a quart of paint, wrapping paper, travel expense, parking, etc.

As with the record of sales, these expenditure totals—by month and years—can be transferred to a summary sheet and, as the months and years go by, will be invaluable for comparative purposes and as a tool of management.

ADVERTISING

Advertising is designed to draw *buying* customers to your shop. In this lapidary business · we have the problem of promoting the acceptance of the hobby in addition to drawing customers to a particular shop.

Considering our competitive status we should support the gem shows in our trade area and provide interesting displays of the lapidary art at every opportunity, not only for our rock hound customers but for the information of the general public. Provide the local newspapers with human interest stories and pictures of outstanding accomplishments of your rock hound friends. Don't push yourself or your shop into the story. Reporters are under constant pressure from publicity seekers and they will cut the whole thing if they have the slightest idea you are trying to obtain free advertising. Take advantage of every opportunity to build goodwill for the rock hobby.

A listing in the classified section of the telephone directory is a must. Perhaps two or three listings such as Lapidary, Agates, and Jewelry would be advantageous.

Advertising is another of your managerial duties which requires planning, direction, and purpose to fit your individual conditions. Don't plunge in spasmodically and intermittently with an advertisement now and then. Plan your campaign, set up a budget for the year. (Some retail stores spend 3% gross income for advertising.)

Decide what people you want to reach and what goods or services you wish to sell. Your budget will be small and space limited so don't try to sell everything and spoil an ad with too much detail. Elsewhere we have suggested a specialization in one or two items or the development of a unique product to make your shop distinctive . . . here is a chance to "cash in" on that specialization. Use it in your advertising.

Advertising in our rock hobby magazines is effective over long periods of time. Those magazines are saved and read and reread. You will be getting replies from advertisements two and three years after they are issued.

Look through the rock shop ads and pick out one that appeals to you. Then copy its style and layout. Most of the advertising outlets will help lay out your ad and make suggestions.

Advertising is a full-time profession requiring alertness to new opportunities and new techniques. Here are a few do's and don'ts that may be helpful.

Don't ever tell a half-truth or misrepresent in any way.

Don't try to say too much . . . keep it simple.

Don't use stock phrases, clichés, and stereotype phrases.

Do try to make the ad interesting and easy to read.

Do try to make answering easy. If you are selling mail order, make your price postpaid if at all possible.

Be sure all conditions of sale are listed. If there are minimum or maximum or sizes or number, list them distinctly.

Don't brag or boast. Your item may be excellent, large, complete, or first grade, but be very cautious with words like *the biggest, the best, the only, world famous.*

Do stick to your advertising budget. Set aside a few dollars for emergency use for unexpected opportunities.

Keep records of your advertising expenditures and compare with sales and profits. You will learn which type of advertising brings the best results and eventually you will be able to make the best possible use of the advertising outlay.

Perhaps this is a good place to mention books and magazines, not only as profitable merchandise for sale but as help in building public knowledge and increased interest in the hobby. Always carry a good supply.

Another item of goodwill and possible profit is formal class instruction in the lapidary art. You should not have secrets about how to cut, polish, and mount stones. Encourage classes in all phases of the rock hobby under whatever sponsorship.

COMPETITION

The hobbyist will visit more stores and spend more time negotiating the purchase of a $10.00 gadget than he will in spending $500 to put a new roof on the house.

Rock hounds are no exception. Don't ever get the idea that you will become the sole source of supply for anyone. Your customers are going to visit your competition and they all read and study the catalogues. You can't sell everything to everybody; all you can hope to do is attract a portion of the trade. There is no need and you are not obligated to advertise your competition, but if Joe Blow wants an 8" saw blade and you don't have one in stock, send him down the street or, better, call up your competition and tell him you are sending a man to him for a saw blade. Your first consideration is the convenience of your customer, not to prevent your competition from selling a saw blade.

If a customer asks about other rock shops, tell him where they are and say something good about them. If you can't think of anything praiseworthy say something about the lovely shrubbery or the nice picket fence or the lovely pink paint on his storefront. Whatever you do don't knock competition—it's a deadly boomerang.

Try to be something above just another rock shop. Specialize in something; become known as the shop with the big display of bookends, or findings, or maybe good slabbed material. In other words, excel in one or two items. Don't try to specialize in the same thing the other fellow features. For example, if your competition has a big and beautiful supply of mineral specimens, don't try to outdo him, but feature something else, like findings . . . have a complete line. You may soon have him sending customers to you for findings, and you will be sending customers to him for specimen material, and both of you will be doing a nice business. Thus, you will find more and more ways to cooperate to build goodwill.

APPRAISAL AND IDENTIFICATION

As the run of the mine rock hound you probably helped many people identify their finds and discussed at length locations and hunting areas. Now as a rock shop proprietor you will discover that that activity is increased a hundred times.

Don't consider it a profitless waste of time. Remember back when you started rock hunting. Perhaps you can recall those who helped you, and haven't you had a warm spot in your heart for those people? You may also remember the gruff "That is nothing but junk" answer that others gave you.

You will find many customers know a lot more about stones than you do or they may have vast and detailed knowledge of a specialized field, so don't try to fool anybody. You will learn a lot more by just listening.

From these beginners who seek your help will come the customers for machinery and supplies in the years to follow. Don't forget a satisfied, friendly customer is your best advertisement. A dollar's worth of time spent to make a friend of a potential rock hound may be far better advertising than a $10.00 ad in a magazine.

WHAT'S IN A NAME?

Shakespeare said it, but Bill lived long before these days of high pressure selling and psychological advertising. Give a little thought as to how your shop name will sound to a complete stranger. All your friends may call you Fred or Jack or Pinkie but how many are there with similar names. Even the most common names of Smith or Johnson are better than a first name. Smith Brothers made a cough drop famous . . . would Fred & Joe's cough drop have been as effective as Smith Brothers?

Ordinarily thumbnail-sized operations should take the name of the owner with one or, at most, two descriptive words. Smith Agates and Smith's Lapidary Supplies are good. Smith's Rock Shop and Lapidary is too long. Now if you have some big, long, unpronounceable name—even though it be a proud name carried back to the Revolution or the nobility in the old country—better leave it out of the title and call yourself some short combination of descriptive terms such as Lapidary Supply Company, or maybe make up a word or name from some of the syllables in your own or your wife's name. Or the initials of, say, Katherine and Sylvester might be the K & S Rock Shop. Or Frances and Thomas might be combined as was done to make the well-known Frantom Lapidary Company.

We never know what the future growth will be, so select a name suitable for use if your business grows beyond its little circle of friends or the city or state.

HONESTY

The finest asset any rock shop can possess is a reputation for just plain common honesty.

Describe your merchandise truthfully. Your customer may have little knowledge of values now, but he will eventually learn. You may think you are a "smart businessman" when you sell someone a fifty-cent stone for one dollar, but that little trick may cost you the sale of a $400 saw at some future date when that customer discovers he was "taken". If he does come back he will examine every purchase with a cautious, suspicious attitude.

Don't "oversell" a customer. Don't try to sell him ten pounds of expensive polishing oxide when you know he will not use two pounds in a year. And don't reverse the process and "undersell" him. Don't tell him the 12" slab saw you have in stock is adequate to cut the bookends he wants from those

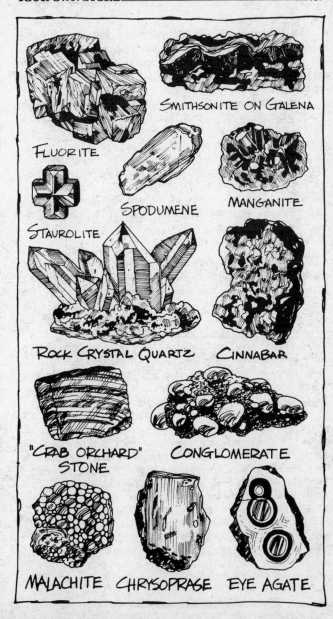

FLUORITE

SMITHSONITE ON GALENA

STAUROLITE

SPODUMENE

MANGANITE

ROCK CRYSTAL QUARTZ

CINNABAR

"CRAB ORCHARD" STONE

CONGLOMERATE

MALACHITE   CHRYSOPRASE   EYE AGATE

big petrified logs.

Know your equipment and machinery well enough to be familiar with its limitations as well as its strong points. *Do not sell machinery or merchandise unless you are willing to supplement the manufacturer's guarantee with your own reputation.*

The small community rock shop for whom this book is intended must depend upon the repeat customer—the fellow who spends five, ten, or fifteen dollars a month and occasionally buys a piece of machinery.

A repeat customer only returns because of his confidence in your advice and guidance and in the assurance he is getting his money's worth in quality.

Another point: So many of us have such poor memories that we should stay very close to the truth at all times.

CONCLUSION

Starting and developing your own business can be a most gratifying and pleasant experience and we have endeavored to encourage those who have a reasonable chance for success. On the other hand, we hope those whose only qualification for starting a rock shop is unbounded enthusiasm will be stimulated to find a specialized field for their venture.

To those of you not in business we hope we have given a little insight into the problems and frustrations of the rock shop operator to the end that you may be a little more tolerant of their "shortcomings" and perhaps a bit more appreciative of the fine service so many are providing.

We hope we have revived the memories of some of the suppliers, wholesalers, manufacturers, and importers. Recall those few short years ago when you, too, considered an order for ten gross of caps, a hundred pounds of stone, or a slab saw as a major decision, requiring a consultation of the entire family and a long look at the bank balance. These are little shops now but some of them will grow, and they will grow because they fill a need for friendly, helpful service.

MAGAZINES DEVOTED TO
THE LAPIDARY AND RELATED HOBBIES

Earth Science Digest
P.O. Box 550
Downer's Grove, Illinois 60515

Gems & Minerals
1797 Capri Avenue
Mentone, California 92359

The Lapidary Journal
P.O. Box 80937
San Diego, California 92138

Rocks & Minerals
Box 29
Peekskill, New York 10566

Desert Magazine
74-109 Larrea
Palm Desert, California 92260

The Australian Gemhunter
40 Seymour Avenue
Armadale, Victoria, Australia

The Australian Lapidary Magazine
11 Robinson Street
Croydon, N.S.W., Australia

ADDITIONAL SOURCES OF INFORMATION:

American Gem and Mineral Suppliers Association
P.O. Box 176
Downey, California 90241

Gemological Institute of America—Los
   Angeles, California
11940 San Vicente Boulevard
Los Angeles, California 90049

Small Business Administration
Telephone book ●

The above article originally appeared in THE MOTHER EARTH NEWS® NO. 7 . . . along with a great deal of other live-better-for-less and self-sufficiency how-to information. For further information about the magazine—and other books and periodicals devoted to home businesses, self-sufficiency, and related subjects—please see page 367 of this handbook.

MABLE SCOTT:
YOU CAN MAKE FIRST-CLASS PROFITS
WITH A SECONDHAND BUSINESS

It's high time that someone told MOTHER's readers about a truly flexible be-your-own-boss moneymaking venture . . . one you can start for a small bag of jellybeans, and—with time and effort—build up to something big. I'm talking about the business that keeps my own family in winter boots and oatmeal: a secondhand store. (In a way I'm rather reluctant to give away the deep, dark secrets of the trade. Then again, I welcome the chance to sort out some of the public's weird beliefs about dealers in used goods.)

Our introduction to the secondhand business came about through necessity several years ago. We were living on a 40-acre tract and my husband drew around $700 a month from a lumberyard in a nearby town. Then we bought a quarter horse for our kids to use as a 4-H club project and that mare turned out to be—for us, anyhow—the world's most expensive animal. Less than a week after the papers were signed, she kicked my mate in the face with both hind feet. It was a miracle that he lived through the experience.

Once out of the hospital, our breadwinner found that the lumberyard had changed hands and the new owner had brought in his own crew. So there my husband was: no job, no strength to look for another, and five mouths to poke vittles into.

At that point I suggested that we borrow $500 from the local bank, rent a cheap building, and purchase a pickup load of furniture at a nearby auction and sell it . . . the idea being to take the money we made, buy more stock, and repeat the process. (We already had a garage full of the odds and ends I kept pouncing on at sales, fixing up, and reselling elsewhere.) My husband admitted later that he thought this to be a ridiculous plan. All the same, he went along with it . . . because there was nothing else in sight and you can't lose if you have nothing to start with.

Well, the bank's officers (bless 'em!) went along with the idea and loaned us the money. And we soon found a building where another secondhand store had formerly operated (a boon since many of the old firm's customers came to us). Then we got the first load of furniture and The Jungle was in business.

Now I'm not going to sit here barefaced and claim that that's all there was to our fresh start. Not at all! We suffered through days and days of sitting on our small stock and praying that somebody would buy just a dollar's worth. The store was listed as belonging to me, but my husband was able to help as his strength increased. Meanwhile he was drawing unemployment (which provided our groceries), and I clerked at an auction one night each week and spent one morning cleaning our church's rectory. There was little time to worry about whether we were on the right track or out of our ever-lovin' minds.

Slowly, though, our trade picked up. One of the best gimmicks we had for building business turned out to be a more or less weekly ad in the local paper. I tried to make the wording catchy . . . and succeeded, I guess, since the editors gave us much more space than we paid for and threw in some showy typesetting. They said people bought the paper just to read our notices!

A typical ad went like this:

The Jungle has stalled off creditors for another month

and is still doing business under the fair trade system: Buy low, sell high. Remember . . . antiques made while you wait. Puppies given all children unaccompanied by parents. Free Coke with every $500 purchase. Browsing privileges extended to animals and people.

Or sometimes we'd paraphrase the advertising of the leading furniture stores. One firm's publicity said:

When you see the big green truck go by, you know another lady has been made happy with furnishings from

_____ .

Our version:

When you see the old beat-up pickup go by, you know another lady has been made happy because we bought her junk to sell to her neighbor.

(Incidentally, out of this experience has grown a weekly column of nonsense which I've now written several years for another paper. They even pay me. That's nice!)

Whether our ads really sold papers I don't know, but they did sell our goods. People started coming into the store strictly from curiosity and stayed to buy.

As time went on, our business grew . . . but not quite enough to both finance the increasing amount of stock it required *and* pay us a decent wage. We kept the bookkeeping department at the local bank busy renewing old notes or tearing them up and making new ones. (Of course, you wouldn't necessarily need to do the same if you ran such an enterprise from your garage or didn't need a full-scale income. With three kids in grade school, though, we had to make money in quantity.)

I'll pass over briefly what was in fact a lot of blood, sweat, and tears. My husband did carpentry work when the unemployment ran out and helped at the store as he could . . . and—finally!—we began paying off our notes. Then we found a large Quonset with three lots for sale outside the town's main business section on a well-traveled street. This was a steal at $8,500 and the Scott family (with a big assist from the bank) bought it.

Most regretfully we said goodby to our 40 acres, purchased

a two-story house, and had it moved to one of the parcels adjoining the store. This worked out fine because we could keep an eye on the children while working next door. (Of course, we've never sold our dream of returning to the land when the offspring leave the nest . . . and, meanwhile, the business has kept them in pretty good feathers as they grow up. They've also developed self-reliance by assisting in the store and running the house.)

That's the surface history of our venture . . . but you're probably more interested in the do's and the don'ts, the profit possibilities, and some of the side benefits. So here goes:

I should say, first of all, that buying is really more important than selling. You have to get back twice what you give for most items in order to average out a living in the long run . . . and that's where your ability to size up salable merchandise comes in handy.

True, you can't win 'em all: You'll sometimes find yourself taking what you can get for an article or tossing it out the back door. On other goods, however, the margin of profit will be sensational. Suppose you buy a table for a dollar and sell it for ten. According to my bookkeeper husband you'll have made 900% on your investment, and where else could you match that?

Then again, right now is a good time to dispose of the prevalent myth that all secondhand dealers get rich by picking

up costly items like carnival glass for next to nothing. Not very often! People now recognize the worth of most such articles. Sometimes, however, when you buy a package deal—a complete houseful of furniture—you will get a few valuables in the collection. A certain number of antiques will come to you in the same way. These help draw customers, but won't sell for as much as they would in a strictly antique store and won't give you the return you get from plain "used" pieces. (Profit on junk beats the good stuff all to heck . . . which means, incidentally, that it's wise to let the buyer do the refinishing. Anyhow, he has more fun that way and you do less work.)

Buying secondhand items in quantity is almost always a good idea whether or not you get any antiques as windfalls. Keep your bank balance as healthy as possible so you'll be able to take advantage of such bulk purchase opportunities as they arise. We once bought the contents of a local hotel that was to be torn down—furniture, rugs, plumbing, light fixtures, dishes, etc.—and did very well on the transaction. The wash basins, for instance, cost us 25¢ apiece and sold like hot cakes at $2.50 to $7.50. (Used plumbing is always in demand among owners of rental property.)

There's also a certain sentiment about anything that belonged to an old landmark. People will buy an unmarked glass simply because it comes from a particular hotel. The same is true of an historic house. Customers will practically beg you to tell them that some object was purchased from the Jedediah Plunkett mansion . . . until you're almost tempted to bring out all your "clinkers" and palm them off as part of old Jed's estate.

We've always resisted such temptations, however, and made a special effort to remain honest. In the long run, we feel, a Straight Arrow policy pays off better than tricks . . . and brings the same customers back time after time. Some games, though, are fair enough . . . like the gimmick of rearranging your merchandise. If something doesn't sell, don't let it sit in one part of the store. Shift it to another location, and the folks who overlooked the article before will discover it and think it's just come in.

It's also quite legitimate to take advantage of garage sales. Since you can select what you really need and leave the rest, this is a good alternative to bidding for whole lots that contain many unsalable items. Even if you make a tidy profit on some castoff later on, the householder did after all set his own price

and can hardly claim you "stole" those old fire irons or whatever. This convenient source of stock has consoled us for the loss of our line in secondhand clothes, which we gave up when rummage sales started springing up everywhere and selling used garments for practically nothing.

One thing we do miss about the clothing end of the business is that we used to keep our own family dressed from the store's selection (while still making a profit on the articles we didn't want). The secondhand trade has many more fringe benefits of the same kind. There's scarcely a thing we need that won't show up if we're patient enough to wait for it: toothpaste, hair oil, canned goods, combs, permanent wave kits, even groceries. True, they may not be the brands we prefer . . . but who can't switch if the price is right?

You may also have guessed that our home furnishings constantly revolve as we find articles we like better than what we already have and exchange them for our old things (which, in turn, become stock for the store). It breaks my heart to think of the new TV, washer, and kitchen stove we bought shortly before we went into business. We could have purchased such equipment, scarcely used, at one fifth of its original price if we'd just waited a little longer.

We recently enclosed our front porch with four large casement windows—framed, with screens to match—for which we paid $3.00 each. The boxing was odds and ends of boards we had accumulated, including some from the tops of several 25¢ tables. The doors were used, out of our stock. Even the paint was economical (we got it wholesale), since we're a dealer for the Old South line of preservatives.

One more extra: Our dealer's license—which cost nothing—comes in handy for private purposes . . . at auto auctions, for instance. Our '63 Plymouth station wagon cost us $650 in '65, and that sure beat the lot price.

Speaking of licenses, we advertise that "we buy, sell, or trade anything but elephants". That's not quite true, because there are a few things secondhand dealers can't handle without a special permit: plants, food, used mattresses. That last restriction really isn't fair, by the way, since mattresses can be sold by individuals or at auctions or garage sales . . . which pretty well cancels the health protection angle. Nobody can forbid us to *give away* those items, however, and we do: We sell a bed, a cup, even a safety pin and throw in the you-know-what as a bonus.

Finally, a word about the "trade" in our slogan. There's one class of transaction which we handle in that manner, to save taxes: the occasions in fall or winter when a customer brings in, say, a cooler that he wants to exchange for a stove. To keep the government happy we count that as an even swap . . . something you don't want to do in the ordinary course of business. (The rule of thumb is, "Always draw some cash difference.")

Well, that's about it, and I hope it helps. If you'd like to know more, we'd be glad to give you pointers or discuss your entry into a similar venture. Believe me, this is a perfect business for those who want to regulate their income to their desires. If you need a lot of money (as we did), you can work for it . . . but if you want to close up and go fishing, you can do that too. And don't worry about location! A cabin in the country is fine. Customers love to drive out to a quaint setting when they're buying secondhand items . . . and it won't hurt a thing if you're a little quaint too! ●

The above article originally appeared in THE MOTHER EARTH NEWS® NO. 31 . . . along with a great deal of other live-better-for-less and self-sufficiency how-to information. For further information about the magazine—and other books and periodicals devoted to home businesses, self-sufficiency, and related subjects—please see page 367 of this handbook.

GARY HOLMES: HOW TO START YOUR OWN SMALL-TOWN BICYCLE SHOP

Here—for all the folks who want to get out of a big city and start a little business in a friendly, peaceful spot—is yet another small-town self-employment suggestion: become a bicycle dealer in the small town of your choice. My wife, Sharon, and I have run a bike shop for a year now and feel sufficiently expert to pass on a few basics (enough, we hope, to help you decide whether or not this trade will suit you as well as it suits us).

First, why a bicycle shop? Because—as you probably know—a "bike boom" is underway. In 1972, two-wheelers outsold automobiles for the first time in modern history . . . and someone has to market and service all those millions of machines. (Incidentally, one satisfaction of the business is the knowledge that you're providing your customers with non-polluting transportation.)

And why a small-town location? Partly, of course, to give you that relaxed, pleasant life you're after . . . but also because the smaller community is a good potential market for well-made bicycles, and one that's been neglected because of the direction the boom has taken.

Increased demand for bikes has brought more and more manufacturers into the field: some with fine products and some with junk designed to be sold cheaply to Americans who don't know what makes a good machine. These larger producers—with a few exceptions—seem to be concentrating on urban sales, with much of their output retailed through department stores and discount houses. So it happens that the resident of the average small town can buy a bicycle only through the local chain outlet . . . and in most cases his acquisition will be of poor quality.

Which adds up to a fine opportunity for you, the independent small-town dealer, to profit by offering—without competition, usually—better goods than those in the department stores. You won't have a monopoly on local bike sales, of course: Many people will buy the cheaper products from large outlets just to save money. But when their purchases fall apart (as they inevitably do), *you'll* get the repair jobs.

CAPITAL

The amount of money you'll need to start a bike business depends on the scale of your plans. Ten thousand dollars will launch a very large operation, $5,000 an adequate one. Sharon and I began on $3,500 and could probably have got by with a little less.

Whatever your initial grubstake, it's best if you don't have to borrow the money to start with. Today's interest rates could easily make the difference between success and failure.

LOCATION

Before you rush out to open a shop in some village with a population of 49, let me say that by "small town" I mean a community of at least 10,000. Independence, Kansas—our own location—has about 12,000 people and provides enough volume to support our business . . . but I wouldn't want to try it anyplace much smaller.

Although almost any building will do (at least to start with), it's best to find one that can be divided easily into a small showroom and a service area. *When* to start looking for that ideal place is a tricky question: you don't need a store until you have goods to sell . . . but you don't want to fill your house with bicycle cartons while you hunt for a shop, either. Sharon and I initially chose to live with the boxes and I used our living room as an assembly area. After three or four days of tripping over bike parts, however, we found a location for our soon-to-be business and moved frames, wheels, pedals, and all over there.

A bit of hindsight: If you aren't native to the town in which you open your shop, it's easy to choose a poor spot. Our first building (which was small and rented for just $60.00 a month) was only two blocks from the main intersection of Independence, and—since that's a short distance by city standards—we assumed we were "downtown". To the local people, however, our place was on the outskirts of the community and we had very little walk-in business for a few months (until we moved to a roomier, better-located shop that costs us a monthly $125). What you want is a small building in the very center of town. An old gas station (easy enough to find these days) on a good site would be perfect.

SUPPLIERS

Before your Grand Opening, you will—of course—have to line up wholesale suppliers to furnish you with bicycles, parts, and accessories. This, too, calls for careful timing: During the summer months you may have trouble finding sources whose merchandise hasn't been sold out to existing dealers.

For this reason, I think it's best to open a new bicycle shop in the fall when the height of the season is over and most distributors will welcome new business. That way you'll also have time to become familiar with the operation before spring rolls around, and the local people will have some months to get used to the presence of your store.

The easiest way to find suppliers is by going to your local telephone company office (which probably has, or can get, phone books for every major city) and thumbing through all the Yellow Pages. Start with centers of commerce close to you, because the nearer your wholesale source, the less you'll have to spend for freight charges.

We've dealt with several supply houses and have found that they range in quality from excellent to terrible. The following are the best we've traded with:

> Gitane Pacific
> 4925 West 147th Street
> Hawthorne, California 90250
>
> Alpine Distributors
> 328 Link Lane
> Fort Collins, Colorado 80521
>
> Beacon Cycle Supply
> 1801 East Bolivar Avenue
> Milwaukee, Wisconsin 53207
>
> D-I-N Industries, Inc.
> Stierlin Road
> Mountain View, California 94043

INITIAL EXPENSES

Right! You've tracked down a building and contacted your suppliers. Now, how do you spread your money around so you'll have the best chance of making that new bicycle shop a going concern?

Let's say you begin with a total of $4,000. From that

amount you should set aside $500 to cover your non-merchandise overhead for the first couple of months. (After that length of time the shop ought to be generating sufficient income to pay these expenses as they arise.)

Next, reserve another $200 for initial advertising. This isn't much, but it goes a long way in a small town where rates are generally low. We spent about that amount—mostly on modest-sized, straightforward newspaper ads surrounded by heavy borders—just to let everyone know we were open for business. Now that we're established, we find that the same simple, direct advertising approach still works best for us.

STOCK

With the remaining $3,300 of your original investment you'll buy everything else you need, including $1,500 to $2,000 worth of bicycles. This should get you 17 to 21 medium-priced 10-speed machines which will retail for about $125 each.

The average markup on bicycles is 30 to 35%, not a lot compared to that on other types of goods. Fortunately, you'll do considerably better on parts, accessories, and service. Other dealers have told us that new bike sales pay their expenses while all their profit is derived from other areas. Not so with us . . . we place a priority on selling new machines and let the sidelines develop in proportion.

Your initial supply of bicycles should allow the customer a choice of at least two brands. Your suppliers can help you decide on the best colors and frame sizes to start with. As long as you're dealing with reputable firms, you shouldn't have to worry about being oversold on any style. The wholesalers may, however, try to sell you their more expensive bikes (which retail at $200 to $500 each). In the beginning it's best not to tie up your limited capital in such items . . . but do get brochures on the distributors' lines in case someone wants a higher-priced model than you have in stock.

PARTS AND ACCESSORIES

You now have $1,300 to $1,800 left to invest . . . about $400 of which you should put into parts and accessories. That's not a lot, but it will buy most of the items your customers are likely to want at this point. Since the usual markup on such merchandise is 100%, this expenditure *can* bring you a return of $800. In our shop, however, we think it helps business if we hold our percentage down a little. (You'll find this wise, particularly if other stores around you sell cyclists' supplies.)

Space doesn't permit a list of the specific parts you'll need but here's a good working principle: Especially at the beginning, don't try to stock every component for every machine made . . . it can't be done. Concentrate instead on replacement items and accessories for the bikes you handle and—maybe—one other popular brand sold in town. They'll probably fit other lines also, since many parts are interchangeable among good 10-speeders. Remember, if you don't stock a certain article you can always order it when you need it. That's better than having odds and ends gathering dust on your shelves.

If possible, assemble a couple of bicycles before you order parts so you'll be familiar with the various bits and pieces. Then—if you still have trouble selecting from the wholesale catalogs—talk to at least two of your suppliers. They should be able to give you plenty of help (and may even go so far as to make up lists of suggested merchandise for you). After a while you'll learn what to order and what not to, and your inventory will grow until you can give your customers just about anything they need. And don't neglect the parts-and-accessories end of the business: Such sales will make up a large part of your income.

TOOLS

Obviously, you'll need tools to put bicycles together and keep them that way . . . but there's no need, in the beginning, to spend more than $100 on this equipment.

First, get a set of metric wrenches, some adjustable wrenches, and a few screwdrivers. You'll be amazed at the repairs you can do with these few items alone. You'll also need some tire repair tools, plus a few gadgets made especially for bike work. The rear gear cluster (or freewheel) on a 10-speed model, for instance, can be removed only with a special piece of equipment . . . and different variations of the tool are necessary for various brands of the cluster. Again, your supplier can tell you what to order. The more expensive articles, such as movable repair stands and air compressors, can come later as your business grows.

ASSEMBLY AND REPAIR

When you're just getting into the trade, putting bicycles together can teach you almost everything you need to know . . . except the best way to go about it. At the outset, just to assemble a modern 10-speed machine may seem an impossible task. The first one I tackled took me the best part of two days before it was fully adjusted and ready to go. Now I can do the same job in about 15 minutes.

The best solution to assembly and repair problems is to get a good book on bikes and read it as you go along. My own favorite—and the manual I learned from—is *Derailleur 5, 10, and 15 Speed Bicycle Repairs* ($4.95 from XYZYX Information Corporation, 21116 Van Owen, Canoga Park, California 91303). Some distributors hold regular "repair schools" and if you can get in on one of these, so much the better.

Since a good portion of your income will come from bicycle service, you'll need to know how to charge for the jobs you do . . . and that's where some outside help comes in handy. You'll find it well worth $25.00 a year to belong to the National Bicycle Dealers Association (29025 Euclid Avenue, Wickliffe, Ohio 44092). Among other advantages, your membership will bring you a service rate book that tells how long a specific repair or adjustment should take and how much you should ask for the work in your area. The Association will also send you a listing of bicycle and parts suppliers all over the United States. By all means, join . . . you'll save yourself hours of frustration.

RESERVE FUND

What's left of your original $4,000 should be held in reserve just in case you need it. If a customer walks in and wants five or six bikes for his grandchildren, for instance, and you don't have that many in stock . . . at least you'll be able to order the machines.

While most businesses are new and growing, it's usually best to plow every penny of profit back into the operation . . . and a bike shop is no exception. In fact, it's a good idea not to try to depend on your fledgling enterprise for a living until it's firmly established.

PROFITS

How much can you expect to make from a small-town bike shop? It's hard to say. We've always felt that a good part of our income isn't measured in dollars, but in the satisfaction of meeting the good people who ride bicycles. That much we can promise you: The rest depends on how hard you work at learning and operating the business. Unless you open a large establishment in a big city, you can't expect to get rich . . . but if you're satisfied to work hard at your trade in quiet, peaceful surroundings, good things will come your way. ◆

The above article originally appeared in THE MOTHER EARTH NEWS® NO. 26 . . . along with a great deal of other live-better-for-less and self-sufficiency how-to information. For further information about the magazine—and other books and periodicals devoted to home businesses, self-sufficiency, and related subjects—please see page 367 of this handbook.

FRANK LEAVITT: FEEDBACK ON THE BICYCLE BUSINESS

As a bicycle mechanic with a fair amount of experience, I'd like to add a few words of warning to Gary Holmes' "How to Start a Small-Town Bicycle Shop".

[1] Gary says: "If possible, assemble a couple of bicycles before you order parts so you'll be familiar with the various bits and pieces." It seems to me that if you aren't already on speaking terms with those bits and pieces, you shouldn't be in the bicycle business.

Get some experience first: either work with an established dealer for a while, or start off—as I did—just doing repairs out of your own home and buying parts as you need them from the local bike shop. (You may be able to persuade the owner to give you a small discount.) I operated that way for several months before I was offered a job in a shop. Now, a year later, I'm just about experienced enough to open my own place (which I would do were I not more interested in home-steading).

[2] It's very hard not to get burned ordering bicycles, even if you're a veteran in the business. The inexperienced dealer hardly stands a chance. Most of the 10-speeds now manufactured are absolute junk and will take up much of your time and money with "guarantee" work (when you—not the

factory—must do the guaranteeing). This is true even of makes with good reputations . . . the big companies have cheapened their products incredibly in the past few years. Making many of these machines work involves everything from replacing parts (usually at your expense) to frame-bending or redesigning the drive train.

[3] Gary says he can assemble a 10-speed in 15 minutes. I don't believe he can do this without cutting corners. I'm pretty fast and it still takes me an average of 50 minutes per bike . . . but that includes checking and usually adjusting hubs, bottom bracket, and headset, truing the wheels (and sometimes dishing the rear one), making the gears work perfectly, and checking every nut and bolt on the bike.

Incidentally, the best handbook for a bike shop is the Schwinn dealers' manual. Try to get a copy from a friendly Schwinn agent (it's not available to the public). Second best is *Glenn's Complete Bicycle Repair Manual* by Clarence W. Coles and Harold T. Glenn (1973 edition, hard cover $7.95, paperback $5.95, Crown Publishers, Inc., 419 Park Ave. South, New York, N.Y. 10016). This books bears a strong resemblance to the Schwinn guide . . . it even contains some of the same mistakes. ◗

The above article originally appeared in THE MOTHER EARTH NEWS® NO. 28 . . . along with a great deal of other live-better-for-less and self-sufficiency how-to information. For further information about the magazine—and other books and periodicals devoted to home businesses, self-sufficiency, and related subjects—please see page 367 of this handbook.

LOUIS V. BIGNAMI:
ANYONE FOR A COFFEE-HOUSE ?

Are you gregarious, a good organizer, and in search of a business that will let you be your own boss? Then maybe you'd do well to consider running a coffeehouse. If you like the life and manage your cafe efficiently, you can make enough to support yourself and your family . . . and you'll have the additional satisfaction of providing an important service to your neighbors.

I'm serious. All successful coffeehouses have one point in common: They fill the need for companionship which, in our mobile and impersonal society, too often goes unmet. People want to go to a place where they're recognized and liked. The corner bar has served this purpose for years, and if you offer a similarly warm environment to a different clientele, you're well on your way . . . as long as you observe certain rules.

Rules for a coffeehouse? That's right! Such an establishment is a business . . . admittedly an unusual one, but still a business and subject to the same laws as any other. The many cafes that don't make it fail because their owners refuse to recognize this fact.

The first rule for successful operation is that you, the owner-manager, must like people. Sounds elementary, but I know of two places that foundered because the proprietors thought only of money and didn't try to make their customers feel welcome . . . which should have been their main concern.

The second rule is that you should find out whether you really like running a coffeehouse *before* you make a large investment of time and money. One establishment I'm familiar with was sold by its previous owner because he wasn't sufficiently businesslike to keep the place going, and because his efficient wife felt demeaned by working behind the counter.

Moral: Anyone who plans to open his own cafe should first get at least a couple of months' experience working for someone else. If you're already handling a full-time job, try a weekend or night shift. Keep your eyes open while you're on duty and form your own opinions about kitchen layout, menus, ordering, and other potential problem areas. If, after a couple of months as a part-time employee, you still like the business well enough to tackle it on your own . . . then, and only then, is the time to move on to the next step.

And that next step is mainly just thinking . . . about the type of coffeehouse you'd like to run. You're going to have to spend a lot of hours there—especially at first—you know, so you'll want to make absolutely certain your place is exactly what you want.

An essential part of this brainwork should concern *theme* . . . the idea or concept that will set your cafe off from the hot dog stand down the street. Your menu, decor, and music must blend to set a mood. When a patron steps through the door he should get an impression of unity, a feeling that everything has always been just as it is. All successful coffeehouses have this quality . . . plastic imitations do not.

Your own ethnic background—Spanish, Greek, Italian, or whatever—can give you the central idea you need, or you can build your establishment's atmosphere around one of your own interests. A lover of classical music, for instance, could call his place Beethoven's Last, hang pictures of composers on the walls, provide constant classical music on a good stereo with the record jackets prominently displayed, post recital notices on the bulletin board, make scores available, run special programs of live chamber music, feature European specialties on the menu . . . and so forth.

Other musical motifs could be country and western, English, Irish, Spanish, hard rock, or modern . . . anything that's not too esoteric for your area. In a large population center there are sure to be enough people who share your taste. The only "must" is that you follow your central ideas closely. Give your customers credit for being able to spot a phony!

With your theme in hand, it's time to start looking for a location. This is the most important decision that still remains to be made. Your coffeehouse must be within a densely populated part of the city (or possibly in a rural area where there's already a demand for this type of gathering place). Remember that people won't make a long trip to visit you until you're established, and your first regular customers will be walk-ins . . . so select your neighborhood carefully. Areas near colleges and universities, and other spots where there are large numbers of single adults, are the prime locations. Your choice of theme will influence your choice of location: Beethoven's Last, for instance, would do well near a music school, opera house, or symphony hall.

Check any general area you like for possible competitors. If there's a well-established cafe nearby, can you live off its overflow, or will you attract a different type of clientele?

If you seem to have a clear shot in your chosen neighborhood, check with local realtors for a building. It's wise to set up in an area of small shops and plenty of foot traffic . . . or, if you expect your customers to be driving, make sure that parking is no problem. Also, be certain your place is easy to find. One of the best ways to fail is to locate on an obscure side street. A busy corner would be ideal.

Eventually, your search will narrow down to a couple of buildings. Best of all would be a former restaurant or coffee shop (which would already have gas, electricity, and officially approved restrooms). That last point is important, by the way: Before you sign any lease, make sure the Health Department will OK the johns! Plumbers are expensive, as we all know from Watergate, and if you have to bring in utilities and install toilets the costs can be astronomical.

Ask the realtor a lot of questions. Find out why your predecessor left the building. Check out the landlord and your future neighbors. Try to get a renewal provision on the lease so your rent won't be bumped up substantially the second year.

In particular, be sure to *get down in writing* all the duties of each party to the agreement. Don't try to rely on a verbal understanding, since the human memory can be conveniently weak at times.

A word about the law: Good relations with the Health Department and the police are a must, and both can tip you off to possible problems *in advance*, if you ask. (Remember, the person who gives you advice feels a sense of involvement and identification with your business.)

Try to visit the local cops before you open. Let them know you aren't going to stand for any drinking or dealing on the premises, and ask them for suggestions. If your neighborhood has a beat patrolman, it pays to be pleasant to him.

OK. You have your building. Now you can start turning the bare interior into the warm, inviting spot you see in your mind's eye.

The kitchen is the heart of an efficient operation. It should be set up so that one person can both prepare food and do cleanup work in slack periods, but two or more can work at night when you're crowded.

What kitchen equipment you need varies with your menu. As a coffeehouse employee you will have formed a definite idea of the necessities. Accumulate your supply gradually, if you can, in the three to six months after choosing a theme and before opening. Be careful not to overbuy! You can add additional stock once you're in full operation.

The company that supplies your coffee will usually provide burners free . . . so if you serve only sandwiches, soups, coffee, and pastries you won't have to buy a stove. You should, however, have two refrigerators just in case one breaks down.

Used equipment is, of course, much less expensive than new. A small ad in the local newspapers may locate everything you need . . . maybe even a refrigerator or other major item free for the hauling.

How about your cafe's public area? Coffeehouses are so infinitely flexible that almost any arrangement will serve, as long as live entertainment can be seen from all parts of the room. Tables should be small, and will harmonize with your theme if you cover their tops with pictures or sketches and then people-proof them with coverings of transparent fiberglass. Their lower parts should be painted an inconspicuous color. Try to place your tables in rows that point toward the kitchen so that your waitresses can get in and out easily.

Around the tables you'll need chairs . . . fifty or more, depending on the size of your room. So many, purchased new or even used from a supplier, can be a great expense . . . but an ad asking for free chairs and a swing through your area's garage sales should do the job.

You're going to have to move your establishment's seating a lot every time you sweep the place, so "light but sturdy" is the word. If the chairs you find are made of wood check them for loose parts, glue them carefully, and sand them well. Then rent a sprayer and paint the whole batch at once.

Benches placed around the wall are excellent for handling overflow crowds at peak periods, and are out of the way the rest of the time. Build them yourself or look for old church pews at a wrecker's warehouse.

How much money does it take to open a coffee-house? That depends, to a large extent, on you. The New Unicorn—the San Francisco establishment you see in the illustrations—was set up for less than $1,000 . . . but the owner did most of the work himself and bought all his equipment used. If you have to hire professionals to fix up your building, you may need upwards of $3,000 to open its doors. If this sounds expensive, remember that—on top of fixtures and stock—you'll have the costs of repainting and installing water, gas and electricity. The lease, the state and federal taxes and the deposits for phone and utilities will also eat up a lot of cash . . . so it's wise to have a cushion.

Remember, too, that it takes time to build up a clientele (and that also means money). You can try to stretch your start-up bankroll by keeping your daytime job and operating your new coffeehouse only at night in the beginning . . . but you'll really feel the strain if you do. A couple can manage such an arrangement much better than a single person.

The best method of weathering your cafe's early period is to have enough money on hand to run the place for the first couple of months after you open. Keep the costs down . . . but *don't* try to save by letting your bookkeeper go. He's the only person who can tell you how you're really doing.

"Light and clean" is the rule for the toilets. Your whole establishment should be well kept, of course, but the restrooms must be spotless. Nothing turns people off faster than dirty johns. Make it a policy to check them every hour. Paint the walls of these rooms a light color: That will make them easier to clean . . . and let you collect a number of interesting graffiti in no time at all.

With the physical part of your operation in hand, you can start thinking about the entertainment. People will leave the tube only if you can offer them something better . . . and although records and tapes appropriate to your theme are adequate during the day, only live attractions will draw well at night.

Vary your programs as much as you can, while trying to remain true to your theme. For example, Beethoven's Last could appropriately offer opera, *Lieder*, classical guitar, chamber music, or traditional English folk songs . . . but should still try to work in an occasional ethnic night— flamenco, fado, or Greek—to add a change of pace. A regularly posted weekly schedule is a must, to help your customers plan ahead.

Notices at the local schools, music stores, and conservatories will help you find performers at the outset, and the musicians' grapevine will do the rest once you're in operation. Set aside one afternoon or evening for auditions, get the best people you can, and pay them what they're worth. You won't regret it. Nothing clears out a place of entertainment faster than a lack of talent.

When you're just beginning, of course, you'll probably be strapped for money. Tell the musicians what you can afford to pay and why it's not more. If they draw well, increase their rate . . . if not, get someone else.

A tip to remember when you hire musicians: A single is always preferable to a group, because the costs of the act are lower. Further, you should have a spare who can come in on short notice if a scheduled entertainer fails to show.

Coffeehouses that can't afford live music every night can schedule other events. Poetry readings, funky old movies, radical theater, or puppet shows can all attract audiences . . . at varying costs to you.

Whatever entertainment you offer, the rule is "Keep it short". Run a twenty- to thirty-minute set and break for a record. This period gives your customers time to talk, order, visit the john, etc., and the result is a quieter house during the performances. Also, try to set up the coffeehouse lights so that they can be turned down for the show and raised for intermissions.

Now we come to an area that can break you: employees. At first you won't be able to afford many, but at least two are a definite necessity. The first—a bookkeeper—is a must so you'll know where you stand, and so you won't have trouble later with the IRS and local tax agencies. Hire one before you start and he or she will save you more than his/her salary the first year.

Your second employee should be a five-nights-a-week cleanup man. You just won't have time to scrub the place down every morning and still do all the ordering of supplies and other work your coffeehouse will require. Two nights a week, however, you should handle the cleanup detail yourself. This gives your helper a five-day week and lets you see what the place looks like after a full evening.

Later on, once your business merits them, you can hire waitresses. Until you reach this point, however, you should arrive at your place about ten in the morning to do the ordering and get the food ready to serve at lunch. If you open at 11:30 for the lunch trade, you'll have a busy period until about 2:00. In the slack time until 5:00 or so you can get caught up on paperwork, take deliveries, and audition new talent. Then you'll have a busy period that will slack off about 6:00 and build after 7:00 to closing.

This is a brutal schedule for one person. I know, because I

ran a cafe this way all one summer. Nevertheless, these are what your hours will be until your gross is high enough to let you hire more help. You'll get tired and bored with the menial labor . . . but stay cheerful and remember that to run the place efficiently in the future you must be able to do each of your employees' jobs well.

When business does pick up, you càn have a day man and one waitress to run the place during the afternoon, and several waitresses and a kitchen helper at night. The people who serve your customers must be spotless, gregarious, and dependable. Check them carefully and replace any that aren't first rate.

You may find it hard to discharge the help that doesn't work out, but remember that your first duty is to your customers and your *long-term* employees. If you go out of business, everyone loses. Remember, too, that only faithful, experienced helpers make it possible for you to leave your coffeehouse for any extended period of time. Weed so the flowers may grow!

One of the best ways to form a loyal, efficient staff is to pay the going rate. Let your employees know what you're making and give them a share of the rewards of good business. But don't let your profits be eaten up in salaries, especially during those first critical months: Once your business slacks off each night, let your help go on home and finish up yourself.

So far, I've said nothing about the items that pay the freight in a coffeehouse: the food and drink you offer. The appeal of this fare starts with the printed menu itself, which should reflect your theme. Beethoven's Last, for instance, might offer various traditional coffees and dishes named after composers. If your decor allows, you can also post daily specials on a wall blackboard to help your patrons make a decision at the counter.

The specialties you serve should be part traditional and part a unique reflection of your tastes. Coffee, tea, Italian sodas, and cider are all top sellers and should be available in several varieties. My favorite coffeehouse—The New Unicorn at Hayes and Ashbury in San Francisco—offers ten types of tea, several coffees, eight sodas, and a special spiced cider. Whipped cream, rum and vanilla extracts, and a selection of spices will let you add variety without a huge inventory.

Soup—especially homemade—served with a slice of buttered bread is both easily prepared and a popular item. More

extensive hot dishes require a stove with a ventilated hood, which could cost more than you're likely to take in. Most cafes, therefore, are better advised to make sandwiches and cheeseboards the backbone of their menus. Salami, corned beef, tuna, and cheeses are standards . . . and the raw ingredients are easy to store, prepare, and serve.

Pastries and cakes—if you can get good ones—are also profitable items for a coffeehouse to handle.

Supermarket-quality goods, however, won't do. This is true of all your offerings: People won't buy more than a cup of coffee if they can get the same sandwiches, cake, etc., in a store. In food, as in entertainment, search out the special and charge a fair price for it if you want a successful operation.

The rates you list on your menu depend on the prices of your raw materials, which vary regionally and seasonally. You may also want to check what your competition is charging. Just be certain not to underprice! All your costs must be covered or you'll soon be out of business.

The effort and energy you expend setting up your cafe, of course, is wasted if potential customers don't know you're there . . . so start your publicity campaign with a good location and a big sign. If you set up near a school, run off some circulars and post them on campus. Perhaps you can think up an effective stunt to let people know your coffeehouse is open.

When you do start attracting business, move around among your guests and ask them what they like and dislike about the new establishment. You'll get lots of free advice, some of it quite useful. The old saying is perfectly true: Your best advertisement is a satisfied customer.

That, in fact, is the secret of coffeehouse management: You can be as independent as you like in the running of your place if you just make your customers feel welcome. If you and your employees treat the chance drop-in as a guest, he's yours for as long as you're open. When he's asked about your cafe, he won't say, "I've been there" . . . he'll say, "I go there." Once you reach this point you're set up for good as your own boss in surroundings designed to your own taste. What better way is there to earn your daily bread? ●

The above article originally appeared in LIFESTYLE! NO. 8 . . . along with a great deal of other live-better-for-less and self-sufficiency how-to information. For further information about the magazine—and other books and periodicals devoted to home businesses, self-sufficiency, and related subjects—please see page 367 of this handbook.

JACK MC CLINTOCK :
GRASS-HOPPER FLATS

Donn Stoffer left Brown County, Indiana rather hastily in 1962. In an orgy of youthful exuberance he had siphoned some gasoline from a school bus, and a judge had suggested that Donn might prefer life in the U.S. Navy to life in the county jail.

Today, Donn is 27 and back in Brown County. Thanks to that judge he's a veteran, and thanks to himself he's one of the most successful—and independent—businessmen in Nashville, Indiana.

Donn minds a store called Grasshopper Flats, which has paid for itself five times over in the last year, and now owns an inventory worth $15,000. The same business establishment has made Donn Stoffer the third largest retail depositor in the local bank and is the main reason that Donn and his wife, Joyce, now live the Good Life on a nearby 190-acre farm where they're 75% self-sufficient ("We do everything by MOTHER").

In short, Donn Stoffer has freed himself from the system and now lives as he likes . . . and he says that you can do it too. There are many ways to accomplish this end but if you want to do it the way he did it, Donn says you should start by choosing a place.

The place Donn chose was Nashville . . . partly because it's his home and partly because it's an art colony. Because of that second reason, Nashville—even though it's a small town (about 800 souls)—draws tourists from the big cities. And that's why the tiny Indiana town can support Grasshopper Flats—a combination head shop and crafts store—in such royal fashion.

The right small town, in other words, can be a better location for a New Life shop than most large cities. The secret? No competition.

The second ingredient you'll need as you brew up your heady new way of living, according to Donn, is "an idea, not money". Donn's idea was jewelry (since he happened to be a silversmith) . . . which meant he automatically had something to sell. But Stoffer didn't stop there and you probably shouldn't either. He combined silver with other crafts (brought in on consignment) with head shop gear with a MOTHER dealership. "Diversification", the captains of industry would call it.

And then of course, yes, you *will* need some money . . . but not much. Donn started small, with just a few hundred dollars. A silversmith, you see, equipped with only a pounding block, ball-peen hammer, and pliers can magically transform $100 worth of wire into pieces of jewelry that will sell at colleges and stores for maybe $400. If he then invests the entire $400 in more wire and repeats the process all over again . . . he'll have enough cash to start his own store! And Donn did.

Donn was lucky when he located his shop . . . it's right on Main Street and surrounded by other attractive small business establishments that invite visitors and tourists to stop and browse. Donn was double lucky: his is the most striking building on the street . . . so he laid down his $200 rent, laid in some more silversmithing supplies, and began to scavenge old showcases.

Stoffer picked up his shop's fixtures at junk shops. He also found some of his merchandise there (you can paint junk, make jewelry out of it, or turn it into sculpture . . . and sell it).

Donn also filled his mini-emporium by spreading word that he'd accept craft items on consignment at "the lowest possible markup" . . . about 25%. Such an anti-greed business philosophy, Stoffer soon found, gave his contributor-craftsmen a good feeling of participation and prosperity while making his customers feel they were buying handmade items at bargain prices. That's the way to develop volume.

Volume indeed! Strange as it may seem, one potter actually sells more of his work through Grasshopper Flats than through his own store *right across the street*. Why? Well . . . if your shop is stuffed with the work of many craftsmen, you've got yourself a one-stop shopping bazaar. Folks who wander in to see a belt walk out—like as not—with a belt, a pair of earrings, a painting on an old barn board, a jar of preserves, and a copy of MOTHER.

Donn and Joyce sell paintings, macrame, leatherwork, metalwork, pottery, clothing, apple butter, pumpkin butter, honey, beaded chokers, sterling silver rings, roach clips, pipes, knitted dresses, ponchos, scarves, hats, collages, tie-dyed items, candles, and lots and lots more. Grasshopper Flats thus becomes a place for freaks (the tape deck was playing Sly and the Family Stone the day we stopped in) and for straights (a matronly lady was inspecting jewelry between side glances at Donn's rather luxuriant hair).

At first, Stoffer took anything on consignment he could get . . . just to fill out the bare corners of his new store. "In the beginning," he says, "the thing to do is to get your shop open, the people coming, and the income flowing. Don't start out with just junk or no one will ever come back . . . but do be prepared to accept somewhat less than an ideal selection of consignment goods. Strike a fine balance. Once your new enterprise is safely launched you can begin improving your stock."

Now that Grasshopper Flats has come of age, Donn's policy of upgrading the merchandise sold in the store is clearly apparent. Unlike schlock shops—where one glance tells you there's nothing in the place you want—Grasshopper Flats invites you to take your time and look around at everything . . . because most items in stock are fine work. "Now, if a craftsman brings in something of poor workmanship, we tell him what's wrong with the piece, urge him to fix it, and *encourage* him to bring it back. We're constantly trying to enrich the store with things that look good."

The consignment merchandise is also expected to pay for its space and Donn says he's figured out a formula for computing the exact markup he must receive on each item. The formula varies with overhead, however, and what works for Grasshopper Flats won't work for anyone else . . . so Donn advises you to calculate your own sliding scale. Just remember that you don't want to rip off your customers and you certainly don't want to rip off your craftsmen-suppliers (many of whom will be your friends).

A major secret of Donn Stoffer's success is the $1.00 set of earrings. Seventy-five percent of his store's stock is products made by Donn and his apprentices . . . and about 35 percent of *that* is $1.00 earrings. The earrings cost 2¢ apiece (plus labor) to make and they always sell. They're the staple that Donn can count on to bring Grasshopper Flats a consistent income. If you're into another kind of craft, you should know of a comparable staple—such as ready-made sandals or a series of paintings on a simple theme—in your field on which you can base a business.

Donn pays his apprentices $20.00 per week, plus a commission. If he paid them $21.00, he'd have to begin withholding taxes and otherwise start down the government's road of enormous hassles and time-consuming red tape. Unless you hope to become a second General Motors, Stoffer feels that it's easier (and more fun) to keep things simple.

But do keep thorough books, Donn advises, and write *everything* down . . . even those 10-mile shopping trips. "That way you'll see what you're doing. You'll know whether you're going in the hole or pulling yourself out . . . whether you can buy more silver or leather or whatever, or ought to tighten your belt for another week until you *can* afford it."

Stoffer handles Grasshopper Flat's income in just as straightforward a manner: He puts nearly everything back into the business. The store grosses maybe $600–$800 a week. One hundred and fifty dollars of that is used to replenish the inventory and another $50.00 covers the overhead . . . which leaves about $450. And does Donn squander that $450 foolishly? Not on your life. He pays himself and Joyce $20.00 per week apiece (which is all they need to live on) and puts the rest back into the store.

By plowing back the shop's earnings this way, Donn is able

to finance inventory and expansion directly from Grasshopper Flat's cash flow and he's developed rather a disdain for the fix that most modern businesses mainline: credit. Matter of fact, Stoffer recommends staying completely away from the habit if at all possible.

When Donn first opened his store he bought all his supplies C.O.D. (because he had to). Then, as credit became available to the shop, Stoffer tried using it . . . but found the "courtesy" to be a hassle. Bills always came due when his cash was low . . . or when Donn wanted to buy something else . . . or when he had an opportunity to pick up a real bargain. So he

CHEAP SILVER

Donn Stoffer says the best place to buy silver (at prices something like one-third less than New York outlets charge) is from the company listed below. If you're a silversmith you might like to write for prices and compare.

Cincinnati Gold and Silver Refining
316 W. 4th St.
Cincinnati, Ohio 45202

learned to pay cash and keep the accounts straight as he goes along. When a Dun and Bradstreet questionnaire arrived in the mail recently, Donn just scribbled "DO NOT WANT CREDIT" on its face and sent it back.

Perhaps because he always knows where he stands, Donn can afford to be far more generous than most businessmen. If a customer walks out of Grasshopper Flats with a purchase and accidently drops it on the sidewalk . . . Stoffer gives that customer a free replacement. He also provides free tea and a sympathetic ear to all the students and freaks who drop in to talk. They seldom buy anything but Donn feels he meets a lot of good folks this way and that his easy way of running the store helps attract the paying customers.

Although Donn usually rationalizes his generosity ("I feel

good doing that and, besides, it's good publicity"), one gets the feeling that—good publicity or not—he'd do the expansive things he does anyway. If he happens to notice a little girl staring at a silver barrette, for instance, it's not unusual for him to take the piece of jewelry down and give it to her.

Stoffer is also famous for not charging sales tax to freaks or local folks. He pays it himself. "Aw, it doesn't amount to much," he says. "Keep the customers happy and they'll return the favor."

The other side of the coin, however, is *not to allow yourself to be taken* . . . and Donn is hard-nosed about theft. Signs all over the store warn that "If no one would steal, no one would have to be watched." Once, when some kids came in and lifted $300 worth of merchandise, Donn immediately called the sheriff. "If you let it get around that you can be ripped off, you'll become a constant victim . . . and so will your customers who have to pay higher prices to support the thieves."

Being honest, Stoffer says, isn't only right, it's also good business . . . especially when you're a longhair and vulnerable to community-relations problems. "When I came back to town, the first thing I did was get a haircut. Then I went around to Nashville's influential citizens, reintroduced myself, and explained what I intended to do. Putting it all up front that way did an untold amount of good in smoothing the way for Grasshopper Flats."

Donn also believes that "good business" means using every penny to the utmost. Even today—success that he is—Stoffer doesn't waste wire and he still takes the time to shop around for everything. Donn gets rock-bottom prices on beads, for example, by buying these simplest of items from a half dozen different sources.

Perhaps, though, the most important ingredient of all in Grasshopper Flat's success is Donn's attitude. He says, "I'm not interested in piling up a million dollars. The main reason I opened the store is because I like to make things with my hands. Though I haven't 'worked' for six years, I've put more hours into what I do than a factory does. But I *enjoy* it."

It's certainly nice to make a satisfying living while "playing" at the hobby you enjoy. Ask Donn Stoffer.♥

The above article originally appeared in THE MOTHER EARTH NEWS® NO. 15 . . . along with a great deal of other live-better-for-less and self-sufficiency how-to information. For further information about the magazine—and other books and periodicals devoted to home businesses, self-sufficiency, and related subjects—please see page 367 of this handbook.

CARTER RHYS:
HOW I STARTED A SILVER SHOP

When I was asked to write this article I had grave doubts as to whether I could be of much help to anyone. If considered as a real business, Renaissance is actually very backward and poorly done. In fact, it's the most unbusinesslike and informal shop I've ever seen—including "hip" establishments—and it certainly isn't making us rich. Nor have I any intention of correcting these shortcomings . . . I'm just not into making more money than we need.

We named the shop Renaissance because it is just that . . . a rebirth, back to using my hands, back to devoting my energies and thoughts to the creation of beautiful things. This change came after a ten-year sidetrack which began in the seventh grade when Sputnik was launched, took me to Princeton where I was supposed to major in mathematics (but wound up in philosophy), and ended over Thanksgiving dinner in 1967 at a prep school where I was teaching math and feeling useless and misdirected.

I see Renaissance as a long-term, transitional phase. It's the road I've chosen to getting into the country, painting, making very special silver pieces, and following all my other interests . . . surrounded by sunlight and space.

This is a long road because I want to be fully prepared for the end of it. I believe in slow organic growth and in following the natural order. There is something destructive and disharmonious about the shock of getting anywhere too fast, whether the vehicle be jet plane, acid, or a too-abrupt change in lifestyle.

This is what I believe. And the reason I put it all down before getting into the meat of the article is to allow you to see the attitudes behind what I write, attitudes which clearly are not best suited to the establishment of a permanent, profitable business.

You can see now why I had misgivings about writing this article. But it must be written, because the story of Renaissance is yet another story which can show you the two things which I believe this beautiful magazine is all about: You can do it, and it's worth it. I hope also to show you how.

MAKING THE BREAK

Perhaps you are now where I was that Thanksgiving: secure in a well-paying job but not very happy at it . . . with numbness creeping in over the frustration. My wife and I had no capital, not even a savings account. We wanted "out" but we had no idea where we would like to go. On top of that—if I left teaching—I would lose my deferment and force the draft board to rule on my claim of conscientious objection . . . a decision not likely to go in my favor.

It took tremendous courage and much soul searching to say "no" every time the headmaster urged me to sign a contract for the next school year. The one thought which prodded me into making the break was this: Of all the forty- and fifty-year-

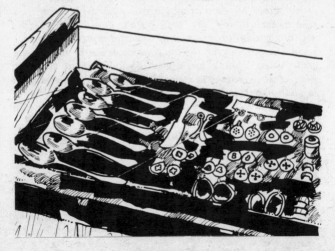

old men I knew, nearly every one was suffering from the illness known as *middle age*.

Middle age, as commonly observed in the American male, is only the realization that he is really never never going to do the things he dreamed of in his youth: never have an exciting job, never spend his vigorous years at what he likes to do, never write that book or paint the picture that takes twenty years of preparation. Now it's too late. Now he has *responsibilities*. And, worst of all, now he is so used to spending forty hours a week in irrelevant activity that he doesn't really care that much any more.

It's tragic to see such men shrug off fifteen years until retirement when they'll try to get down to living . . . but will have forgotten how. Fifteen years is a long time to shrug off and I've heard these men say, "Sometimes I wonder if I should have done thus-and-such with my life."

You see—easy as it is to put off the plunge for one more year while you're young—it gets even easier as you get older. If you're waiting one more year to save another couple thousand dollars, it won't be long before you'll be a rich, listless, and callous man of fifty waiting fifteen more years to retirement, wondering if you should have done it when you were twenty-five.

If my venture did fail, I decided, and I had to go back to a conventional career . . . at least when I was fifty I wouldn't be tortured by doubts. I would, at least, have tried. As far as the draft was concerned, I would just have to stand up for my convictions.

Of course the whole thing did work out and it took me an entire year to realize that I wasn't on vacation but was actually earning my living!

Even my claim to conscientious objection was accepted and Cathy, my wife, found she could keep the store open while I worked both there and in a hospital. This arrangement would have been acceptable for the entire two years of my alternative service, but the birth of our son took me entirely out of the draft picture . . . a nice break but not a necessary one.

The whole point is this: Whatever is hanging you up, whatever little excuses you have for knocking your head against the wall "for just one more year"—be it job security, money, fear, lack of training, even the draft—you CAN do it. You're never too young and *you're never too old* to make a fresh start. You CAN do it.

THE PROPER TRAINING

You can do it even if you're still a little unfocused about how you'll make it happen. The main reason I'm into silver work today is because that was one of the first classes to become available in the area where I was teaching. Perhaps your plans are a little more specific and you're already proficient in a craft. If so, fine. If not, let me put down some unproven impressions of my own.

There are two kinds of teachers . . . and they're both bad: The first is the man whose primary love is teaching instead of the field in which he instructs. The second is the individual who loves his subject matter . . . but not enough to go out and work at it; a teacher's salary is more important to him than working as he pleases.

A third kind of instructor (whom we won't even consider here) is the man who both works in a field and is employed by an institution to instruct others. He usually is "teaching" only because he's greedy for the extra money and he probably doesn't pay much attention to his students.

It is my personal opinion that you probably will not find a teacher who loves working in silver as much as you do—or *should*—if you are reading this article seriously. What you're looking for is a man who will teach you technique. By that, I mean the bare minimum of design and a lot about working. Your instructor should sit you down for a short lecture on the use of every tool he introduces, he should make you practice, and he should make you do any shabby job over until it is right.

I strongly advise you to seek out the second kind of instructor, the one who is teaching because he doesn't have the courage to make it on his own. He's the best compromise and you'll find him in craft centers and the like.

Avoid adult education classes held at night in high schools unless you are *sure* the instructor is not the artsy-craftsy type who only digs teaching. I would also avoid art institutes because instructors there are usually indifferent to teaching. And if they *do* instruct, they may very well try to teach you a style as well as techniques.

While you're taking lessons, read every book in the library which appears to be useful. And keep a notebook. Take notes in your class on everything you learn from books and doodle new designs all the time.

Of course you are not going to learn everything about jewelry making before you open your shop, unless you're willing to wait several years . . . which you don't want to do. If you've made three or more pieces which you consider really good—and are confident that you can turn out work of that quality consistently—go ahead. You'll get plenty of practice while stocking your shop for opening day. You can also experiment with ways of finishing pieces in less time.

GETTING FROM NOWHERE TO SOMEWHERE

We started with $1,000, no silver, no tools except a set of needle files, and one finished piece of jewelry. Within two weeks the car broke down and we found that we owed two months' security deposit plus a month's rent in advance on our new apartment. After deducting that, a month's rent on the store, and living and moving expenses . . . we had $100 left for the shop. We had hoped the $1,000 would last two months.

Cathy got a job which netted exactly enough for the two rents (home and shop). No food, no laundry, no gasoline, just rent. She drove a couple of other girls to work, which paid for gas and, since the shops in our area were staying open late every night, I offered to bring the shopkeepers a hot dinner for $1.50 each evening. Two of them accepted and there was just enough left for us to buy our vegetables (we're vegetarian, thank God) six nights a week. On Sunday we fasted or ate popcorn.

I couldn't believe the indifference with which people tossed around five dollar bills in the supermarket. When I took down one of the walls in the shop I saved and straightened every nail, pulled off the fireboard so as not to break it and used the wood to rebuild the interior and my workbench.

Of course we had no merchandise and no hope of buying silver to make any. But we had to open the store if we were to survive. Fortunately, we had a wire necklace Cathy had made in an adult education class. With her permission I borrowed a drawplate and drew the necklace out as thin as ear wires, then cut and bent it into shapes that could be worn in the ear. These were to become our $3.00 earrings.

I made papier-mâché bracelets, pendants, helmets, head-dresses, and lamps, embedded them with bits of broken mirror and bathroom chain, and painted them bright colors. We blew all our eggs and painted them and I covered the walls with my drawings. A month after renting it, we opened the shop: August 1, 1968. By mid-October, Cathy was able to quit her job and we have been supporting ourselves ever since.

It sounds scary as hell but it was really fun. The things to remember are: Make bits and pieces of money any way you can, have somebody—spouse, partner, even you—work while you're putting the shop together, and expect to be poor. If you can possibly avoid it, don't start without tools or materials as we did.

As for saving to finance your venture, that really depends on how long you're willing to wait before breathing free. More important than having a lot of capital is being able to make your assets grow, once you get started. It also does very good things for the head to start from nowhere and get to somewhere.

One more word about money: Don't ever, no matter *what*, ever go into debt. Don't even borrow a dime for a Coke. I've seen many shopkeepers on our street go into one form of debt or another and there isn't one of them who didn't emerge an unhappier person for it. Being in debt—not being your own man—brings on pressures from without and conflicts from within which can destroy you. Often the *one thing* which kept us working and kept us happy was that—broke as we were—we never owed anyone a penny.

WHERE WILL IT BE?

Choosing a location is a highly personal matter, and the shop you finally select will probably depend more on your personality than on considerations of good business. But don't be too hasty. In our case, we wanted a "hip" area but one that was not yet tourist-laden and commercialized. On the other hand, a hip area may look great at first, but turn out to be only a place where college kids play "dress up".

Every Saturday I'm appalled at how many of the beautiful young people walking up and down the strip are really only snotty know-it-all rich kids on a heavy ego trip. Remember, you'll be seeing these people day after day. The clever remarks they utter for the first time, you'll have heard a hundred times before. Many of them have dabbled in this or that and figure they can do everything you can do. They'll be sure to tell each other so loudly . . . just to put you properly in your place.

Though it may not seem so, this is an important point and I want you to think about it for a moment. Remember that you'll be hearing the same comments once or twice a day, month after month. The area you choose will predetermine the comments. If you pick a hip location, especially in a college area, you'll be amazed at how intolerant our generation is of people who sell their own work rather than factory-made Mod items. How many times have I smiled to myself at the comment: "It must be nice to have a shop for your own things . . . if you have the money!"

Of course I'm speaking from personal experience and can't really recommend a sure-fire location. But I can tell you this: On the whole, the rich ladies that everyone puts down (Why? Because they're rich?) are more tolerant, more interested, more interesting, more pleasant, and have better taste than many of the young adults who come into my shop. Like the college kids, many of these ladies have taken courses in silver. Unlike the college kids, they recognize that that's not the point and will appreciate your work because you did it as only you can.

Think about that.

Naturally you will also want to talk to the owners and clerks of existing shops to find out whether the area you're considering is growing or declining, and whether there will be any interest in a shop such as yours. It might not be a bad idea to stand in front of the location you have in mind and count passers-by over a given period of time. You want the most passers-by per dollar spent for rent. Thus, if one shop has double the traffic of another the same size, but rents for only 25% more, it's the better deal.

Once you're ready to start, find the county auditor's office and buy a vendor's license. If you're doing any renovations, you'll also need a building permit from the Building Department in your city. For simple jobs (like tearing down partitions, etc.) that do not involve electrical work or plumbing, you'll most likely be allowed to do your own work. Once you're finished, an inspector will come and look over the job to check for fire hazards or other violations of the building code. Be nice to the inspector; he's only trying to keep you out of trouble. When your place is approved you'll get a Certificate of Occupancy.

The last bit of red tape we had to go through was a sign permit, as there is a limitation on size and construction. Only the big outfits, with the really ugly eyesores, are granted variances. Try not to be too upset with the strange inconsistencies of your city government. Government is an organic thing and you will find an occasional tumor. Stay happy.

HOW TO PRICE YOUR WORK

It took me over a year to figure out how to price my work, and I suspect my fumbling around in this area has done more to hurt my business than any other single factor.

Every person who makes objects of beauty and offers them for sale probably has five or six friends who constantly tell him his prices are too low . . . regardless of how high they are. You must not listen to such people. It *is* possible to price your work too low but, chances are, you'll notice that these same friends won't be willing to buy your work at the prices they recommend. If they won't buy, why should a perfect stranger?

The first thing you have to do is figure out your costs, excepting materials. How much rent do you pay each hour you're open? Add on hourly rates for lights, phone, heat, and water if they're not included in the rent. What is an hour of your time worth to any average employer in your area? Or, if you intend to hold income to a subsistence level, determine your minimum expenses and calculate how much you must realize per working hour to cover them.

Total your basic wage or per-hour living expenses and the out-of-pocket costs (rent, etc.) of doing business. Add on a small percentage for growth, such as buying new tools and improving the shop. The result is the rate you should charge for your labor when you sell your goods wholesale. Let's see how this charge will be applied to the work you do.

Always make a prototype when starting a new design. This will give you an idea of the most expedient way to properly make the article. It will also help you judge the salability of the finished piece. If you're not sure it will sell, try it at a price that seems reasonable compared to your other prices. Chances are it won't sell very soon and you won't be making any more.

If you are certain a new piece will sell, set about making a number of them. Say six. For each step in the construction, time yourself and record the time in a notebook. This information will be useful later when you are estimating custom orders. Unless you stop working completely—to wait on a customer, for example—keep the clock running. Changing saw blades, rinsing the pickle from the soldered work, washing your hands, etc., are all part of the job.

Now compute the value of your labor per piece and weigh the finished work on a scale to calculate the value of the silver. The weight of the piece times your selling price for silver plus the value of your labor equals the wholesale price of the new design.

But, of course, you are not only a craftsman. You are also a shopkeeper. If you sold your work to a shop they would double your price to cover their expenses. You should do the same. You will find that nearly half your time will be spent talking to customers, sizing rings, and keeping books. So, to pay yourself for doing the shopkeeping, you must double the wholesale price. This gives you the final retail price. If you are a fast worker, as I am, it should be quite reasonable—less, in fact, than commercial silver jewelry—though you will inevitably overhear an occasional customer tell her friend, "This stuff is really expensive."

There are two exceptions to the above procedure. First, if you find yourself selling faster than you can produce but you don't want to hire an assistant, you must raise prices until business slows down to a level you can handle . . . unless you want to take all the fun out of it and work yourself to death to get rich.

Second, you should have one—or even a couple—bread and butter lines. These are designs which are fairly easy to make and which consistently sell at prices higher than the price you establish by timing yourself. Choose styles you enjoy making and which sell regularly.

The reason for a bread and butter line is that actually, unless you are a much better businessman than I am (and that's entirely possible), you won't be making as much per hour as you need. Now, of course, you could hold the prices low on these good sellers and spend all your time on them but that would leave no time for experimentation and an occasional super beautiful piece. It would, in other words, allow you no margin for the growth and development of your skill, and that is unfair to both you and your customer.

CUSTOM ORDERS

I spend roughly a third of my time making up custom orders. People who wish to have custom work done rarely buy the stand-ard styles, but they keep coming back for special designs and they bring their friends. For this reason it behooves you to do special jobs and—sometimes—even charge less for your time when doing them. Aside from the long-run financial gain, we have made some good friends through custom work.

Further, these custom jobs will help you grow and develop as you try new things. If you are careful to accept only those jobs you figure you can do but have never done before, you will learn something with every assignment. Just be sure you can handle it.

By custom work I do *not* mean repairs. If you have read this far, then I must assume that you are seeking a pleasurable occupation . . . and doing repairs most assuredly does not fall into that category. But it is very easy to get trapped.

People bring in non-sterling jewelry, jewelry they have tried to solder with lead (short of very careful filing, lead is impossible to remove and it permanently clogs files. If left on, lead will eat right through the silver when you heat it), glued pieces, and pieces which have been repaired before with soft solder (which will fall apart as you solder the new break and then you will have *two* repair jobs).

A creative jewelry maker has neither the tools nor the training for repair work and he has no business doing it. If a customer becomes insistent or starts begging—and they often do—emphasize that you are *not* a jeweler but a silversmith (or any other title of your choosing). This usually works.

Back to custom designs: There are two pitfalls you should

be warned about. First, never never start work until you have taken a deposit of roughly half your estimate. *Every single customer* from whom I have failed to take a deposit has disappeared and never returned. Every single customer . . . from friends to total strangers.

The second pitfall is one which you can avoid a number of ways (one of which works). This is the selection of a design. Many people will offer you close to total freedom, others will want you to sit down with them and do drawings. Very few will come in with any specific idea of what they want.

I am especially wary of those who offer me freedom to do what I want. After all, if none of my standard designs suited them, what assurance have I that they will like a special design done just for them? My experience has shown that such customers rarely like the special pieces any better than my other work. I've found that a person who offers you total freedom is really a person who has a definite idea way in the back of his head. What he is asking you to do is to come up with that design without making him go to the trouble of fishing it out and communicating it.

The same is true of those who want you to "just sketch some designs" for them. You will very likely spend well over an hour drawing only to have them finally get up and say, "Well, I'll think about it." In customer language, this always means "forget it".

Whenever a customer requests a custom job the first thing I do is tell him to go home and make some sketches. Nothing perfect, just an idea I can refine with him during his next visit. His next question is "how much will it cost", and I reply that I can't possibly make an estimate until I see his sketches. I spend absolutely the minimum time on this first visit. If the job is something I either cannot or do not wish to do, I tell the customer I am sorry but I do not do that type of work . . . and I refer him elsewhere. He is usually very understanding.

During the second visit—if the customer returns—I go over the designs with him, making whatever practical and artistic suggestions seem appropriate. I make absolutely certain that each of us completely understands every aspect of the design of the finished piece. I then offer an estimate (which is nearly always accepted), take his name, phone number, and deposit. We also agree upon the day he will return for the work.

If you wish, of course, you can accept total freedom on a custom job, but make *sure* that you'll be paid for the work . . . perhaps by charging the entire estimate in advance. And don't be disappointed when your customer doesn't seem very enthusiastic about the finished piece . . . or when he never returns.

You can also sit down on the first visit and draw for a prospective customer, but I strongly advise that if you do you charge him your hourly wholesale rate for the time so spent. Chances are, you'll realize no other financial gain from the session . . . and it won't really be much fun either.

There are exceptions to the policy I recommend. With some customers you can sit down and draw, depending on the job and how well you know the customer. You will learn these exceptions by trial and error. The only rule from which I never deviate is the 50% deposit.

MISCELLANEOUS TIPS

As you get into your shop you will find that some questions are asked over and over again: Do you have peace pendants? Would you make one? Do you have ankhs? Will you make them? Do you have zodiac symbols? Would you make one?

Peace pendants, ankhs, zodiac symbols, and the like have no place in a studio devoted to the creation of new designs. At least not in my opinion. They are also boring to execute and smack of commercialism. To spare myself and my customers the embarrassment of telling them this, I have found that a sign, strategically located and briefly stating my policy, does wonders.

I have signs discouraging the comment, "Oh, I could do that," signs discouraging repair work and peace symbols, and a chart showing where the money goes for people who complain that the prices are too high. The signs make everyone a little happier and that's what we're after.

Growth is, perhaps, the most important ingredient of success. If every time a person walks into your shop he sees the same old stuff, he will soon stop coming. Try your best to have a new design at least every week so people will learn that it is worth their while to stop in every now and again. If you're in a rut—always making the same old thing and never enjoying the creative end of the art—your store will suffer, your head will suffer, and you will lose your happiness and your customers.

WHERE TO ORDER TOOLS AND SILVER

The following company is sometimes very slow and seems to have grown to the point where it is indifferent to its customers, but it has the best selection of tools I've found anywhere:

Allcraft Tool & Supply Co., Inc.
100 Frank Road
Hicksville, New York 11801

or:

Allcraft Tool & Supply Co., Inc.
204 North Harbor Boulevard
Fullerton, California 92632

Allcraft's catalog costs $1.00 and that dollar is refunded with a purchase of $5.00 or more. You might also wish to order the $2.00 catalog (money refunded with an order of $10.00 or more within a year) from:

William Dixon, Inc.
Carlstadt, New Jersey 07072

I order all my metals from:

Hoover & Strong, Inc.
119 W. Tupper Street
Buffalo, New York 14201

Hoover & Strong is prompt, reasonable, and reliable . . . the best I've dealt with. The folks there have friendly vibrations. As far as I know they have no minimum.

Now you know everything I know about opening and running a shop for your own work. You know much more than I did when I started. The only obstacle which can possibly deter you is a lack of courage.
"And if we fail?"
"We fail! But screw your courage to the sticking place and we'll not fail." ⬥

The above article originally appeared in THE MOTHER EARTH NEWS® NO. 6 . . . along with a great deal of other live-better-for-less and self-sufficiency how-to information. For further information about the magazine—and other books and periodicals devoted to home businesses, self-sufficiency, and related subjects—please see page 367 of this handbook.

CLARENCE P. SOCWELL:

MY PAPERBACK BOOK EXCHANGE BUYS ME BOTH LEISURE AND PROFIT

Hey! Look at me! I just received a couple of awards in a poetry competition, sold a piece of my writing to a national magazine, and am now working on a novel, some stories, more poems, and still other articles. In between times I paint pictures and make ornaments out of driftwood, dried flowers, weeds, and other odds and ends. Am I independently wealthy?

No . . . but I can afford to indulge my creative interests because I've found a way to sit back and—quite easily and pleasantly—let enough money come in to keep the wolf from the door.

My "secret source of wealth" is a paperback book exchange. I started the business with a few books and very little money less than two years ago, and it's really beginning to thrive . . . but not so much that I have no time for writing and artwork. When that day comes, I'll sell the enterprise and start over in another town.

My reasons for wanting time to spare are probably not the same as yours. Perhaps you'd like to practice organic gardening, work with young people, or just commune with nature. Whatever you have in mind, though, you probably need to get away from the job that ties you down all day, five or six days a week, month in and month out. A paperback book exchange can give you that freedom.

Something else to consider is the service you'll be giving your community. You have only to look in any regular reader's garage, basement, or shed to find his old books . . . bought, read, and stored. He doesn't want to discard or destroy the volumes, but he really has no further use for them. A paperback exchange can put that library back into circulation and reward its former owner with new reading at a nominal price.

My own secondhand paperback establishment was started because of my wife's 87-year-old grandmother (whose primary entertainment is reading). After making a number of 80-mile round trips to such an exchange in Salt Lake City, it occurred to me that Ogden needed its own book-swapping center . . . and, since the town and its surrounding area have a population of over 100,000, I thought the venture would be profitable.

(Incidentally, more than a year of operation has convinced me that a smaller community—or even a rural area—should have enough readers to support a shop like mine. The more individuals you can reach easily, of course, the bigger the business . . . but location doesn't seem to be all that important. People will drive many miles for such a service. Some of my own customers live in Logan, about 60 miles away.)

What I needed first when I began my enterprise was a vacant store and, although Ogden's business rentals run pretty high, I found a good building—somewhat off the beaten path—for $150 a month. You might be able to do better in your own area. Then, too, there's always the possibility of operating out of an extra room in your home, a garage, or a roadside stand. Once readers find you they'll return repeatedly, wherever you are.

My own exchange is somewhat out of the way for shoppers in my city's center. Then again, a downtown location—which might give me more drop-in business—would be less convenient for people who must park a vehicle while they carry in their sacks of books. As it is, I know when someone walks in that he's probably there to buy . . . not just to browse.

And what about stock? In my case the answer to that question was easy: The owner of the Salt Lake City concern I'd been visiting told me he'd provide me with enough books to launch my enterprise, and that I could pay for them as my business progressed. The approximately 5,000 volumes I obtained in this way were more than enough for a beginning.

If I *had* lacked merchandise, though, I could have obtained it by other methods . . . perhaps at even less cost. For instance, some of my customers pick up old volumes at garage sales and turn them in to me for credit so they can choose the titles that they really want to read. A prospective dealer could obtain his goods the same way. A classified ad would probably bring in additional books for small fees, and you might induce youth groups to gather others for you in return for a small donation . . . say 5¢ a paperback. Now that I'm open, I've even been contacted by people who give me books just to be rid of them.

Whatever stock you get will have to be put in shape before you offer it for sale. To begin with, the paperbacks' covers often have to be washed. Many come in with spills on them, some are dusty from storage, and most are marked with body oils and dirt from normal handling. I spiff them up with a terry-cloth rag dampened with water and a liquid cleaner (or sometimes cleaner alone, on very dirty books).

After washing my new arrivals I check their covers for tears (which I repair with transparent tape . . . the kind that becomes invisible when pressed on). Loose bindings or pages are glued back into place. I don't accept an offering that lacks a cover or has leaves missing, by the way, but I'll take anything else . . . even if it's so shabby I have to throw it away. The resulting customer credit brings in money, and—eventually—I'll have too many books anyhow.

I display my merchandise quickly and inexpensively on 1" X 6" boards laid across 4" X 6" X 18" split cinder blocks that are set on end and spaced four feet apart. Books are stacked flat on the shelves so that [1] the titles can be read easily and [2] the full 18 inches between boards is utilized. Any kind of display can be used, however, as long as the paperbacks are accessible and their spines are in clear view.

Customers like my store because they can readily find what they want. I made this possible by arranging books under the following categories: general fiction, westerns, suspense, light romance, gothic, war, adult, science fiction, history, biography, classics, youth, poetry/stories/plays, and non-fiction. Within each class the books are shelved alphabetically by author.

I built my own counter from 1" plywood (a heavy table would have done just as well). Apart from stationery, the only other equipment I needed before I opened the used-paperback exchange was an adding machine. I filled that gap with an electronic calculator that cost me about $100 (these days they can be found for even less). Finally I painted my big storefront sign on a piece of 3/4" plywood and made other, smaller ones on poster paper for indoor use.

To let people know that The Bookateria was ready for business, I placed a notice in *The Big Nickel* (a classified ad publication distributed free in local stores). The charge is 5¢ a word, and a dollar or so a week buys quite a lot of public attention. Later I also took advertising space in the Yellow Pages of the telephone directory.

I also considered newspaper advertising at first, but decided against it because of [1] the cost and [2] my own belief that people who read classified newspaper ads are looking for something specific like a used car or an apartment. Such individuals, I feel, wouldn't be attracted by my notice in sufficient numbers to justify its expense. In contrast, thrifty folks who pick up *The Big Nickel* will scan several pages searching out bargains.

When a salesman for a local radio station tried to sell me air time, I asked him how large an audience he could guarantee. The report he quoted from described a survey in which the station had called 304 people and found 164 home, with 31 listening to the radio. An additional 133 said they were occasional radio listeners... *but only 16 claimed that they tuned in to that particular station.* The odds that possible customers would be listening at the particular time my announcement was read appeared negligible ... and the rates for a package of ads ranged from $75.00 to $130 for a ten-day period. Needless to say, I didn't subscribe. I'll leave radio and TV advertising to big concerns with large advertising budgets.

My wife and I did have several hundred fliers run off by an inexpensive "instant" print shop. We had some boys and girls leave the sheets on doorsteps ... and even put quite a number on automobile windshields in various downtown parking lots before we discovered an ordinance against flier advertising in the city center. At any rate, we got better results from the notices we tacked to bulletin boards in laundromats and at the local college.

We always have some of our fliers available for new customers to give to their friends or to post at their places of business. We never suggest that anyone do so, but our patrons

are so pleased with The Bookateria that they often volunteer to help us in this way.

On the whole, my publicity and ad campaign has worked quite well. Although I haven't advertised in *The Big Nickel* for weeks, new customers come in every day because they've seen the notice in the Yellow Pages or heard about us from other people.

Would-be buyers, of course, need to know *when*—as well as where—they can find me doing business . . . so I've established regular hours. Inasmuch as my hobbies can be enjoyed right at

FIG. 1		FISHER, JOE			
Date	Books In	Trade Value	Books Out	Value	Balance
Aug. 28	11	4.40	6	3.75	.65
Sept. 17	12	6.10	4	4.65	2.10
Oct. 1	7	5.30	5	3.30	4.10

the store, I keep to quite a full schedule: 10 a.m. to 7 p.m. six days a week. At first—out of consideration to late shoppers— we stayed open until 9 p.m. on Mondays and Fridays, but the few people who took advantage of the extended hours didn't make the time profitable. You may want to open your own store only a few days a week or a few hours a day . . . but whatever timetable you set up, you should stick to it out of respect to your clientele.

We expected our exchange to produce income the day it opened (it did), so we had our bookkeeping methods figured out in advance. When a person brings in books I give him 70% of the volumes' list price as trade value. Example: if he hands me $10.00 worth of old paperbacks, he can take out other titles worth $7.00 *plus 10¢ in cash for each "new" book he chooses.* If the value of the titles he picks doesn't equal the *trade* value of those he brought in, the customer's balance is entered on a 3" X 5" card (Fig. 1) that I file alphabetically for easy access.

If the customer wants to take out more books than he has credit with The Bookateria, or if he has no goods to exchange, I charge just half the list price on each item he buys. In this way I needn't do any special pricing and my patrons know what any given title will cost.

To keep my accounts in order, I make an entry of each sale on a daily record which is divided into trade and straight transactions. With the help of my calculator I fill in each column as the deal is made. The 70% figure is rounded off to the nearest 5¢ (See Fig. 2).

I tally up the "charge" columns at closing time so I know just how much the day brought in. For tax purposes, I keep track of all expenses and income in a ledger.

I should mention that I'm required to collect state and local taxes, which necessitates getting a sales tax number (free) from the state and sending in the appropriate amount of money every three months. (This is the procedure for Utah . . . it may be different in other states.)

You'll have to wade through one more bit of red tape, of course, to get your city or county business license. Its cost will vary according to your firm's gross income. In Ogden, any concern which grosses less than $5,000 per year is charged $12.50 annually . . . which isn't too bad.

How about the profits? Well, they're pretty good for so little effort. We grossed approximately $6,000 during our first 12 months and will probably reach about $9,000 the second time round. That's certainly not all profit, to be sure, but the overhead I have to deduct from this figure _is_ extremely low: I never have to replace stock (because it replaces itself) . . . most advertising—apart from my space in the Yellow Pages—is by word of mouth . . . and I have no need for hired help.

Perhaps more important to me than the money I make is the time I have for other activities—my writing and art—and the satisfaction I get from such comments as, "This is wonderful! Now I can read all I want," and "I wish I'd known about this sooner."

Furthermore, as a member of a very wasteful society, I enjoy the fact that I'm helping to recycle knowledge and enjoyment (as well as the paper on which it's printed). It's also amazing how many friends I've made among the customers who return week after week.

A book exchange is just the right business for me. Try it. It might be just right for you too. ●

FIG. 2			MONDAY, OCT. 1, 1973					
TRADE						STRAIGHT SALES		
# In	Value	70%	# Out	Value	Charge	# Out	Value	Charge
13	12.30	8.60	2	3.00	.20	1	.50	.25
11	10.65	7.45	9	7.70	.90	3	2.50	1.25
47	28.10	19.70	41	22.75	4.10	1	1.50	.75
7	3.50	2.45	5	2.45	.50	2	1.35	.68
			1	.95	.10	3	2.85	1.43
7	7.55	5.30						

Note: The customers of the second, third, and fifth trade sales in this example already had balances due on their customer cards. The sixth trade customer brought in books but didn't buy any at this time.

End-of-day totals are not tallied for the "value" or "70%" columns. Those figures are used only in calculating the transaction and the credit or charge entered on the customer card.

THE ECONOMICS OF A PAPERBACK EXCHANGE

You may have thought, as you read my article, that $9,000 a year is an awful lot of dimes . . . and you may not have seen at first glance how I can make *any* profit on that gross when I offer my clients a trade value that's higher than my selling price for the volumes they bring me. A further explanation may well be in order.

The reason I can't lose money by giving a customer 70% of list price as trade value on the books he brings in—on merchandise which sells at 50% of the same figure—is that the

50% is cash and the 70% credit. And even though the patron is entitled to purchase books to the limit of his allowance . . . he *still* has to pay me 10¢ cash for each one he chooses.

Most people use their full trade values and perhaps take a couple of extra books at half price (a practice I encourage by giving only 70% of the goods' worth in exchange). Other folks are collectors and always pay the 50% rate because they keep their purchases.

Last year I did some figuring and discovered that each volume which went out brought an average of 27¢ into the store. In reality, though, every book in stock has much more potential than that . . . because it may pass through my hands a number of times. An initial sale often is just the start of my gain.

Let's say, for example, that a customer buys $10.00 worth of my stock, at the 50% rate, for $5.00. Later he brings the books back for exchange, at which time he receives 70% of the list price in trade value and takes out the full $7.00 worth of reading matter. That's maybe 10 titles or so, at a dime each . . . another dollar in cash for me. Then someone else purchases the returned volumes, either at half price ($5.00) or at 10¢ apiece ($1.30). He, too, may turn them in later, and they'll circulate yet again . . . leaving still more dimes or half-price payments in the store.

Maybe by this point you're finding it easier to believe my $9,000 gross income. Last Saturday, for example, we took in 256 books for trade while 161 went out at 10¢ each ($16.10). Meanwhile, 42 volumes sold for half their list price and brought in $19.88. The day's sales totaled $35.98. Business varies, of course, but if that rate were constant we'd be grossing over $11,000 a year. Note also that the day's transactions *increased* my stock by 53 items. Our policy of giving 70% trade value makes this a typical occurrence.

Incidentally, my friend at the Salt Lake City book exchange is now—after five years in business—grossing about $20,000 annually. I doubt that his overhead has increased much in that period . . . apart from the fact that he now hires some help so he can enjoy more free time. That's the way to live! ◗

The above article originally appeared in LIFESTYLE! NO. 8 . . . along with a great deal of other live-better-for-less and self-sufficiency how-to information. For further information about the magazine—and other books and periodicals devoted to home businesses, self-sufficiency, and related subjects—please see page 367 of this handbook.

PAUL ENCIMER:
USED BOOKS CAN GIVE YOU A NEW LIFE

Is it still possible—in this age of computerized frustration and urban crisis—to live a meaningful, satisfying, ecologically sound, and fairly low-pressure lifestyle in the city? Yes. I've done it for years . . . as owner-operator of one of the world's oldest kinds of recycling centers: a used-book store. The business worked out well for me (even though it did come close to making me the perfect Small Shopkeeper) and it might be the answer to *your* quest for "A Good Life and a Good Living".

I expect that my experience can be applied to any metropolitan area of some size although I should note, before I begin, that all my own used-book store experience has been on the West Coast. The communities I've worked in, however, have varied considerably (three years intensive browsing and buying in the Bay Area, five years of shop ownership in the lower-middle-class family community of Inglewood, and five years split between a semislum in western L.A. and a more solidly middle-class and academic section of Santa Monica). This article contains the distilled wisdom of that 13 years spent dealing in used books. It should, I believe, contain enough facts to put any determined and reasonably capable individual into the business in almost any urban area of the country.

THE ESSENTIALS

OK. To open a used-book store, you must have:

[1] A steady supply of cash with which to buy books as you come across them.

[2] Enough free time to work out a route of thrift stores, junk shops, and booksellers from which you will begin to accumulate the stock necessary to start your store. Given that stock you must have:

[3] A location in which to do business. Its rent, book capacity, and area will help to make or break your enterprise. But in order to open your doors you will need:

[4] Licenses from the city and perhaps a permit from its police department.

[5] The go-ahead from the State Board of Equalization which (as in California) may demand a deposit of several hundred dollars before issuing you a license to resell merchandise. When you've obtained the city and state permits you will require:

[6] A rational and accessible arrangement of books on stable shelving. This is the essence of your merchandising. Given a well-organized store, you will need:

[7] A posted schedule of days and hours. An ad in the Yellow Pages is the most helpful form of ongoing advertising but word of mouth and plain chance will be your biggest source of customers.

[8] Motivation sufficient to keep you from walking off the job in the middle. This incentive can be a starving family, a love of money, an unholy passion for books, an intense hatred of real work, a desire for a minimum of independence . . . anything to keep you coming in five or six days a week.

In the process of expanding on the preceding points, this article should succeed in raising most of the questions you'll need to think about before embarking on your career in used books.

MONEY

Money—which is listed Number One—may well be your greatest stumbling block. As you know, they named the system after the fact that you need a certain chunk of capital just to take your first breath. If you have a big pile of bread to fall back on, great. You can go out scouting for stock five days a week and be in business within the year. In fact, a friend of mine hunted up his opening-day stock of 2,000-plus books in half that time.

LOCATION

The perfect area for a book dealer is many-faceted. Ideally, you might have a university and/or a counterculture contingent on one border of your neighborhood, a choice piece of real estate containing a healthy sampling of the well-to-do on another . . . with a large population of highly literate and highly mobile (*moving* is a prime reason people give for selling their books) middle-income apartment dwellers surrounding you. The store itself might sit on a well-traveled side street that leads into a large and thriving business district or beside a main drag which sends thousands of cars and/or pedestrians past you daily.

Such an area would maximize your chances of selling your fabulous stock and should disgorge a varied surplus of books with which to replenish your supply. This is crucial. Your community's reading habits and interests will be reflected quickly within your shop. If the intellectual horizons of the community are limited, your store will show it.

IF YOU RENT A SHOP . . .

When you rent, your landlord will want a lease. Ideal for you would be something like one year cheap, with a ten-year option at the same terms. What the landlord asks for, however, depends on the degree of his desperation, how much he wants to nail you down, and what sort of plans he has for raising the rent later on. I consider anything under $200 reasonable—all things considered—but established used-book stores have been known to survive rents of $800.

ZONING

It's the "used" nature of your business-to-be that causes certain areas to be zoned to exclude you. In these sections, used-book stores are classed with junk, thrift, and secondhand clothing stores. Though this is actually very pleasant company, you may want to represent yourself—for strategic reasons—as a dealer in scarce, rare, or out-of-print volumes. This would put you more on the level of an antique store and open the better zones to your shop. It's more likely, however, that high rents would exclude you from the best districts long before zoning ordinances.

POLICE PERMIT

In some cities there is an added penalty for dealing in used merchandise in that you may be required to have a police permit before you can do business. Theoretically, the guardians of the law are afraid that you'll use your operation to fence stolen goods. The police, of course, know better, but the permit may give them a lever to harass you if you've ever been arrested. In that case, you may have to hire a local attorney (for instance, the D.A.'s brother-in-law) who's familiar with the political situation.

CITY LICENSES

Local permits are usually dirt cheap—$12.00 to $50.00 a year—and hardly significant in terms of your overhead. The Chamber of Commerce will try to sign you up at another $50.00 to $100, but there's no penalty for not joining.

BUSINESS EQUIPMENT

Don't burden yourself with useless machinery. A cash register takes up a lot of desk space and, along with an adding machine, is really a case of overkill. Since you set your own prices, you can make them all end in zeros and fives, while a simple lockbox in your desk drawer will do fine to hold your bills and change. Business cards are a good investment, however, and one designed for use as a bookmark can carry your advertising far into the future.

SHELVES

Wood is expensive and carpenters even more so. If you have any inclination in that direction, you'll save a lot of money by building your own bookcases. Since I'm no handyman, my only advice here is to consider carefully how tall the individual shelves are going to be.

I recommend an arrangement something like this: top and bottom shelves 13 inches high with five more—each 11 inches in height—in between. This puts your highest row of books within reach as well as allowing for different volume sizes. A section of 15-inch-high shelves should be set aside for art and other oversize works. Since the optimum way to display paperbacks (aside from a rack) is on their sides, spines showing, a shelf 7-1/2 inches high works and will allow you to set the paperbacks upright if you choose.

SPACE

A large store—which means, to me, in the neighborhood of 2,000 feet—has its advantages. Remember, first of all, that in a couple of years, your opening stock of 2,000–3,000 volumes may increase fivefold and more. Also, ample space takes pressure off you and gives you room to experiment with what sells and what doesn't in your particular area.

This reasoning, of course, can be taken to a ridiculous extreme. I've done it myself. In fact, my earliest ideal in store size was a warehouse of a place where the unwary customer could get lost in the labyrinths. (The truth is, I'm a junk dealer by first instinct and like to have enough space for everything I find.)

Over the years, interestingly enough, I've drastically moderated my earlier thoughts on space. While I still believe that the simpler customers are impressed enough by the sheer bulk of a Queen Mary-size operation to spread the word in awe, recent experience has taught me that a store of not much more than 1,000 square feet is perfectly adequate. Adequate, that is, if you use discrimination in your book-buying forays. Most of the rest of this article is designed to help you develop that discrimination.

ROUNDING UP THE ORIGINAL STOCK

To begin with, there are your own books . . . at least some

of which you will undoubtedly donate to your cause, along with whatever reading matter of your friends' and relatives' you can get your hands on. It's a start, but still far from the 2,000–3,000 volumes you'll need to open your doors. The major part of that first stock, then, you'll get from three sources: scouting, house calls, and buying across the counter.

SCOUTING

For the beginner, it's scouting which will bring in the bulk of the books. The search begins in thrift shops, Goodwills, Salvation Armies, junk stores, and so on where the price per book is around a quarter.

Scouting in established bookstores is expensive but it can pay off in terms of education. If you've acquired a field or fields of special competence, you may hope to pick up a bargain here and there to salt the stock of your store-to-be. Beware of becoming a premature specialist, though, unless you really know what you're doing. Later your location, as I've said, will dictate specialties to you.

If you plan to do much buying in established used-book stores (in spite of the higher prices you'll pay there), it might be wise for you to get your Board of Equalization license (where needed) early in the game. For one thing, this permit will release you from the necessity of paying sales tax. Also, book dealers tend to respect such permits and—since it's traditional in the used-book business for one dealer to offer a discount to another (normally 20%)—your license may give you sufficient standing to qualify for this trade courtesy.

You'll want to work out some sort of rhythm in visiting your various book bargain centers. If you put together a regular route you'll begin to discover helpful facts: for instance, which days new shipments of books are likely to arrive or be displayed. You'll also get to know the clerks who work at your customary stops. They may be appreciative of a steady customer who buys in quantity and offer you a discount . . . or they may give you first crack at a new load of stock as yet unboxed in the storeroom.

HOUSE CALLS

At this point in our imaginings, you have no store but, if you're geographically stable, you can use your current home phone to attract sellers with a small ad: *Bargain Book Shop,*

Books Bought under "Books" in the business section of your local telephone directory. Prospective sellers who notice this listing (and, later, additional potential sellers who see the same kind of sign in the window of your shop) will—sooner or later—begin to contact you and ask you to come look at their books.

The results, at least in the beginning, may not pay for the cost of your ad . . . but, if you're lucky, two or three good libraries could give your store depth in surprising places. Such richness can elicit word-of-mouth advertising. It may also prevent your first browsers from mentally crossing you off as a junk-store operator, and lead to their curious reappearance later. This is more important than you now realize.

Once you're established, you'll be choosy and refuse to travel to view any library that contains less than X number of titles. You'll be looking, as well, to avoid certain types of libraries . . . such as ones made up of book-club offerings, general fiction, and school texts. At this point in your career, however, you're probably wise to follow every lead that you're offered.

BUYING ACROSS THE COUNTER

After your business is really rolling, buying across the counter will supply you with more than enough books. People will voluntarily come into your store during operating hours with bags and boxes of possible stock. This is an advanced stage of the operation and I'll deal with the specifics of that kind of buying later in the article.

HOW TO RECOGNIZE GARBAGE

You'll have to handle a certain amount of garbage before you begin to recognize it. You may even have to live with rows of trash books, sitting on the shelves of your finally opened bookstore, for months or years before you begin to pick up their peculiar odor.

Of course, if your book-scouting days are to be productive you must be inoculated against accumulating too much garbage in your system or bankruptcy will result. Discrimination is quite a task, too, considering that 99% of the books you'll be seeing in your thrift store rounds will be worthless. Luckily for simple instructors like myself, useless items fall into large and distinguishable categories.

To begin with, a book is worth nothing when no one wants to buy it . . . and a prime example is the bulk of book-club fiction. Why? For one thing, millions have already bought these various novels and the market is glutted. Then, too, those looking outside the book clubs for cheap leisure reading prefer paperbacks these days (and even that area is glutted). The book-club novel, moreover, is a mail-order item and it isn't very attractive in the flesh.

You can help yourself recognize these unsalable works by buying a $6.95 novel at your local bookseller. Carry it around with you on your various rounds and compare weight against weight: The book-club edition is light, like white bread. Compare dust jackets: The mail-order jacket is thin and flimsy and, to make it easier on you, often has "book club" stamped on the front flap. Compare bindings: The cheap volume has a smooth, cardboard cover while your expensive hard-cover is bound in rougher buckram or cloth. Also, the book-club publication sometimes has a little circle stamped into the lower right-hand corner of the cover.

Even without book-club novels, a good deal of what you'll see in the secondhand stores will be fiction . . . but my advice is to go easy on it since most of what you'll find on your scouting travels will be old and outdated best sellers. (See my remarks on fiction under "WHAT PEOPLE BUY".)

There's no market, either, for books people were forced into buying in the first place. The textbook in particular was bought under constraint and so is detached from the "real" life of your customers. This means that you'll see many more schoolbooks in your scouting tours than you'll later find a market for. The salable exceptions are mentioned in "WHAT PEOPLE BUY".

WHAT'S IT WORTH?

What makes it worth your time and money to handle a book? The first and most obvious rule of the game is for a title's publisher to offer the volume at a fancy price.

Let's say that the new price on a particular in-print title is $20.00. Any copies of the book you have, then, should be salable to a bargain buyer at some fraction of that amount . . . usually around half the listed value.

To be even more specific, my rule of thumb has been never

to pay more than 20% of a title's new price. If I think I can get $12.00 for a $20.00 art book that's offered to me, I'll happily pay $4.00. This rule—also known as "Triple Your Money"—goes into operation primarily after you've opened your bookstore doors. In thrift shops you'll pay the price marked inside a volume's cover (which should be a bargain), but when people begin bringing books into your establishment, they'll want more than just a quarter for each one.

PRICING IN-PRINT BOOKS

Now, to discover the in-print, new prices of the books you accumulate, you'll need that most invaluable of all reference guides: *Books in Print,* in two volumes arranged by title and author and published by R.R. Bowker Co., 1180 Avenue of the Americas, New York, N.Y. 10036 for $20.00. In your early days of scouting you can get away with a year-or-two-old copy—if a local used dealer has one for sale—but when your own doors are open, a current edition of *Books in Print* is a must. I've always made a habit of using the guide to check doubtful titles while I'm buying. It gives me a precise reference from which to work.

Condition is another crucial aspect of book pricing and each volume moves along a scale somewhat like the following: Mint, Fine, Good, Fair, Poor, Ratty.

"Mint" is a term borrowed from the coin collector and refers to an item as fresh and crisp as the day it was issued. A mint copy in its original dust jacket has an irresistible appeal to the true collector.

"Ratty", on the other hand—a label that will never turn up in dealers' catalogs—means damaged, dog-eared, and underlined. You want to keep such volumes out of your store . . . they detract from and drag down everything around them. For the average in-print and out-of-print book, it's enough that it falls between the extremes of Mint and Ratty. Your price should relate to any individual copy's place on the spectrum of condition.

You must also take into consideration demand or shelf life of a given title. The longer it's going to sit on your shelf, the less—proportionally—you want to pay. It takes some experience to sense the possible shelf life of a book (will it move fast, slow, or at all?), although the title's category will soon give you a reliable hint.

To figure your markup on in-print books, return to my "Triple Your Money" formula. This rule of thumb was pounded into my head as dogma when I first entered the business and is definitely in line with the standards of the field. In fact, some dealers even like a margin that is multiplied by a factor of five or more. Your "Triple Your Money" guide, then, should at least keep you competitive.

The rationale behind the 3-for-1 rule, of course, is 1/3 to the seller, 1/3 to overhead, and 1/3 to you, the dealer. However, in my ten years' experience, I've found that my cut ends up as at least half the gross. Furthermore, as you build your stock of books, customers, and experience, the profit will keep going from plateau to plateau just as if it were being guided by Adam Smith's invisible hand, and will stabilize at ever more comfortable levels.

Despite the fact that I could tell my customers to their faces what my markup was without having them go into convulsions, I have come to believe that you can carry "Triple Your Money" beyond the point that brings you a just price. If I were to return to the used-book business tomorrow, I'd settle for double my money as a base, *though I don't recommend this as a safe policy until you master the business.* And, of course, no formula can substitute for the sliding scales which operate according to the condition and shelf life of a particular book. I'm merely suggesting that—as you, too, increase your skill in the business—you'll no longer need the security of profit margins which were originally created to protect you from the unforeseen and from your own mistakes.

After you've mentally (and spiritually) settled on a price for each in-print book, I recommend penciling in the new book price, only to cross it out and put your used price below. No, this is not a bargain-basement merchandising trick. You're giving your customer one of the important facts he needs to make up his mind by telling him just how much he's getting off the original cost. This stops many price hassles before they start and gives you more time to read.

PRICING OUT-OF-PRINT BOOKS

So much for pricing in-print books. What about out-of-print volumes? First, many that are of recent vintage can be treated with the same standards we applied to the in-print book, making necessary adjustments for inflation.

For instance, suppose that a book in question was printed in 1961 and its dust jacket says $4.00, but its equivalent price nowadays is $10.00. Condition and demand being equal, price it at $5.00 as you might if it were a current title.

Most books, you see, are no more impressive to customers because they're out of print. The prospective buyer is usually looking for a title on a certain subject and it doesn't concern him whether or not a particular edition is still available new. Because he's probably not a book collector, he won't pay a price that he considers out of the normal range for books of a particular topic. Instead, he'll merely look elsewhere.

The book collector, on the other hand, has already looked elsewhere. He knows roughly the range of prices at which an individual title may be offered and how hard the book is to get. This buyer is either someone filling out spaces in a private collection or a public employee doing the same for a college or city library. He may also be a special case: a book scout looking for underpriced bargains.

THE "UNUSUAL" TITLES

As literacy in America increases, so do private and public libraries and it's the plentiful numbers of book collectors—as much as the objective qualities of the book itself—which create the high prices that get attached to certain works. The whole process, indeed, may often resemble nothing so much as the lowly fad.

Nevertheless, there are—as I've said—objective qualities which have something to do with determining the price of books: irreplaceability or scarcity; the quality of the prose; the beauty of the binding, printing, or plates; the fame or notoriety of the author; the scholarly nature of the book (research quality, footnotes, bibliography), and similar indications of intrinsic value. After sufficient volumes pass through your hands, you will develop a keen sense for the unusual. Something about it will catch your attention, and there's nothing wrong with setting such a book aside until you can figure out its possible worth.

THE REFERENCE LIBRARY

In strictly practical terms, $20.00 has been the highest price I've thought I could put on a book with my unaided eye and mind. To write "$75.00" or "$300" in pencil on the front page of a volume definitely calls for the prop of an outside authority: a reference library of some sort.

The most "objective" of these references is the *Auction Record*, a list of books followed by the prices they sold for at public auctions held in London or New York. The records are issued yearly, or in five-year accumulations, by the auction houses, and they're expensive. The most recent *Five Year Auction Record* sells in the neighborhood of $100 a copy. Out-of-print older editions of these listings are hard to come by and can also be costly.

When I was in business, my own reference library included two five-year records covering the '40's. Given my limited experience and interest in rare books, the auction records were particularly useful in helping to approximate prices for English and European books. I found that it gave a real authority to the figures listed in the auction records to know that someone in the flesh had stood up in public and paid the money. Of course, inflation and prices in English pounds can make translation into the present a chancy business, but the information at least serves to warn you that the 16th-century book by the King of Spain that you hoped would be worth $1,000 went for auction in 1944 at $5.50.

Another source of book prices are the many dealers' catalogs on every topic. The prices in these bulletins are based first and foremost on the dealer's experience: He knows of someone, perhaps, who paid $8.00 for Saunder's *Social System of Fowls* last year, so he lists the work at $12.00 or $15.00. The dealer will also use auction records, other catalogs, and price guides to augment his own experience.

The price guides have the benefit of an overview, being the result of an editor's comparisons among different catalogs and auction records within a particular field in the light of his own experience and judgment. This results in a reference work that's a little more dependable than the single dealer's catalog. Unfortunately, it's easy to invest hundreds of dollars in such price guides and not fill a small shelf. I've found the following handbooks of value:

Roskie's *Bookman's Bible.* Three very compact volumes, skillfully arranged and covering a hundred years of publishing.

Heard's *Guide to Americana,* fourth and fifth editions.

Valuable reference for Western Americana and American history.

Used Book Price Guide. Three volumes. Aviation, American firsts, etc.

Boutell's *First Editions and How to Tell Them.* Surveys both English and American publishers and will settle almost all doubts.

At this point, let me caution you against becoming the kind of premature antiquarian dealer who projects "rarity" into everything he touches. Bear in mind that damned few really valuable books will fall into your hands by chance. Rare editions are already owned, in most cases, by people who know their value because they paid a lot for them and only ignorant used-book dealers fill their stores with highly priced garbage.

You should also guard against becoming so paranoid about underpricing a book that you "cover" yourself by marking up almost everything. Five or ten dollars extra won't guard you against the real mistakes and you'll only depress your customers with your irrational figures . . . thus making it hard for them to spend money with you.

WHAT PEOPLE BUY

What I need to pass on to you now is a concrete idea of the variety of people's tastes in reading matter . . . a diversity that I can best convey by running through the categories book dealers use to classify works for sale.

The classifications arose from the used-book seller's need to organize his store efficiently so he could set his stock in order and keep better track of individual volumes. Putting books of one theme together in the same area serves the customer too, of course, and protects the busy browser from exhausting himself prematurely. However, the system's special value to you—at this point—is to sharpen your buying eye. Indeed, just the bare names of the genres should give you some notion of what to expect and what to look for in your scouting travels.

I'll start my survey of book categories with some sections that are often of interest to collectors, and end it with paperbacks, the favorites of the idle reader.

COLLECTORS' ITEMS

FINE EDITIONS are books that are especially well bound or illustrated. Some are in print and should be priced accordingly. Also, many are available through expensive book clubs and their prices can be monitored through the advertising pages of quality magazines.

LEATHER BINDINGS are collectable even when the book itself is insignificant. Clever plastics have replaced hide in current production and bookbinders charge a fortune for the real thing, so there are plenty of eager buyers of old leather. When you price a volume for its binding, consider the condition of the material, the amount used, and the quality of the workmanship.

ILLUSTRATED WORKS. Many older volumes contain lovely color plates, woodcuts, and other ornaments which can increase the editions' value manyfold. This is especially true of children's books and of publications from around the turn of the century which follow an *art nouveau* style. Keep your eyes open, also, for books with good paper, tooled bindings, and exceptional printing.

When you price in the above areas, as elsewhere, you'll have to rely on your own judgment and on experimentation. Handy rule of thumb: Think to yourself when you're handling a choice book, "When am I going to see another one like it?"

FIRST EDITIONS. For purposes of collection, these are mostly American novels but can include any literary item of merit. Since fads and fashions are important in this hobby, current catalogs can be a help to the dealer . . . but a friendly fellow bookseller or a couple of good customers will be your best sources of education.

WESTERN AMERICANA. The emphasis in this field is on the settlement of the local area (*your* local area) and on the Western movement in general. Western Americana is not to be confused with American history, which is primarily political in conception and offered in textbook form. (The Civil War is the exception that straddles academic history and Americana.) Books on this theme are generally priced below $10.00.

ART BOOKS. Although big books with fancy prices and color plates are the cream of this section, overproduction, remainders, discounted prices, and collectors' book clubs have created something of a glut. Avoid textbooks of the art appreciation variety and handle art books without color plates cautiously. Artists' handbooks and technical aids are in some demand if clean and current.

A brief interjection on the subject of remainders: Several New York firms offer bargains which are the genuine result of publishers' overstock. For example, if demand for a certain title has died in the middle of the third edition (or, unfortunately, the first), the publisher may then turn over the remainder of the unsold copies to wheeler-dealers at spectacularly reduced prices. Years later some of these books may become valuable. Be careful, however, of publishing companies which produce phony remainders, specially printed and "marked down" from front flap prices never meant to be charged.

Before leaving the area of oversized and fancy volumes, let me add to the list architecture, city planning, travel, and photography collections . . . customers seldom queue up before these sections.

THE ARTS

POETRY. Avoid anthologies, but *not* the collected works of single writers. Poetry, high and low, is a living art and authors of every type seem to have their followers . . . so, as you scout, buy whichever poets your budget will allow. Although modern works sell fastest, the old classics should be kept in stock at reasonable rates (1/3 to 1/4 of the new price, for instance). Remember that the shelf life of other verse will be longer, and pay accordingly. By the way, I suggest that you eventually alphabetize your poets for convenience.

LITERARY CRITICISM. I've found it handy to put studies of particular writers in among the author's creative works. Otherwise—though individual critics can receive tiny amounts of popular attention—this is a pretty academic section. Don't go out of your way, either, to stock criticism of the mass media.

THEATER AND CINEMA. Except maybe in New York, theater books move slowly. (Most of what you'll see in scouting is college drama-class stuff.) Even the play, which is a respectable literary form, collects dust. Movies, though, may have their fans everywhere, so be alert to the interests of your area.

MUSIC. Classical scores, sheet music, and instruction books move well, but school texts on appreciation and understanding are useless. There are feeble cults for opera, jazz, classical, and—coming up—rock. The best sellers are works intended for

musicians . . . handbooks on instrument making go immediately.

And what about records? The ones you'll see on your
thrift-store rounds—and even those offered later by your
customers—are usually the quintessence of garbage. Since
people worry most about the condition of discs, I've found it
necessary to give an unconditional guarantee—money back if
not satisfied—on any I sell.

If you handle recorded music, you should have reliable
taste in the rock, jazz, and classical fields, and should keep up
to date on local discount rates. Here are a couple of hints that
may help you in this area: Remember that some record
collectors are looking for choice 78's . . . and bear in mind that
tapes (the coming thing in musical recording) may prove better
suited to the used-book operation than plastic records cur-
rently are.

RELIGION AND PHILOSOPHY

RELIGION. Beware of the garbage in this category:
"inspirational books" bought as bland gifts from Aunt Mary to
Cousin Sue and vice versa, but *never* bought used . . . or any
doctrinal, official, catechismal, and historical books put out by
the Western Standard Brands. Books on Protestantism, Cathol-
icism, and Judaism are purchased strictly within the context of
the churches themselves, never outside that setting in a place
like a used-book store. Nevertheless, religion can be one of
your finest sections if you're careful about what you're doing.

For instance, never pass up a Bible if—and you must excuse
my crass manner of expression—the price is right. (The New
Testament, however—taken by itself—is not so attractive as the
Bible as a whole . . . or even as the Old Testament alone.)
Likewise always buy Bible commentaries and dictionaries,
Holy Land archaeology (including Dead Sea Scrolls material),
and any other Bible study aids, especially concordances.
Scriptural learning is very much alive and if you build up a
good section it will be avidly patronized by students and
ministers.

There's another, intensely American, area of religion which
is a center of attention in the used-book business: mind power,
sometimes labeled "metaphysical". The best sellers of mind
power include books from Christian Science, Unity, Norman
Vincent Peale, and Dale Carnegie. These works have sold in the

millions, so don't try to corner the market. What's more, dozens of newer authors have since come along to preach the Miracle of Mind Power, the Magic Within You, and the Power of Prayer. Avoid inspirational books: You want practical manuals that promise Success. "Condition yourself to be God's Winner" is the common theme, and its popularity depends—as far as I can tell—on how close your store is to the doorstep of "middle America". (Writings on hypnotism and salesmanship are loosely allied to the mind power books, although they're rarely as popular.)

OCCULT AND METAPHYSICAL. A convenient label under which to group all the religious and philosophical currents excluded from the Western mainstream. In this section, Eastern thought is rapidly becoming respectable and is very popular. Equally in demand are witchcraft and magic, which stem from the remains of Celtic and European paganisms and prove how thrifty we have been in retaining our own Western heritage of beliefs.

The influence of Egyptian and Babylonian religious thinking, mediated through Hellenistic, medieval, and Renaissance sources, is still strong in such areas as astrology, the tarot, alchemy, cabala, Rosicrucianism, Egyptian magic, and so on. Another group in this category, occult sciences, includes numerology, phrenology, handwriting analysis, and palmistry.

Established science has taken a great interest in the field of psychic experience, but such formal study hasn't hurt its popularity. This subject covers a lot of ground: telepathy, out-of-the-body experiences, communication with the dead, precognition, dreams, prophecy, even flying saucers.

WESTERN PHILOSOPHY. Concentrate on the philosophers themselves: Your list will include Greeks, a few Romans, and many modern Europeans . . . Descartes and his colleagues. Since philosophers have almost as good a following as poets, you'd do well to alphabetize this section, too. On the other hand, pass up textbooks, surveys, histories of philosophy, and studies of philosophical problems like free will, ethics, epistemology, etc.

SCIENCE AND TECHNOLOGY

NATURAL HISTORY (LIFE SCIENCES). Biology, botany, and zoology are academic subjects and their textbooks accumulate without the intercession of customers. However, books on animal observation, experiences with nature, ecology, and so on are more sought after. Guides written to help the reader identify birds, trees, plants, animals, rocks, stars; books on wild animals, on training animals, on animals as pets; books on the sea, the earth, fossils and evolutionary history, the mountains, deserts, lakes, forests, and the unique flora and fauna of your locality . . . all these have select audiences.

PHYSICAL SCIENCES. This category includes physics, electronics, astronomy, chemistry, engineering, more or less in that order of importance and with the subdivisions each may contain. Avoid computer and space science: The material you receive is almost always already out of date, even when only a few years old.

SOCIAL SCIENCES include anthropology, sociology, history, political science, and economics. The last-named topic is almost as grim a collection as education, and political science can be equally dismal. The trouble is that both are the subject of a lot of "popular" writing, the very currency of which ruins it for resale.

History is a more complex category. You should be looking for journals, source books, super-scholarly items with vast appendices, bibliographies, and footnotes . . . works that appeal to the collector. Remember that the idle reader will depend on the drugstore rack and the student wants only *the* book required for his course. Ancient history and archaeology are exceptions to this rule, however, because of the quality of many of the works.

As for anthropology and sociology, these fields—though primarily academic—have some popular appeal and may be worth experimenting with.

Occasionally, an elderly lady will ask you for your biography section. What she wants is your *royal* biography section. Good luck.

PSYCHOLOGY. There's much interest in the various psychoanalytic schools built around the works of such figures as Freud, Jung, Adler, Reich, Fromm, Horney, etc., and in the writings of other therapists in this area. As you move away from therapy, self-help, and self-understanding and enter more academic realms, observe my standing caution against buying textbooks.

BUSINESS AND TECHNICAL. These are two popular offshoots of the social and political sciences respectively.

Business works deal with practical ways of making money, most notably through speculation in stocks and real estate. The practical acquisition of specific skills is the subject of technical books: carpentry, shopwork, metalwork, home-building, care and repair. Auto maintenance is worth a shelf to itself. Craft books count as technical, too: Leatherwork, pottery, printing and printmaking, model shipbuilding, weaving, and the like are all good subjects to come upon when you scout.

SPECIAL INTERESTS

AVIATION. This is a weird section and sometimes hard to price. Collectors—who seem to be everywhere—are on the lookout for all sorts of historical material with World War I aviation (aces, planes, balloons) in the lead. Moreover, technical manuals on old planes are hunted up just like old car manuals.

SPORTS. Directions on how to become proficient at a particular sport should be kept in stock. Also, people sometimes collect books on bullfighting, boxing, baseball, and football . . . and guides to horse racing and other forms of gambling will be called for on occasion. Don't ever be eager, though, to pay top dollar for any sports book . . . its shelf life will probably be long.

GAMES AND HOBBIES. Chess books are excellent sellers, and books on cards, checkers, or party games are useful to have in stock. Bridge guides, however, back up on you unless you know the state of the art. Because hobbyists have stores of their own, writings on such subjects as coin and stamp collecting rarely sell (though handbooks on magic are OK).

COOKBOOKS. A good cookbook section is a must, but you'll have to be quick to pick up bargains while scouting because the housewives are bidding against you. As a result, the prices may be outrageously high . . . but plug along and buy what you can. Book-club entries abound, however, so pay close attention to the weight and quality of the volume (as such) before you squander your fortune. The size and importance of your eventual cookbook section will depend on the population of homemakers in your area. Forget diet books, home ec., etiquette, and such . . . no one is much interested in these subjects at the used-book level.

HEALTH AND MEDICINE. Look for medical dictionaries,

but avoid the run-of-the-medical-mill textbook and ignore school hygiene manuals. There will always be customers for books on chiropractic and body massage, as well as Hatha Yoga. Some health-book writers—like Adelle Davis and Gayelord Hauser—have produced best sellers and their works are common, but not worthless. Otherwise, look for authors of the 19th and early 20th centuries who wrote about fasting and nature cures, raw eating, and pure food. These old-fashioned purists now have an audience among those of us who are turned on to a lifestyle that flourished prior to the chemical revolution.

FARMING AND GARDENING. People almost everywhere are interested in gardening . . . books on flowers, lawn care, or the handling of trees, plants, and shrubs will be sought after even where the apartment house reigns supreme. And, as with health books, there is now the potential of an expanded readership for books on farming and country living.

LANGUAGES. Because people are always brushing up their foreign languages and often depend on old schoolbooks to help them out, this is one good-selling section that's made up primarily of textbooks. The same is true of mathematics except that the teaching of this subject was revised in the early '60's, a cutoff date you should keep in mind when you scout.

SEX BOOKS. You won't see much useful material of this kind in the thrift shops. If you feel that the nature of your store's area justifies an investment in these works, take a tour through one of the local "adults only" bookstores to see where the popular taste is at. Remember, you'll have to keep up with fashion.

ENCYCLOPEDIAS AND REFERENCE WORKS

Encyclopedias are a business in themselves. You want to stay with the name brands—*Britannica, World Book, Collier's,* and *Americana*—since other sets need either a hard sell or a combination of recent vintage and absurdly low price. Of these standard titles, *World Book* (a concise children's set) sells best and almost any year and edition of *Britannica* will bring some price over $20.00. The remaining two are best when no more than five to ten years old.

Although there's a slow, steady demand for English dictionaries, more recondite reference works may end up behind your desk . . . at least for a spell.

JUVENILE

CHILDREN'S BOOKS. The book club has struck here as a convenient way for parents to get reading matter into the hands of their youngsters, but when the book-club "classics" get to the used stage no one is terribly interested.

Children themselves are after *Mad* paperbacks, comics, and cartoon books (like *Peanuts* and *B.C.*). There's a continuing cult among boys for the Hardy Boys, and among girls for the Nancy Drew series. Adults are always looking for books for the very young . . . the kind that have five or ten words to each picture. Works of the Dr. Seuss variety are in great demand.

You generally have to sell children's books cheaply to move them . . . 1/3 to 1/6 of the new price is the range I worked within.

COMICS. A lot of dealers don't think this field is worth their while. After all, half price on a comic book doesn't come to much . . . and the kids shuffle through the pile vigorously (and noisily) enough to disintegrate a percentage of the stock. On the other hand, there's a cult of comic book fans and some of these publications are worth outrageous amounts. The children themselves will pay cover price and more on recent numbers they think worth collecting, but you have to get into it, too, to find out what's going on. Story values and artwork pretty much determine what's collected and what isn't.

MAGAZINES

Whether or not to carry periodicals is up to you, but most dealers try to avoid them on the theory that the majority of people subscribe to the ones they want. If you do stock magazines you may end up depending on the collector with his odd tastes.

FICTION

In fiction, paperbacks of pocket size will be your most dependable item, but the thrift stores you scout as a beginner won't be your best source of supply because the selection there is poor and overpriced. Later, across your desk-to-be, you'll be able to buy most paperbacks in bulk for pennies (though you may offer a good price in a pinch until you sort out what you're doing). Soft-cover novels can become a glut—just like book-club releases—unless you know how to distinguish what's salable. Helpfully, fiction can be broken

down into genres, a number of which are worth investing in.

SCIENCE FICTION. This moves so well you can pay thrift-store prices for works in good condition (unbroken spines, undamaged pages, and crisp bindings). In paperback you can get up to 60% of cover (my top rate for anything). In hard cover, beware of book-club offerings but pick up any original and first editions you see, since these are collected along with fantasy, supernatural tales, ghost stories, and fiction in the manner of Lovecraft and Poe.

MYSTERIES. A broad category, but if you stick to the pure detective fiction in the hard American style and whodunits in the English manner, you'll do all right. Authors are important here, so alphabetize them (and science fiction writers too). The hardcovers you'll see will be mostly book-club. However, some writers (Hammett, Chandler, etc.) are collected as firsts ... so keep open and expand your knowledge in this area.

GOTHICS. The Gothic novel, a slight genre which appeals almost exclusively to women, can be recognized by the melancholy cover on which a girl shrinks from the menace of a louring castle. Buy what you see when you're scouting and pay up to 15% of cover. The Gothic and its related subspecies—

nurse-doctor, suspense-romance, and horror thriller—are non-existent in hardcover.

WESTERNS. Westerns as a literary form are slowly dying . . . along with the old men who read them. Go easy until you see how many of these prospective buyers are around your store-to-be. Hardcovers are not common and are in some demand, but your price should be low (which means, for me, the range between 75¢ and $1.50).

WAR NOVELS. During World War II, a generation of males shared a trauma and a lot of them—maybe most of them—wrote novels about it. It's also this generation that buys the works (and war non-fiction as well). Business, however, is very slow, and other wars don't count. Except for the great creations by Mailer, Heller, etc., let the hardcover war novel pass.

HISTORICAL NOVELS. Apart from the romance type—which is of interest to women—historical novels are a drag in both paperback and hardcover. Know your authors instead of buying these works as a category.

SEX NOVELS are another male genre. Not surprisingly, you won't see any hot items of this type at the Salvation Army. Your store's area (and maybe your upbringing) will determine how heavily you specialize.

THE CLASSIC NOVEL means the works of Dostoyevsky and his friends, alphabetized for convenience. In paperback, the category may be extended to contain any fiction that's not included in one of the genres which a customer might ask for specifically. Again, the idle reader and the student depend almost exclusively on the soft-cover editions, which will easily outsell the hardcover in your store. In fact, you should use great discrimination when you select permanently bound classic fiction: The harsher your literary judgment the better. Remember that—in this age of paper—buying a clothbound novel is the act of the serious book collector.

THE BEST-SELLER NOVEL. In paperback, this is whatever is now selling on your neighborhood drugstore rack. The cover is all-important as the prime indicator to your customer that the novel in question is indeed current. Even though having a drugstore rack of your own will help immensely in moving the best seller, it's obviously pointless to go after such books in any quantity while you're in the scouting stage. In hardcover, by the way, this category exists mostly in book-club format . . . and you know what I think of that.

OTHER PAPERBACKS

THE "POCKET-SIZE" NON-FICTION PAPERBACK. You'll see a lot of these in your scouting travels, but most of them will be garbage. First of all, the titles selected for this format generally lack sufficient breadth or depth to make it worthwhile to shelve them independently (as can be done for genre and classic fiction paperbacks) . . . yet such books also go poorly in the hardcover section because of disparity in size and because—like the best-seller novel— their intellectual horizons have been limited by the drugstore rack. In most categories, indeed, these non-fiction paper-backs go stale quickly and if carelessly accumulated will require a bargain table, a bait rack, or a trash can to relieve the pressure.

QUALITY PAPERBACKS. The quality paperback is a larger (sometimes only slightly) and more expensive soft-cover book. Since it's often printed from the same plates as an earlier clothbound edition, it belongs among the hardcovers. As a cheaper reprint of a valuable work, it sells well to students, scholars, and in some cases even to collectors.

One last note on paperbacks: According to an article in a special issue of _Daedalus_ magazine on book publishing, the difference in manufacturing cost between the hardcover and the paperback comes to something like 80 cents. Thus the retail price disparity between the two doesn't reflect produc-tion expenses so much as costs of advertising promotion and distribution. It's the hard sell, not the hard cover that makes the difference.

BARGAINING FOR BOOKS

Scouting will get you accustomed to buying books for a lot less than they are eventually worth, and also entails very little dickering over price. Therefore, once you're established in your store you may find it hard to get used to buying books as they come across the counter at you, hauled in in cartons by their owners. Nevertheless, this is the final, make-or-break point in your venture into the used-book business.

Over-the-counter buying will be hardest at the beginning when you're still not _precisely_ sure what books are worth and so lack that air of authority so necessary to a smooth transaction. This isn't to say that most people are hard to deal with . . . they may be even more embarrassed at the thought of bargaining than you are. Some will be happy to accept any price you offer or, if they can't, will wordlessly pick up their cartons and split.

You don't want to see your visitor leaving, however, with any good books. Therefore I recommend that you make it a practice to separate all incoming potential stock into three piles: [1] the books you know you want and can sell, [2] those you consider garbage, and [3] items that are in between. Go through the good volumes carefully, book by book, using *Books in Print* or a reference guide if you have to, to arrive at a price for each one in line with the rules of "Triple Your Money", shelf life, and condition. Then go through the stack of "maybes" and figure out a minimum sort of shelf life and condition. Then go through the stack of "maybes" and figure out a minimum sort of price. Finally, look over the garbage to see if you missed a jewel.

Now you're in a position to offer an overall price to those people who want to sell everything regardless. And, having separated the good from the bad, you're also prepared to deal with objections that your price is too low, since you can point out that you're willing to give, say, 80% of what you originally offered for 25% of the books.

Actually, you'll have to dicker less than you may expect. Most people understand something of the mechanics of the used-book business, enough at least to know that they won't get a lot of money from a dealer. And, basically, they're selling their books because they no longer have any use for them . . . so they'll be sympathetic to any attempt on your part to maximize the value of some of their offerings. The normal reaction, then, will be to accept your overall figure. A few of the folks who offer you books may be enterprising enough to sell you the good items at the good price and wander off with the remainder to freak some unsuspecting dealer. And—in a few cases—the owner's reaction will be to sweep up all his books and say, "I'd rather give them away than sell them at that price."

The hardest people to deal with are those to whom a book is a foreign article that fell into their hands accidentally. If the titles are current, they may want 80¢ on the dollar . . . or, if the books are 20 years old or more, they may be convinced that *any* price you offer them is peanuts compared to the real value of their treasures. With these people it's wisest not to strain yourself. They won't part with their volumes until they've been buffeted by X number of dealers like yourself. Sometimes fate will be kind and put you at the end of the series.

In America, there are comparatively few people who will want to argue your price up. Remind these tough ones that you're in business to make money, not to swap even . . . let alone trade for a loss. (But stay loose, since it's possible that the profit system itself is doomed.) Remind yourself in the interim that—during a buy in your store—*you* have to be the world's greatest authority. Don't be afraid to point out the flaws in the books, physical damage, lack of buyer demand, and the control your eventual markup exerts over the price you pay.

Sometimes a seller (perhaps in the hope of rattling you) will start rapping at you from the moment you touch his library, telling you how valuable his books are and so on. It's important not to let him upset you at such a sacred moment in the buying process. In such a case, it's good to plan ahead by fixing your price at less than normal to give yourself bargaining room. A lot of the time such a seller is a compulsive extrovert who just can't bear to take you at your word and wants the pleasure of forcing your price up. By preparing yourself in advance, you avoid a rigid "I won't bargain" stance which could kill the sale.

About 1% of the people who sell you books will do so because they need the money. *Really* need the money. You can recognize them instantly by the feeling of anxiety they will communicate to you. When you meet such a person, you might use the opportunity to put another jewel in your heavenly crown by paying him or her somewhat more for his or her stock than you really should.

Fortunately for your peace of mind, though, 99% of your contacts are selling their libraries because they are moving, or because they're out of space in their apartments and/or can't stand to look at all that junk anymore. You can pay these sellers a realistic price with no qualms, feel good about recycling the printed word . . . and, at the same time, enjoy a reasonably good and hassle-free living from your venture into the used-book business. ●

The above article originally appeared in LIFESTYLE! NOS. 3 & 4 . . . along with a great deal of other live-better-for-less and self-sufficiency how-to information. For further information about the magazine—and other books and periodicals devoted to home businesses, self-sufficiency, and related subjects—please see page 367 of this handbook.

FEEDBACK ON THE USED BOOK BUSINESS

I much enjoyed Paul Encimer's article, "Used Books Can Buy You a New Life", especially since—after a few years of collecting and also working part time in a used/new bookstore—I'm putting out (with a friend) my first mail-order used and rare book catalog.

May I add a few remarks that Paul, perhaps because of space considerations, didn't get to?

[1] The leading trade journal in the field is *A.B. Bookman's Weekly* (Box 1100, Newark, N.J. 07101, third class subscription $20.00 per year). *A.B.* lists hundreds of books that other dealers and libraries are looking for, and anyone can answer these ads . . . provided, of course, he has for sale any of the titles that are being "searched". The normal terms are cash-with-order, and if your "quote" on a particular work is attractive enough, you're in business.

As with the issuing of a mail-order catalog, you don't even have to have a full-fledged shop to begin with and can start a book operation with practically no investment. One point, however, should be made: On the relatively common titles (experience will tell you which they are, I guess), the advertiser will receive many quotes, and some will be very low. It's better, I think, to experiment with a few works that strike you as unusual and perhaps scarce.

[2] Paul suggests using your current home phone and placing an ad in the Yellow Pages. Be advised that in my state, at least, you can't do this . . . you must pay the fee

for an official business telephone. No business number, no ad, says Michigan's Ma Bell.

[3] About supply: A fruitful field in this neck of the woods and elsewhere is the used-book sale . . . usually sponsored by a "Friends of the Library" group or by college alumnae associations or American Association of University Women branches. The price is usually right, and you'll get to know the collectors, readers, and, of course, hoarders in your area.

[4] A few additional reference works: Merle Johnson's *American First Editions* is still the standard short work on American (literary) authors, but is slowly being superseded by Jacob Blanck's multi-volume *Bibliography of American Literature* (BAL for short). The Johnson title is, I believe, out of print but is occasionally offered in the "For Sale" section of *A.B. Bookman's Weekly* and in used/rare bookshops. Among the price guides, Van Allen Bradley's new *Book Collector's Handbook of Values* (Putnam, $17.50) is worth the investment as a basic—though, of course, incomplete—reference. Finally, the title of the auction record mentioned by Paul (or, to be more precise, the one usually most readily available) is *American Book-Prices Current*, or *ABPC*.

[5] Finally, regarding Britannicas: The *older* edition most in demand is the 11th, which brings (if in good condition) anywhere from $30.00–$100, depending on which binding and size is offered, etc. The reason for the 11th's appeal seems to be a combination of excellent authors and valuable material in the humanities, which had to be cut in subsequent editions to make way for more "modern" information.

Thanks again for a most interesting article.

> Tom Nicely
> LEAVES OF GRASS (Rare Books)
> Whitmore Lake, Mich. ⊜

The above article originally appeared in LIFESTYLE! NO. 5 . . . along with a great deal of other live-better-for-less and self-sufficiency how-to information. For further information about the magazine—and other books and periodicals devoted to home businesses, self-sufficiency, and related subjects—please see page 367 of this handbook.

PUT IT ON WHEELS

But what if you don't want to be tied down? What if you'd prefer to own a little business that allows you to freely roam over your city, county, or even state? What if you're looking for something that will let you work hard for six months or a year . . . and then close the whole shootin' match down for a like amount of time while you live off your profits?

If that's the case, I've got just the thing for you. *Two* things, in fact.

First, a fellow by the name of J. Winike is going to let you in on how he runs an ole-timey produce-out-of-a-truck business (and does it today!) up Chicago way. And then Catherine Lesley will really open your eyes with a fascinating explanation of the method she and her man used to make their beat-up VW van foot their rent for eight months, buy all their food during that period, pay a year's college tuition, finance a move to the country, and still leave them with $8,000 in their pockets. And it was all done in expensive New York City too!

That's not bad, and either Winike's "come and go as I please" lifestyle or the Lesleys' "work eight months and retire for a year" way of doing business is worth copying. Maybe this is the part of the book you've been waiting for! ◗

J. WINIKE:
HOW TO START
A PRODUCE
BUSINESS

With food prices what they are, it should become increasingly less difficult to convince people that vegetables are the best buy on the market today. The economics of the way most Americans eat will catch up with them sooner or later . . . and some of them will then discover that a fruit-and-vegetable-based diet is much more than just a bargain.

That in itself is reason enough to go into the produce business, if you've been considering a small, low-overhead enterprise as a means of liberation. There's more to this occupation than good financial prospects . . . its aesthetics can get you higher than a kite in a desert.

The basic idea of my business is to buy fruit and vegetables at wholesale cost and sell them wherever I can. On weekdays I work door to door in neighborhoods where I have established routes. My customers appreciate the delivery of fresh produce (at road-stand prices) direct to their homes, and I enjoy the benefit of a paced, predictable income. On a given summer weekday, when I'm offering no specially priced leader items, I can expect to make a profit of $30.00 to $50.00.

Then there are the weekends . . . when business prospects are unlimited. Fairs and festivals, centennials, holiday picnics and gatherings, motocross and road rallies, and sporting events of all kinds abound in the summer. I've done a good trade at rock concerts, rodeos, art fairs, and craft shows. You can sell just about any place your imagination and salesmanship can get you into . . . and expect to make $75.00· to $100-a-day profit.

I started in the vegetable trade with a Ford Econoline and $80.00 cash. With some concentrated effort and very little time, I built up my income to a $100-a-day turnover . . . working only on the days I chose. Careful buying and distribution give me a high level of control over my profits: The amount of money I make depends directly on how much of a truckload I buy and how much effort I put into selling. I've found no other work situation in which I felt my income was regulated so fairly.

GETTING STARTED

The formula for a produce business is simple, really. You'll need the following:

[1] A truck you're sure of. It has to be reliable enough to haul up to two tons of vegetables wherever you want to sell them. An unexpected breakdown could mean the loss of a day's produce (up to $100 worth) because you'll probably have no place to store and cool the stock while the vehicle is repaired.

[2] At least $100 cash to set up . . . $60.00 minimum for your first load, plus some incidentals: paper and plastic bags and a scale, perhaps.

[3] A neighborhood with no competition. My first route—in a suburb of Chicago—consisted of four or five square blocks of residents who relied on supermarkets for fruit and vegetables. They lived too far from the city to benefit from wholesale produce dealers and found farm roadside stands inaccessible or, at least, inconvenient. All I had to do was offer better-quality truck than the chain groceries and at lower prices. (I found I could still maintain a wide margin of profit because my overhead costs were so low.) My only competition came from the small backyard gardens some of my customers

kept . . . and I gladly moved over for them.

To begin with, then, you'll have two areas to research: where to buy your produce and where to sell it.

WHERE TO BUY

In Chicago and cities of similar size, the buying of fruit and vegetables offers no problem. I visit the Southwater Street Market at 4:00 a.m. before the big buyers and supermarket representatives arrive. That way I get the best bargains and don't have to hurry to make my selections.

One thing to remember when dealing with a wholesale house is that their margin of profit is very slim. You can't haggle with their prices, and you can't waste their time. On my buying trips I make it a point to know exactly what produce is selling for in the stores from one day to the next. (Local supermarkets often buy leader items by the boxcar, and if you don't keep track of their specials you can easily be undersold.) Then all I have to do is walk up and down the dock with a salesman and point to the goods I'm interested in. He'll throw a price at me, and I can tell whether I'll be able to turn the article over at a profit or not.

You can also get your stock from farmers' markets or directly from growers. I've bought truckloads of fruit such as watermelons or cantaloupe right off the boxcar at the freight yards. It's just a matter of tracing the supply lines and meeting the people who can give you the breaks. The cheaper you buy, obviously, the greater your profit . . . and a little market research goes a long way.

WHAT TO BUY

The produce you handle will depend on your customers' preferences—which you'll determine from experience—and the availability of a given fruit or vegetable. I sell only what's in season and stock regulars around which my patrons can build their diet.

I cover each route twice a week with the first load heavy on vegetables: lettuce, cabbage, cukes, tomatoes, green peppers, beans, onions, and some breakfast melons. On the second trip I carry sweet corn and a large selection of fruit: plums, peaches, grapes, watermelons, apples, oranges, bananas, and occasionally strawberries and cherries.

Everything is effectively displayed in the truck so that customers can approach the side or back doors to see, smell, and feel their selections. Color and tactile qualities are important in the sale of fresh produce. An attractive item can literally sell itself.

PRICES

I display my prices on a chalkboard over the scale and money drawer on the front seat of the truck . . . and I give those figures very careful thought. I've learned that it's infinitely more acceptable to cut my rates two or three times in the course of a day than to be stuck with a whole case of some item at the end of it. Generally, I find that if I sell for a few cents less than the supermarkets I can still make up to 90 percent profit on a load. That margin is, of course, affected by numerous variables—right down to how hot the weather is—but these variables *can* be controlled with careful market research and produce handling.

WHERE TO SELL

The backbone of your business is the specific area where you sell regularly: your own neighborhood route. I have two—each four blocks square—and serve one on Mondays and Thursdays, the other on Tuesdays and Fridays. The houses are close together and set back only a short distance from the street, which minimizes the amount of walking I have to do. (By now most of my customers know when to expect me, and generally come out to the truck when I pull up . . . but in the beginning I did quite a bit of trudging back and forth knocking on doors.) Another point that led me to choose these territories is that the streets are quiet and shady with a minimum of traffic. This means that I can park my truck anywhere along the side of the road and not have to worry about creating an obstruction.

In the summer the sidewalks are crowded with children playing, and I always make friends with them first. Not only do they herald my arrival and save me a walk to their mothers' doors . . . they often gather around the truck and do most of the selling for me. "Look, grapes! Oh please, we haven't had grapes in a week . . . and strawberries!" Wherever there's a child who calls for fruit instead of candy, there's a mother willing to buy if the price is right.

Next to children, my most enthusiastic customers are old people. They may not use as much produce as a family, but they're infinitely more pleasant to deal with. On each of several streets in my territory live six or seven retired ladies who gather around the truck at the same time every delivery day to haggle, barter, and negotiate for the choicest produce bargains (and they usually have a better eye for a bargain than I do). They give me recipes to pass on and tips on what to buy when . . . and they usually purchase for friends and kin across town who don't have a vegetable man. My elderly patrons help me keep quality up and prices down, because they know, even more than I, what produce is worth.

There are several corner stores on my routes that soon found they couldn't compete with my prices and began to buy from me. They benefit because I give them better wholesale rates than they had been getting from Chicago produce houses, and I make a small, quick profit by turning over cases of

goods. In addition, this arrangement gives me more control over the amount of fruit and vegetables that comes into my areas.

I also serve a nursing home in the neighborhood. The two ladies who do the cooking for the establishment are delighted to have fresh, reliable delivery of the commodities they previously had to spend time shopping for. Not far away is a small private school that uses enough lettuce and tomatoes to justify the petitioning I had to do to get the account.

Another factor to consider in choosing a route neighborhood is the availability of taverns. I have five in each area, and among them I can usually count on selling whatever I have left in the truck at the end of the day. I just pack the remainders in plastic bags and hawk them from table to table or along the bar. It was hard going at first, until I established a good reputation, but even in the beginning my produce spoke for itself. A dozen ears of corn for a buck, two heads of lettuce for a quarter, and tomatoes for 25¢ a pound are bargains in any man's ears.

Most of the guys I sell to in the taverns have just gotten off work, have change to jingle in their pockets, and dig the notion of coming home from the bars with a good buy in vegetables. (There's a psychology to this business, believe me.) I'm glad to get rid of the produce even if I have to take a cut in profit, because I don't want to have to sell day-old truck the next day . . . and I usually accept three or four free beers in the process. Needless to say, this is my favorite part of the route.

Getting yourself established in the bars can lead to other possibilities, too. My regular tavern customers often approach me about buying produce by the case for canning or pickling (or just for special occasions such as picnics). I give them a good cut in price, and I still make a killing.

WHAT TO DO WITH THE WEEKENDS

I make most of my money, and have the best time doing it, on weekends. I'm extremely partial to open-air music, art, and sporting events because fresh fruit seems to complement everything so well and sells like mad at such a gathering. Grapes are hot items at rock concerts, peaches at art fairs. Watermelon goes anywhere if it's cold, even in the parking lots of theaters and carnivals. Plums, apples, and oranges are old reliables: I've even sold them to fishermen I spotted off the road as I cruised home from county fairs.

Some places I work require that I have special permits to sell, others do not . . . so I always carry a peddling license from the town in which I operate my routes. It cost only $10.00 and is official looking enough for most people. Generally, if someone refuses to let me sell on his premises, it's because he's afraid I'll take business from his operation in one way or another . . . by competing with a popcorn or hot dog stand, for example. But I'm a fast talker and—as I seldom turn up at the same place two weeks in a row—I can usually convince *somebody* to turn his back for the afternoon. No one can deny that a peach is a superior refreshment to a hot dog, and that's a surprisingly strong argument.

How much to buy for a weekend depends entirely on the crowd you expect to serve. I sell regularly at a fairground that attracts from five to ten thousand people per event, and I usually unload six or seven cases of grapes, two cases of apples, a case each of plums and peaches, and five to ten watermelons. At smaller fairs and gatherings—say two to three thousand people—I carry more of a selection and a lesser quantity of any one item. Allowing for circumstances, I usually find I can raise my prices 10 to 25 cents per item and not get a complaint. It's not uncommon to triple my investment on weekend ventures.

Here are a few ideas for weekends:

Open-air music festivals: rock, jazz, classical, band concerts. The closer to the bandstand you can locate your truck, the better the sales.

Sporting events: motocross, road, and sports car rallies, hill climbs, Little League, Pony League, and minor league baseball, soccer matches, Sunday pickup football games.

Arts and crafts fairs.

Auctions.

Saturday markets, flea markets, even shopping center parking lots.

Drama presentations, especially big-tent, touring summer stock productions.

Any other tent shows: religious revivals, amateur shows, etc.

VFW or civic league picnics. Sometimes forest rangers will let you sell in state parks, sometimes they won't.

Recreational affairs: boat and air shows, displays of snowmobiles, motorcycles, and recreational vehicles.

Animal exhibitions: dog and horse shows, cattle judgings, grange fairs, rodeos.

Circuses and carnivals. (Permits may be required. Inquire a month or two ahead of time.)

Special event picnics: July 4th, Labor Day.

Dedications, inaugurations, town celebrations, centennials.

Large construction sites or wherever many workers are likely to be assembled during lunch hours.

Roadside turnouts close enough to forest preserves, wildlife refuges, or recreational locations to attract picnickers.

Parking lots of deserted gas stations at busy intersections.

You take it from there. You may not become a produce tycoon, but at the very least you can be a spontaneous entrepreneur who makes a comfortable income at a trade that's healthy and healthful for everyone concerned. ◆

The above article originally appeared in THE MOTHER EARTH NEWS® NO. 33 . . . along with a great deal of other live-better-for-less and self-sufficiency how-to information. For further information about the magazine—and other books and periodicals devoted to home businesses, self-sufficiency, and related subjects—please see page 367 of this handbook.

CATHERINE LESLEY:
UNDER-GROUND MOVING

Student Movers was a child of desperation born when my man and I returned to New York in September of 1970 with barely enough money to take our tired VW bus across the George Washington Bridge. By spring, our moving company had grown from a struggling one-truck outfit into a full-scale, full-time enterprise. That homey little underground operation footed our rent, kept us well fed, paid a year's college tuition, and took us out of the city and onto the land the following June with $8,000 in our pockets.

If you're stuck in the city, underground moving or trucking just might help you earn your way out too. All it takes is a secondhand truck or bus, a stable telephone number, strong arms, and a broad back. Here's how.

WHY UNDERGROUND?

Underground, in the case of moving, means unlicensed and uninsured . . . strictly speaking, illegal. But there are dozens of underground movers in every big city that operate openly—and even advertise in establishment newspapers—without hassles from the police. It amused us to call ourselves the Bonnie and Clyde of the moving world, but we really weren't trying to circumvent the law. Working underground was simply the best way to provide a cheap and efficient alternative to high-priced professional movers.

Our customers didn't mind that we weren't insured . . . our low rates made up for that. We made it clear that we couldn't be responsible for breakage and we refused to handle very delicate or very expensive items. But if we did damage something—as happened a couple of times during the year—we paid out of our pockets rather than make the customer file a claim and wait months or years for reimbursement.

We did have a slight run-in with the New York City Department of Consumer Affairs in late spring over licensing. "You're operating illegally," their inspector told us sternly. "You'd better go out of business right away."

"Yes sir," we said, "right away, sir."

The inspector called back a few weeks later. "Have you gone out of business yet?"

"Yup." And that was the last we heard from him. The forces of law and order, it seems, have more pernicious enemies to wipe out than small-time underground movers.

Incidentally, you might avoid the licensing problem altogether if you call yourself "Joe's Truckers" rather than "Joe's Movers". In some areas truckers don't have to be licensed. You can check with the Small Business Bureau in your city about that.

Underground movers, working on a human rather than a corporate scale, can avoid the huge overhead in offices, vans, advertising, etc., that Allied and Mayflower pay. We worked out of our home, wrote our own ads, and used our VW bus—our "family car"—as a van. That made it possible for us to specialize in light moving at low rates. We didn't compete directly with the big guys . . . we only handled the small loads that they found unprofitable.

The big companies in New York City charge $40.00 to $50.00 an hour for three men and a van, but pay those men only $3.00 to $4.00 an hour. Is it any wonder that movers have a reputation for being gruff, careless, inefficient, and even dishonest? They know they're exploited.

With our low overhead, we charged about one-third as much as the biggies while paying our helpers $4.00 an hour . . . more than union wages and exactly what we charged customers for the men's labor. We still made a fine profit from the use of our bus and from our own labor . . . but not by the sweat of others.

Another advantage of operating underground is that you don't have to pay income tax on your earnings if you don't want to. Just insist on cash payments from all your customers and keep your records to yourself. What Infernal Revenue doesn't know won't hurt them . . . or you. *(Unless you get caught! This time-honored cash-payment method of getting around income tax is, of course, frowned upon by the IRS so, of course, I can't recommend it . . . but, of course, it is done all the time.—MOTHER.)*

GETTING STARTED

Our moving business was launched with a handful of yellow 5 X 8 cards:

STUDENT MOVERS
Light Moving in a VW Bus
Low Rates—Local and Long Distance
364-5744

My husband plastered the cards over every university, bookstore, and supermarket bulletin board in our neighborhood. We were fortunate to live near a university, by nature an extremely mobile community (students are always moving into or getting kicked out of apartments).

The fact that we were students ourselves—and made it clear in our advertising—got us lots of business. Everyone wants to help students finance their education and we even received a number of contracts with the university. If you don't live in a student neighborhood, you still should advertise there anyway.

We also tacked cardboard signs up on the windows of our bus (which was patently illegal because we were advertising a commercial service and didn't have commercial license plates) and we'd hold our breath when cops stared at the signs. No hassles. One of the policemen even jotted down the number and called us up to do a job.

Eventually we had our advertising Xeroxed (at about $3.00 for 100 sheets, three ads to a sheet) and spent a day pasting the pages all over town: at transient hotels, YMCA's, churches, apartment complexes, other colleges, and on outside walls and lampposts. Some got ripped down, but at that price it was no problem to replenish them. We also kept a bunch of these notices in our van to hand out to passers-by who stopped us while we were on a job.

Finally, we began to advertise in the classified sections of the college paper and of other local newspapers. Each type of advertising paid for itself many times over and the jobs started pouring in.

Our office was in our apartment, but the constant barrage of phone calls day and night made the place seem—at times—more like a fortress under siege. A bulletin board over our desk contained rosters of helpers with and without trucks, their phone numbers, and the times they were available to work. A strategic diagram of our mini-van showed its length, height, width, and door dimensions. Would a 5 X 7 bookcase fit in? We could tell right away. Another sheet listed the vital information we had to give our customers: rates, non-responsibility for breakage, etc. We wanted to be sure there would be no misunderstandings at pay-up time.

We set a notebook by the phone, with a page for each day, and wrote down the jobs as they came in. For each appointment we filled in name, address (and how to get there if we didn't know), phone number in case of changes, the time we were to come, the number of helpers requested, and a brief description of the job—like, "two trunks to Brooklyn, five flights up"—or an estimate of the time it would take.

Estimating job times requires a bit of skill. You have to consider [A] what's to be moved (will it take two trips?), [B] from and to where, [C] what time of day (rush hour jobs mean traffic jams), [D] if it involves stairs (they take longer than elevators) . . . and then allow some for broken elevators, acts of God, and indecisive customers. Underestimates can be disastrous when you're booking jobs back to back, so leave yourself lots of leeway in the beginning. You can schedule more tightly once you get the hang of it.

We tried as hard as humanly possible to meet all appointments on time, and we asked our customers to extend us the same courtesy by notifying us immediately of cancellations or changes in the location or size of a job. We absolutely refused to book tentative assignments. Occasionally we'd get requests for special rates or special services . . . we learned, the hard way, to simply turn such jobs down. The people who hassle you on the phone are usually the ones who hassle you on the job, and we didn't need that.

To establish our rates, Chris and I checked the local newspaper (in New York, *The Village Voice*) used by other underground movers, then decided on a competitive price: $7.50 per hour for one man and a truck, $11.50 for two men. (Later on we upped our rates to $8.00 and $12.00 respectively, simply because that made it easier to figure fractions of an hour.) That price included gas but not tolls. We set a one hour minimum for each booking, charging to the nearest quarter of an hour thereafter.

The customer was "on the clock" from the time we left home until we got back (we'd make a reasonable estimate for getting home), obviously with no coffee breaks or dallying on the way. That's called travel time, and all professionals charge for it . . . you're cheating yourself if you drive a long distance on your own time. If a customer was suspicious, we'd invite him to drive along. We *never* agreed to flat rates on local jobs: it's too easy to misestimate the time involved.

We were more flexible on long distance rates. Those jobs were easier—mostly driving—and so profitable we didn't want to lose them. We'd ask for 30¢ a mile (40¢ for two men) round trip plus tolls, and haggle down from there. A 300-mile run might net us $80.00 for a full day's work, but many customers told us that price was reasonable—if not absurdly low—compared to the rates charged by professional movers.

"All terms cash, no checks, no credit." We got damn tired of repeating that, but it was necessary. In the city, unfortunately, you have to be very cautious about accepting personal checks from strangers. By insisting on immediate cash payment we avoided the hassles of billing by mail, bouncing checks, and incriminating records for the tax men. We'd make a rough estimate of what each assignment might cost, then ask the customer to have at least that much cash on hand to cover it.

TRUCK, EQUIPMENT, LABOR

The only major equipment you need to set yourself up in the moving business is some sort of small truck or van, and if you shop around you'll probably be able to find a usable vehicle for a few hundred dollars. Our '57 VW bus, which we bought originally to use as a camper, cost $300. For an additional $450, we had Volkswagen mechanics install a guaranteed rebuilt engine. Although our initial investment was repaid many times over, you should be able to get a much better deal.

Moving furniture is hard on a vehicle, but we kept maintenance costs down by doing our own repairs. John Muir's *How To Keep Your Volkswagen Alive* (which you can order through MOTHER) taught us everything we needed to know, from doing tune-ups to adjusting brakes to engine overhauls. Extra large tires on the rear wheels helped support heavy loads with less wear on the bus.

We were constantly amazed at how much we could fit into that little van . . . from sofas to double beds to small pianos to 2,000 pounds of filled file cabinets to our own mattress and Coleman stove when we just had to get away to the hills for the weekend. VW's are easy to maintain and park on crowded city streets, and they're wonderfully cheap on gas (ours got 27 miles per gallon on long runs).

The small doors on the old bus, however, did present a problem in loading and unloading. After 1964, VW enlarged the back door . . . and after '68, the bus itself was made a foot longer with larger sliding doors. These changes make a big difference in loading capacity. American-made vans (Chevy, Dodge, etc.) are more expensive to buy and operate than VW's, but they have wider doors and a lot more space inside.

If you want to operate on a larger scale, you might buy a good, used mail truck or United Parcel van. Or you could, as one of our friends did, put plywood sides and top on a pickup or flatbed truck. With such vehicles, however, you might be forced to get commercial plates in some states . . . and that means higher registration fees, insurance, tolls, and restricted access to some highways. Larger loading capacity would justify higher rates than those we charged, but you should be careful not to price yourself out of business. Whatever the size of your truck, measure every dimension and keep the figures posted over your phone.

Other equipment that's good to own are a dolly for carrying things on flat surfaces and a hand truck with creepers for going up and down stairs. These will save your back but aren't really necessary at first unless you're moving refrigerators, washing machines, or pianos. You might pick up an old dolly from another mover for a few dollars . . . and you can rent a hand truck from U-Haul for three bucks a day or borrow one from a kindly superintendent for use within his building. You should always carry a couple of old blankets to protect furniture from scratches and it's a good idea to collect a bunch of cardboard cartons or wooden crates to carry small stuff like dishes.

As for labor . . . that's you and your closest friends and you don't have to be a big husky guy to move furniture. You'll develop strength and stamina gradually and a lot of the skill is simply pacing and know-how. For example, anyone can learn to balance a heavy box on his or her shoulders . . . and that's much easier than carrying it in front of your chest.

Two people can get a sofa or dresser up stairs best if the strongest person goes behind, keeping the object level and high up, parallel with the front person. If the dresser's too heavy, take out the drawers . . . if the Castro convertible is killing you, remove the mattress and tie the seat to the frame. Take those screw-on legs off coffee tables and beds and you'll be able to maneuver much easier on stairs and in the van. When you have to move up five or six climbs of stairs, it's best to do a couple of flights at a time and rest on the way down. Customers appreciate a steady reasonable pace rather than a mad dash and the dropping and breakage that may go with it.

And women can do it too! At first we used to apologize to our customers, "Uh, the second man you're hiring is a girl." The response was either hysterical laughter, shocked silence, or a hearty "that's outasight" . . . but no one ever objected. After working daily for a few months, I didn't need to apologize anymore because I could do the job as well as the average man.

A few people became almost apologetic watching me lift and haul (I guess they thought I was straining my ovaries or something) and they'd plead with me to rest, despite the fact that they were paying me $4.00 an hour. I'd wither them with a disdainful grin and keep on working.

I even ran a weekly route by myself, transporting cartons of books to a warehouse in New Jersey. The first few trips, the foreman's ferocious stares told me my female presence was unwelcome in that masculine stronghold. But once he got used to me, the foreman would greet me with a "Hi, sweetheart" and call his men around to watch me heave boxes into the van. I think that the uniqueness of a man-woman moving team even helped our business. People would call up for a job and say, "Make sure the chick comes along. This I gotta see."

We encouraged our customers to help out with the labor too. If they were weak and clumsy, it made them appreciate us more (and was probably good for them) and if they were strong, it made the work go more quickly. Sure, that lowered the bill . . . but it let us feel less like hired help and more like friends.

GETTING BIG

Student Movers began as a two-man, one-truck, part-time operation. By spring it had become a big business employing several vans, a number of our friends, and most of our time. Our reputation had spread through advertising and word of mouth, and we had tapped a vast market in the city and suburbs for a reliable but cheap moving company. When the schools let out and summer subletting began, we were inundated by pleas for our services.

It's hard to turn down jobs even when you're booked solid, so we recruited every bus and truck in our neighborhood to take care of our excess business. We worked on a commission basis, doing the advertising and phone work and taking two dollars an hour off the wages for our time. It wasn't worth it.

Student Movers was our business, and the people we hired simply didn't feel the sense of responsibility that we did. They would miss appointments, confuse schedules, overcharge. We'd get frantic phone calls at all hours: "Where's your truck? I've got to move right now," and it would turn out that the driver we'd commissioned had forgotten, broken down, gone to see his girlfriend, gotten drunk, or (this actually happened) taken off for California. Which meant that we'd have to juggle schedules, maybe rent a truck, and do the job ourselves . . . as we should have done in the first place.

Another type of commission work turned out better for us perhaps because—for it—we hired only our friends, rather than any stranger who happened to own a truck. We advertised "experienced workers to help you move," and found that, miraculously, people were willing to pay $5.00 an hour just for labor, no van. These were folks who needed help loading or unloading a U-Haul and people who were moving from one apartment to another within a single building. Once again our commission was small—$1.00 an hour—but we helped quite a few of our friends earn some extra bread. One truckless pal kept running this ad long after Student Movers shut down, and made several hundred dollars out of sheer bravado. If you can't afford a van right now, you might try hiring yourself out as labor in this way.

During spring vacation and semester breaks we used our overworked bus to run groups of students to the New York airports at $4.00 a head. A comparable cab trip costs $13.00 but by packing in ten people, we earned $40.00 for two hours' work. Since we weren't licensed to carry passengers for profit, this too was illegal. So . . . we removed the signs from our bus, took payment before we left, and instructed our cargo to insist they were just friends being done a favor in case we got hassled by airport cops. We never got hassled but the whole thing involved tight scheduling, extra advertising, and careful co-ordination of meeting times and places. Big money, big headaches.

CALLING IT QUITS

Big money, big headaches. By June that was the story of our lives. Our time was worth $8.00 an hour and the money fever had such a grip on us that we refused to waste a precious hour just breathing or sitting in the sun. We were working nine to midnight, seven days a week! Our bank account was huge but we had become walking zombies . . . or rather, moving zombies. We were exhausted and out of tune with ourselves and each other. It was time to quit.

On June 24th we pulled our telephone out of the wall, carried our belongings down the five flights of our tenement walk-up, and packed them into Old Brown Bus. Then, without looking back, we drove our last job . . . moving our own home to rural Maryland. When we unpacked, the New York cockroaches ran out of the furniture, took a deep breath of country air, and sighed.

Sometimes we wake early in the morning and rush out of the house to work. Then we take a look at the mountains and the river running near our yard and we sit back down again. No more moving ever!

The money we earned last year will carry us through another 12 months of just being. Old Brown Bus rests placidly by the garden. Dried apples and green beans hang from her roof . . . and next spring, maybe, we'll take her tired engine out and use her for a goat shed.●

The above article originally appeared in THE MOTHER EARTH NEWS® NO. 13 . . . along with a great deal of other live-better-for-less and self-sufficiency how-to information. For further information about the magazine—and other books and periodicals devoted to home businesses, self-sufficiency, and related subjects—please see page 367 of this handbook.

CASH IN ON TALENT

Then again, maybe you're the kind of person who expects a self-employment enterprise to—first and fore-most—provide you with an opportunity to use some kind of artistic talent. Good for you!

As a matter of fact, I finally wound up in publishing (after trying a great number of ways of making a living) simply because I too prefer to earn my daily bread in a business that affords me some degree of artistic satisfaction.

And that's why I'm pleased to allow the authors in this section to tell you how to make spare- or full-time cash by publishing a local guidebook, operating a 19th century tintype studio, hand-lettering certificates, working as a cartoonist, and turning wild flowers into framed works of art.

Once again, please note that we've tried to feature slightly "offbeat" ideas that haven't yet been over-done . . . enterprises that in some cases can be kept quite small and easily managed, and in other instances can be built into just as large an operation as you could ever want.

We have, in short, attempted to "bracket the field" of talent-oriented entrepreneurial ventures in such a way that—if you don't find exactly what you're looking for—you can pick and choose among the ideas presented and, quite possibly, come up with a new combination of artistic and marketing concepts entirely your own. Which, of course, is the ultimate expression of talent anyway! ●

BARB MULLEN:
YOU MIGHT PAY THE RENT WITH A GUIDEBOOK

In the early 70's I published *The Mendocino Coast*, a small local history and guidebook. Dreamed it up, did the research and writing, took the photographs, dug for the money, and found a printer to run off 5,000 copies. The undertaking took four months and three days. This year there will be a second edition (with tiny changes) of probably 10,000 copies.

It's a modest kind of success, but ever since I started my guide I've wanted to turn other people on to doing the same thing (only differently) where they live. That way I could get some solid information about the Ozarks, say, or Puget Sound or what it's really like in Vermont or Arizona or the far reaches of British Columbia these days.

You can have the same fun, frustrations, satisfactions of doing, and great feedback that I've enjoyed . . . and make *some* money. How much money depends on a lot of things: the area where you live and how interesting it is to how many people, the competition (there may or may not be any), the kind of job you do getting it all together, and luck. Your success—or lack of it—will also depend on the plain old endless and sometimes acutely boring nitty-gritty things like promotion, tax records, press releases, bookkeeping, chopping up cartons, and packing books to be mailed . . . and the constant, bothersome business of blowing your horn (how else will others know the book exists, however much they want it?).

Potentially, at least, guidebook publishing is a good and flexible business that might help you live where you want to live. The demand for honest, loving handbooks is high, and the supply is surprisingly low. And it's a challenge. There are plenty of places still worth singing about, and that singing is best done by those who really know their areas . . . in fog and rain and whopping winds, in ten feet of snow and 110° of sun.

For the Mendocino coast, there was no question about the demand. It's a beautiful and astonishing part of the world. Twisting, crumbling cliffs and pocket beaches confront the moody Pacific . . . which changes, sometimes in minutes, from lapis lazuli to turquoise or teal or slate and back again.

Each year, thousands of visitors explore the small Mendocino villages and towns where clean little salt boxes and Victorian gothics suggest New England more than California. The tourists wander around, admiring and sometimes painting or photographing old fences and barns and wind-worn lowland firs, rejoicing in the clean air (assured by prevailing winds from the ocean). Hundreds of those visitors ask for a guidebook that—until mine appeared—didn't exist.

Oh yes, the area is briefly included (often with astonishing inaccuracies) in larger guides to the whole region. And someone is always putting together a monstrous "thing", strictly for dollars, with full-color pictures of gas stations and other uglies looming larger than the scenery . . . or a brief, boastful, and somewhat biased Chamber of Commerce brochure. But a simple, honest guide? No, there wasn't one.

MY ASSETS

I didn't exactly go into the publication of my handbook cold. I'd had a good bit of seasoning as a professional writer and bookseller and some photography experience. I'd even taught a little. I knew the lay of the Mendocino land (from ten years of exploring and living in the area), had many acquaintances there, and could draw on cluttered files of my own negatives for some of the pictures I would need. (There's no reason, though, why someone shouldn't start from scratch and learn by doing. Every day, people are learning to milk cows and wire houses and build tipis . . . things that sound harder to me than stringing words together.)

My cash assets were something else: about $5.00. There'd have to be money from somewhere and, since I didn't want advertising, I thought that maybe I could have sponsors listed in the back of the book like a symphony program. With only fifty carefully chosen businesses or people who wanted the book enough to put up $100 each, I reasoned, I'd have $5,000 to cover the cost of research, writing, photographs, and the actual printing of the book.

That notion was overly rosy, and I soon ran up against obstacles to the plan:

[1] The country (and thus the coast) was in the middle of a galloping recession. Money was short. There were fewer tourists, and those that came were "just looking, thanks". Local businesses had to think twice about $100.

[2] There weren't that many businesses in the area I wanted to cover, anyway. At the start I ruled out huge corporations, subdividers, and real estate firms. (They weren't all bad but the exclusion would save me the trouble of sorting them out. It would also leave me free, without climbing on a soapbox, to say what I wanted to say about protecting the coast.)

Other possible sponsors were eliminated because I couldn't imagine the handbook helping their business (auto body shops, the manufacture of toilet bowl cleaner, and such). I didn't approach a restaurant unless I liked its food. This kind of picking and choosing certainly reduced the potential take, but I'd do it again.

In the end I chopped my hopes down to 30 or 35 sponsors . . . and got 23, which wasn't quite enough to do the job in comfort (production of the book—*not* counting film, paper, developing chemicals, gas, or my time—cost just over $2,300).

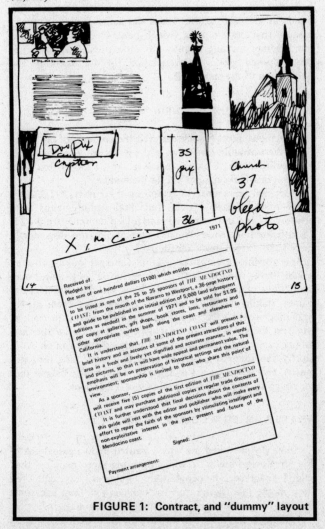

FIGURE 1: Contract, and "dummy" layout

THE BEGINNING

Before starting (except for a couple of trial runs), I wrote up a contract (Fig. 1) which sort of explained what I was about. It worked well, except for two sponsors that I neglected to have sign the paper and which changed their minds at the last minute. I also did some thinking (rough), made a first draft outline (which never changed much), and put together a crude dummy (to show possible sponsors) of the proposed guide as preparation for my assembly and publication of the handbook.

GETTING IT ALL TOGETHER

Geography pretty much dictated the contents of my book. Since there wouldn't be room in the publication for the whole Mendocino coast, I chose to cover the 35 miles that hang together in a fairly natural unit in the middle.

I decided on a size—36 (counting the covers) 8-1/2 X 11 pages—that seemed good for both photographs and printers . . . and cut, trimmed, and folded dummies from 12 X 18 construction paper. When a dummy got too disgustingly frayed and dirty, I made a fresh one.

It is possible—even probable—that a sharper-looking dummy would have done a better selling job . . . but there were restrictions of time (I wanted the book out that summer) and money (taking the final pictures and printing them at the beginning would have meant an expensive delay). Instead, as work on the guide's contents progressed, I wrote in titles and rubber cemented in the dog-eared photographs I had on hand. Slowly the dummy began to look like something (but not much), and it was an act of faith for a sponsor to believe that the rough sample was the forerunner of a real book.

WHAT I WANTED MY GUIDE TO BE

Some people asked me why I wanted to do a guidebook of the Mendocino area. "It will only bring more people," they said. I disagreed. The people were coming anyway, and I felt they might take better care of our coast if they had some factual—but gentle—background about the region.

I planned for the book to have an introduction, a map, a

little general history of the area, a brief guide to looking, and then share and share alike for the communities strung along the coast: two pages each for most and four for Mendocino (the best known) and Fort Bragg (the biggest and most neglected). The little handbook would then be closed out with some final notes for visitors, the list of sponsors, and—because it felt good—a poem on the outside back cover.

My overall goal was to make the small guide as honest, as accurate, and as interesting as possible . . . while emphasizing the importance of preserving the Mendocino coast. For the latter reason I mostly featured the main roads (there are fragile areas best protected by silence . . . those who need them will find them). Humans can be nauseatingly predatory so, unlike some other travel guides I've read, mine would *not* encourage the rip-off of driftwood, flowers, fence posts, abalone, and the other things that make our region special.

To drive home the point that the Mendocino area *is* worth preserving, I intended to focus my book on the coast's fragile beauties rather than the awful neon signs or mish-mosh string towns of body shops, gas stations, wounded cars, and other uglies. Which is to say that I knew in advance that the finished book would somewhat idealize the region. I also wanted my guide to credit the many national groups represented in the Mendocino coast's small population and capture something of the area's cosmopolitan flavor.

To wrap up most of what I wanted my book to be (and to let potential backers know what they might be getting into), I wrote a statement which would appear above the sponsors' names on the inside back cover:

Thanks to these friends who, by their faith and sponsorship, have made this guide possible. With them I share the hope that progress on the coast may be gentle enough not to destroy the beauty, worry the gulls, or deaden the rivers, woods, and beaches!

To me, this prelude to doing and selling the book was necessary . . . but I knew where I was headed when I began, and the advance planning didn't take long.

ANOTHER CONSIDERATION

There *was* one other point to ponder as I considered the

publication and marketing of my guide. The cost should be low enough so that anyone who really wanted it could afford it. A price of $1.95 sounded good . . . and gave me just enough margin to work with.

THE SPONSORS

Selling the first two or three sponsors—by reason of long friendship—was easy. The others were long, hard work with frequent call-backs and "time to think it over". Most of the people I approached, whether they were able to go along or not, were friendly and encouraging. Some were confused by the idea . . . or thought their dollars better spent elsewhere. A couple were downright mean.

In the end, the project turned out to be beautifully self-selective with some great built-in plus factors. The folks who came in on the guide became actively involved and full of hopes for "our book". They formed a community of good people that encouraged me and were proud of the results.

MORE THOUGHTS ON FINANCING

There are, of course, many variations on my sponsorship method of financing a guidebook . . . and some completely

---

A RESEARCH TIP

A while ago, I came upon a new series of small books that might prove helpful to aspiring local guidebook publishers. It's the *Localized History Series* issued by Teacher's College Press of Columbia University and edited by Clifford Lord, President of Hofstra.

The series includes handbooks for many states (most cost $1.50, a few are priced higher), some cities, watersheds *(The Wisconsin Valley)* and national groups *(The Finns in America)*. The list of titles also includes a teacher's guide, *Teaching History with Community Resources.* The books are designed to turn high school kids on to local history and contain ideas and information useful to any regional guidebook publisher.

different ideas for raising the necessary money. A larger number of backers at a lower price each—say, 60 at $50.00 or 120 at $25.00—might or might not be easier to swing. Maybe putting a bankroll together that way would involve so many calls that the book would never get off the ground.

Some handbook publishers might be able to borrow bright new money from friends or their own bank accounts. An advance sale (cash with order) either of the regular guide or a specially bound limited edition is another possibility.

Smaller guides cost less money. You may have to limit the number of pages in your handbook if—try as you might—your fund raising remains stuck at a level a little (or a lot!) lower than you had anticipated.

GETTING IT ON

It might have made better sense to sell all the sponsorships first and then do the book, but—impatient to get on with it—I started the research, writing, and fresh picture taking for my guide as soon as I had three or four firm backers.

RESEARCH

Research was a problem because there wasn't a great deal of reliable material available from which I could draw. The Mendocino area was considered small, remote, and somehow atypical enough to be scanted by the general histories of California . . . and some of the brochures, pamphlets, and newspaper clippings I found contradicted each other about six times to a page.

There *were* three good sources of historical information I didn't tap due to lack of time and space. One, both Mendocino and Fort Bragg have very old weekly newspapers whose files would have yielded far more treasures than I could cram into a brief guidebook. Two, the mountains of data stored away in the museums of a local lumber company and historical society presented the same problem. And three, I would have loved to talk to old-timers but, again, knew that I'd have little or no room for the stories they could tell.

I finally compromised by basing most of my guide's historical research on an 1880 history of Mendocino County which was updated and reissued a few years ago by the Mendocino County Historical Society and on a much more recent—though brief—book about the area done on special assignment for the museum-owning lumber company.

The information in my book is as accurate as I could make it in the space I had available. When accounts disagreed, I said so . . . rather than making my own choice of tales.

THE WRITING OF THE BOOK

Combining history with the here and now gave me more to say than I had room to say it in . . . which is always a good plan.

I have three handy rules to guide me when writing. The first is that old, anonymous quote, "The written word should be clean as a bone, clear as light, firm as stone. Two words are not as good as one." Although one never quite lives up to this adage, it's a good one to have above the typewriter.

As a second rule, I always read my copy aloud to myself. That is, I write as much or more for the ear as for the eye.

My third guiding principle is as much a hope as a rule: I have an obligation to try not to bore the reader.

TYPESETTING AND LAYOUT

Once finished, my copy was set in type on one of those IBM wonder machines. Then, because I felt that technical skills I didn't have were required, I found a commercial artist to do the final layouts and paste-ups for my book. For doing this work, I agreed to pay the artist a royalty on the guide's first edition. It would have been more economical to have had the artist associated with the printer do this . . . but I happened to find the artist I used before I settled on the printer.

THE PRINTER

Printing was the scary part, and I got frightening estimates from three shops before—by happy accident—I found a fourth whose owner was as excited about doing the book as I was. His joy was a valuable plus which made our joint work fun.

My book was printed by offset (very fast and inexpensive) on recycled paper (except for the cover). The recycled paper, by the way, was a calculated risk. People are so used to seeing photographs reproduced on glossy stock with "good blacks and whites" that most I polled before the decision was made thought the recycled paper an act of madness. On the other hand, it seemed somewhat absurd to talk about saving trees while cutting them to print the book. Besides, maybe we were in a photographic rut. Now that the deed is done, a number of folks have written to say they like the gentle result and that it fits the mood of this coastal region.

SNAGS AND FRUSTRATIONS

In writing about the doing, I'm sure that I make it sound simpler and smoother than it was ... because there were hassles without number all along the way.

I was living in Fort Bragg at the time I did the book ... in a very small, one-room cabin which served as living room, dining room, kitchen, office, bedroom, and darkroom. Conditions for printing, washing, and drying pictures were less than ideal.

The printer was 100 miles south—over a slow road—and my car was in the last stages of accelerated senility. During the actual printing, a heat wave with temperatures touching 109° hit Santa Rosa. This was hard on us and very hard on the presses. Water is an indispensable part of offset printing, and the heat played hob with the process. Sheets fresh from the press bore strange globs and streaks. Somehow we muddled through.

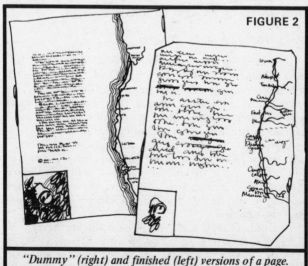

FIGURE 2

"Dummy" (right) and finished (left) versions of a page.

COPYRIGHT

Copyrighting a book is simple. Write to the copyright division of the Library of Congress, Washington, D.C. 20540, and ask for copyright registration forms. Print your book—including the copyright notice in the proper place—and send two copies of the finished publication along with the forms and small fee to Washington.

MAKING YOUR BOOK "OFFICIAL"

There are some standard listings which any publisher should try to get for a book. In addition to the two copyright copies, samples of a new publication should be sent to the Library of Congress for a Library of Congress number. This is a mysterious process, and my book hasn't yet been issued such a number.

Copies of a new volume should also be sent to *Publisher's Weekly* for listing in that magazine's Weekly Record section (they can refuse to list books under 48 pages and, in any case, usually wait for a Library of Congress number before featuring a book). Requests for information should be made to both Advance Book Information, R.R. Bowker, 1180 Avenue of the Americas, New York, New York, 10036, and to Standard Book Numbering Agency at the same address.

GETTING YOUR BOOK KNOWN

In sending out review copies of my guide, I was particularly naive. I blithely mailed the book to all and sundry, expecting immediate response (like the front page of *The New York Times,* for heaven's sake!). Instead, I found that a great many reviewers were quite content to mention the guide in a sentence or two. Even more ignored the publication.

There was also a delay I had not reckoned on. I mailed most review copies in August and early September . . . and one very helpful review (it brought dozens of return orders) was published the following March. Several more mentions are still pending. At that, my book received a number of reviews, and many were generous.

I should further point out that mails are heavy, and packages entrusted to them do go astray. I sent follow-up notes to several reviewers that seemed naturals for my guide, and at least one replied that the first copy had not arrived and asked for another. I'm still hoping for that review . . . any day now.

MAILINGS

In order to qualify for the post office's low book rates, books have to be of a certain physical size. Check with your local postmaster before your guide is printed.

I mail my publication in 9 X 12 envelopes, reinforced with an 8-1/2 X 11 sheet of corrugated cardboard. Invoices can be included without adding extra postage, but if a letter accompanies a book I write "first class letter enclosed" on the outside and add another stamp. When shipping more than two books (two will fit into one envelope), I reinforce the bundle with cardboard and wrap it in heavy kraft paper and tie it with twine. All book-carrying envelopes and packages are stamped *Book Rate* with a handy rubber stamp. I also stamp all outgoing mail with my return address.

THE LOG

I keep track of my mail (there's some, most days) with a simple log. Incoming mail—all of it—is listed on one side of the page and outgoing on the other. When the postage I use differs from that necessary for a letter or statement—or the charge required to mail *The Mendocino Coast* at book rate—I make a note of it.

DISCOUNTS

Most publishers have three discount schedules: [1] wholesale to retailers, [2] wholesale to libraries, and [3] retail by mail (if they handle such orders . . . some do not).

To simplify life, I established one wholesale price for both libraries and the retailers who have a resale number (required in California). I offer no discount on single copies, 25% off on two to four of my books (for a net price of $1.46 each), and 40% off ($1.17 per copy net) on orders for five or more of the guide. That's pretty standard for the book business. When cash accompanies an order, I pay postage.

THE FINAL RED TAPE

Most library orders must be billed in triplicate (and you'll need a fourth copy for your records). One invoice is usually sufficient for retail accounts (plus a carbon for you).

For each retail account I serve, I keep a sheet in a small

ledger. Sales are entered in the appropriate tiny squares from the invoice book. It's important that these records be maintained because all retail sales in California are charged a sales tax, while wholesale transactions are not. It's obviously to your advantage, in such a situation, to be able to prove that every wholesale business deal you make is indeed just that.

It has suited me to deal for cash as much as possible, and a number of retailers are willing to operate on this basis. Consignment works badly. If a store wishes, I agree that the books it buys can be returned for cash in 90 days. So far, none have been returned.

AND *NEXT* TIME

I'm now looking at a second edition of *The Mendocino Coast* . . . which means a second chance. There's just one typo in the first printing, and we'll correct that. A few layouts annoy me . . . I think we'll change them. One or two photographs printed from too-contrasty prints didn't come across. We'll make substitutions.

There's a better quality recycled paper available now than when edition one was printed. The paper (including cover) of number two will be in this new stock.

Financing is still a problem (banks look askance at little publishers, and we're not eligible for small business loans). In part, I'll pay for the second edition with advance orders from regular customers (at a special cash-with-order price of $1.00 per copy, postpaid, instead of $1.17).

I plan to let people know about the second edition with a few ads. There'll be at least a brief announcement in *Publisher's Weekly* and some small advertisements in several other places.

There'll also be a press release going out to as many newspapers and magazines as I have stamps for. The list will be compiled with the aid of two indispensable (and frightfully expensive) paperbacks: the latest edition of *Literary Market Place* and Gebbie's *All-In-One Directory*. The latter lists magazines, daily and weekly newspapers, radio, and TV all in handy order.

THE DIVIDENDS

I'm lucky. Sales of *The Mendocino Coast* have held up well and promise to continue good. If my expenses had been lower,

I'd have come out ahead on the first edition. The second printing should start putting dollars in my pocket . . . and there have been dividends.

As a result of publishing my book, I've spoken to a couple of groups, taped a very local TV show, and received invitations to write other things and take other pictures.

And the letters! They've come from as far as Maine and Israel. Two of the best were sent by a new Chinese friend in San Francisco . . . a descendant of one of the men who'd been shipwrecked on the beach at Caspar. He wrote with great imagination and warmth about what it must have been like for his ancestor and closed, "Thank you for caring about an old American family." I liked that very much.

IN CLOSING . . .

Doing a small, local guide has been a good thing for me. The promotion part gets boring, and waiting for the mail can be discouraging, but—on the whole—I like it. And you?●

GET YER MENDOCINO GUIDE

For those who want a copy of *The Mendocino Coast,* the price is $1.95 plus 30 cents postage and handling for a total of $2.25 (California residents please add an additional 12 cents tax).

If others are inspired to do a local history and want to let me know the area, I'll be glad to keep an informal log so everyone won't be working on the same neck of the woods. No charge, but send a stamped, self-addressed envelope for this service.

If anyone thinks I can help them with their writing, pictures, or red tape, I'd be glad to try . . . but for this I would have to charge something.

BARB MULLEN
P.O. BOX 11484
SANTA ROSA
CALIFORNIA 95406

The above article originally appeared in LIFESTYLE! NO. 1 . . . along with a great deal of other live-better-for-less and self-sufficiency how-to information. For further information about the magazine—and other books and periodicals devoted to home businesses, self-sufficiency, and related subjects—please see page 367 of this handbook.

DANIEL OGDEN
19th CENTURY
THAT YOU CAN

SAYS: HERE'S A
TINTYPE BIZ
START TODAY!

Alternatives are where you find them . . . on a Maine homestead, on a tugboat in the Caribbean, in a craft shop, or home office. Doug Elbinger found his in the 19th century, with the help of a time machine he discovered sitting in a museum: an original Anthony camera, made circa 1860 to take tintypes.

Today, Elbinger is a tintypist . . . a maker of genuine old-time photographs using cameras, processes, and plates developed in the 1880's. At his studio in Harpers Ferry, West Virginia, you can dress in authentic 19th-century costume, pose in front of the big wooden camera, look into the lens for 10 seconds, and have your image recorded on a metal plate. Five minutes later your tintype has been developed . . . and you can see yourself as you might have looked 100 years ago.

Before he found his calling in the past, Doug was a freelance photographer who worked his way through college with a modern-day camera and later traveled the world for the major news agencies. Many such professionals take an interest in the history of their art, and Elbinger was no exception. Less typically, however, Doug didn't just collect early cameras and photos . . . he actually preferred to spend his spare time taking pictures with antique equipment!

Led by his interest in the subject, Elbinger studied early photography at the Smithsonian Institution and spent long hours in the darkroom attempting to translate old emulsion and developer formulas into modern chemistry. In 1972, after many failures, Doug made his first successful tintype. He was then firmly on his way to reviving what had once been America's most popular form of photography.

That's right, "most popular". Over a hundred years ago—before George Eastman came along with the little black box he perversely called "the Brownie"–photography was a wide-open field . . . and the customer had a good many options as to how his image would be taken. The choices included daguerreotypes (silver and copper plates), ambrotypes (glass), photos on waxed paper or wet collodion, and many more. Most of the methods used were invented in Europe, and all of them were expensive.

Predictably, our own country's contribution to the art increased the speed of development, lowered the price dramatically, and allowed everyone to indulge in the luxury of having his portrait made. The tintype–a uniquely American institution–brought photography to the people for the first time.

The earliest tintypes were made by a wet-plate process that is still used by some modern practitioners. One notable reviver of the method is located at Detroit's Greenfield Village . . . a re-creation of 19th-century life and technology complete with working tintype studio. The photo operation is successful, but only because its management called in the Ford Motor Company's chemical division to help with technical problems . . . which are considerable.

The trouble with the wet-plate process is that the formulas of the last century can't easily be converted into modern chemical terms. Some of the ingredients are no longer manufactured at all, and others–potassium cyanide, for instance–are so deadly that the tintypist risks his life every time he takes a picture by the original recipe. *(No kidding. Daniel Ogden knows of one death and another near-death from this cause. The Greenfield Village facility includes an elaborate ventilation system to remove the toxic fumes. You have been warned.—MOTHER.)*

For other reasons, too, the wet-plate process is a challenge even to the professional photographer. Such a tintype is a totally handmade product. You take a thin sheet of steel, coat it with collodion you've mixed yourself, carefully sensitize the plate with silver nitrate, expose it to the camera, develop it with ferrous sulfate, and fix it with hypo. If everything goes well, you have a 50-50 chance of a clear picture. And if you think it all sounds pretty complicated, Elbinger–who made his first tintypes by exactly this method–agrees wholeheartedly.

After a few months of struggling with wet plates, Doug decided to update the process . . . from 1860 to 1880, that is. The "modern" tintype of 1880 utilized a dry plate precoated at the factory with photo-sensitive emulsions. This improved version required no preparation or dangerous and complicated chemical mixtures, and could be developed in about five minutes. Obviously, the dry plate was the way to go . . . especially if the tintypist's art was to be available to anyone other than professional photographers and chemistry majors.

For many months thereafter, Elbinger worked with photo-chemists in an effort to perfect a reliable dry-plate tintype. He ordered steel, gelatin, and silver, coated his own plates . . . and found that they didn't work. They, and many successors, continued not to work for almost a year. It wasn't until the summer of 1974 that the original process was duplicated. The results, however, were worth the trouble: Doug's modern dry-plate tintypes resemble those of the 1880's in tone, texture, contrast, and every other way.

The camera in which the plates are exposed is just as authentic as the tintypes themselves. Elbinger borrowed an original from a museum, took it to a cabinetmaker, and had it reproduced right down to the teak and rosewood plate holder. Equipment like that, of course, begs to be used . . . and Doug soon found himself reviving the old occupation of traveling portrait maker.

At first the newly launched tintypist worked out of a van and hit antique shows, arts and crafts fairs, re-enactments of battles, and other special events. Elbinger and a friend would set up their darktent, display a few sample tintypes . . . and watch the line form. It wasn't uncommon to gross $1,000 a weekend from the sale of pictures at $10.00 a plate. (Once the partners raised the price to $12.00 just to see what would happen. You guessed it: The line grew longer still.)

Doug, however, had dreams of an actual studio . . . a re-creation of those formerly found in every American community. The location he picked for the first such studio—Harpers Ferry—is ideal, an antique in itself. Students of history will remember John Brown's raid on the armory at that site in 1859, and the town's near destruction during the Civil War because of its strategic importance as an arms depot and rail center. There could hardly be a more suitable place to practice a craft of the period . . . especially the making of tintypes, which were enormously popular in wartime as keepsakes for soldiers and their loved ones.

A unique product in an appropriate setting is hard to beat . . . and the Harpers Ferry studio made a small profit in its first half season, with no publicity at all. With the help of some advertising and the reputation built during 1974, the venture is expected to gross well over $35,000 during the eight-month season in 1975. And a second location has now been opened in Franklin Village, Michigan.

That should be the end of the story ... except that Elbinger isn't content to keep the fun and profit of a tintype business to himself. Doug figures that his newly perfected dry-plate process is so easy to master that almost anyone can learn to make old-time photos and use the skill as the basis for a good living: a low-pressure, low-capital enterprise which can be started and operated without a lot of hassle over inventory (and without a rich uncle to absorb losses during the first two years). Elbinger, in short, is offering you the chance to learn and practice a lost art and make money at it.

If you're interested, the Harpers Ferry tintypist can start you off easily with authentic cameras and plates at reasonable prices. He also has access to various pieces of equipment which you may or may not want. The following, however, are the basics:

[1] THE CAMERA. An original made to take 7" X 5" plates would be fine (if you could find one, that is ... and even if you could, any owner who knew the worth of such an item would probably ask a price that ran to five figures). Elbinger has been offered $1,000 for his reproduction. That, he agrees, is a lot of money for a wooden machine.

Doug, however, is able to offer cameras similar to his own at $650. The price includes one standard lens and two plate-holding backs. A stand (likewise a period reproduction) is available for an extra $250.

Elbinger also supplies a very useful accessory that enables you to make copies of pictures. The tintype, remember, isn't made from a negative and therefore can't be reproduced by printing. The original practitioners of the art got around this problem by fitting their cameras with four lenses. Each focused a small image on one quarter of the plate, which was later cut into four sections. Doug uses the same method and recommends the quarter-plate capability as an easy way to give the customer more for his money without increasing your per-picture costs. A set of extra lenses can be ordered for about $300.

[2] THE PLATES. The other major expense for the novice tintypist is an initial order of dry plates. These are pieces of

aluminum coated with a gelatin emulsion and packaged to prevent exposure to light. They have a shelf life of one year and are guaranteed. The cost of $4.00 each includes a supply of developer sufficient to process the number of plates in the order.

Other items are necessary but aren't automatically supplied . . . because Elbinger isn't interested in offering you a big "package deal" full of things you may already have or be able to get elsewhere at lower prices. Such as:

[1] DARKROOM EQUIPMENT. The simplicity of the dry-plate process means that all the necessary developing apparatus should come to only about $50.00.

First of all you must have a lightproof room in which to develop the plates (a van, a tent, even a closet with a blanket over the door will work fine). This space needs a safelight, which can be a 30-watt bulb covered with red cellophane. Add a couple of tanks to hold the developer and fixer, a rinsing system, and some print frames to hold the plates, and you're all set. Don't worry . . . no expertise or split-second timing is needed to finish dry-plate tintypes.

[2] FRAMES. It's good practice to mount your pictures before giving them to customers. The 19th-century tintypist preferred an oval border (for practical reasons, because it concealed the irregular edges of the image). Elbinger uses heavy paper frames of the same shape to give his products an authentic look, and he can help you locate and order a supply of 250 at a price of about $75.00. If you can do better elsewhere, or want to make your own, go ahead.

[3] LIGHTS. If you want to limit your photography to outdoor events, your list of "must" items is complete. Indoors, however, you need lighting . . . and not a couple of 100-watt bulbs, either. Tintypes used to be called "sun pictures" because the process worked only in bright daylight. Today we can create the intensity and "light temperature" of the sun by artificial means . . . at a modest price. A set of lights will cost about $50.00. (Even if your studio has a skylight like its 19th-century counterparts, such equipment still comes in handy on cloudy days.)

That, basically, is all you need to become a full-fledged tintypist. Depending on what gear you've already accumulated, you could get started for around $2,500 . . . and you can reasonably expect to make that much in two or three good weekends.

What about know-how? If all the talk of fixers, safelights, and light temperatures has you a little worried, rest assured that you can learn everything there is to know about dry-plate tintypes in a couple of days. Elbinger has worked for over a year to get most of the bugs out of the operation . . . and he'll train you to be a tintypist at either his place or yours (whichever is easier on your pocketbook).

If you choose, Doug can send someone to your location—at your expense—to teach you the rudiments of the business. Or you can spend a weekend working at the Harpers Ferry establishment. Elbinger prefers the latter approach because it allows better instruction (and gives him a chance to get acquainted with others who want to make tintypes). Several "graduates" of the training program, incidentally, are already running their own studios—at Nashville, Indiana; Georgetown, a section of Washington, D.C.; Alexandria, Virginia; and Scottsdale, Arizona—and a couple more former students are on the road with mobile operations.

I should stress that these are independent concerns. After training, you're on your own to manage your new venture just the way you please . . . and you'll have to make some decisions about what kind of studio you want. This business can be run on many different levels to allow for varying expectations concerning hours and profits. You could easily, for instance, spend over $10,000 to set up a superslick operation on the beach at Fort Lauderdale, including all the options: painted backdrops like those in the original studios . . . Victorian furniture . . . costumes of the period . . . professional publicity and advertising. You *could*, but you don't have to. It's quite possible to do without most of the expensive extras, or to devise inexpensive alternatives.

For example, instead of paying high rent for a prime location, just book yourself into special events. Usually you'll find yourself right on the main drag in a booth that costs you only a few dollars a day.

When you do make such a reservation, offer the sponsors of the show your services in generating publicity for the affair. Art and antique fests, especially, are always looking for unusual angles to catch the eye of the public . . . and tintypes surely qualify. The old craft makes a good story, and Elbinger has found that the media in small towns and big cities alike are happy to give him all the free coverage he can use.

Costumes are optional but desirable and, in Doug's experience, a real help to the business. They add to the period look of the pictures and seem to be especially interesting to the public. They're expensive bought new (half a dozen elegant outfits can run as much as $1,000)... but if you know someone who's handy with a sewing machine, they can just as well be homemade. If necessary, Elbinger can put you onto sources of costumes or authentic patterns. Occasionally, too, a community theater will rent or sell part of its wardrobe. Or you may decide you don't like the idea at all. That's why no clothing is included with the camera and plates.

I repeat, how you run your studio is up to you: no rules, no restrictions, no fancy franchise contract. And how much you make is also up to you. The business can be operated so many ways that there's no saying what the profit potential is. You can concentrate on lucrative special events and enjoy a relaxed schedule (Elbinger was able to make a living while working only two weekends a month, when operating from the van). Or you can go for a fixed location, which means longer hours and more money.

A word about pricing: Doug's projection of $35,000 for the 1975 season is based on an average retail charge of about $10.00 per picture. A higher or lower rate might be appropriate in a different location. Elbinger can help with some quick market research if you need it.

Profits aside, there's something to making tintypes that you can't put a price tag on: the satisfaction—corny as it may sound—of watching your customers actually learn something from the product you sell them. The public knowledge of antique photography is very limited, and you'll find that people generally approach the studio in a skeptical frame of mind. They expect a gimmick... maybe a polaroid camera hidden inside the wooden box. Once they touch the plates and see themselves in real tintypes, though, they begin to have a whole new appreciation for this part of our history. The change in attitude can be a lot of fun to observe.

I could go on... but if you're interested, you'd do better to write Elbinger & Son, 1380 Haslett Road, Haslett, Michigan 48840. Doug can fill in the details... and maybe get you started in a 19th-century business that's just right for today. ●

The above article originally appeared in THE MOTHER EARTH NEWS® NO. 32... along with a great deal of other live-better-for-less and self-sufficiency how-to information. For further information about the magazine—and other books and periodicals devoted to home businesses, self-sufficiency, and related subjects—please see page 367 of this handbook.

R.I. BALL:

HOW TO HAND-LETTER FOR CASH

Hand-lettering is easy to learn, worth money . . . and takes us back a little way toward the days when folks took pride in the graphic arts. Not that modern printing doesn't have its place, mind you (I'd hate to copy whole books by hand as the medieval monks did), but there's something cold about a graduation certificate with your name done in sloppy typing or stark computer printout. Look at your own collection of honors and you'll see what I mean.

You're not the only one who finds mechanized testimonials unsatisfying, either. Schools, honorary and social fraternities and sororities, church groups, social or civic clubs—anyone who hands out elaborate certificates—want to make them as impressive as possible . . . and that's where you come in.

All you need to become a hand-lettering specialist sought after by organizations and printers alike is a steady hand, a slight inclination to the artistic, and some routine self-discipline. If you fit that description, you can earn hundreds of spare dollars pleasantly, at home, in your own time.

I got my own start in the business as an art student at West Virginia University, when a friend rushed up to me in a frenzy. "Know anybody who can do Old English lettering?" he panted. "We've got to have 70 names put on certificates by next week and the printer can't make the deadline."

"Yes," I said, "me! I'll do it for a quarter a name." Much relieved, my friend agreed to the rate (about half the printer's fee) and handed me 75 forms. (I thought I'd need a few extra, since—to tell the truth—I had only a general idea of what Old English Gothic looked like and had never lettered at all except back in high school, when I was the only girl in my favorite course . . . mechanical drawing.)

The following week was a hard one, but the concentrated work paid off. Over the next few years countless organizations—on and off campus—approached me with lettering jobs, and I was launched in a fascinating and profitable sideline.

All the same, I don't recommend such a haphazard beginning to anyone else. Hindsight suggests that it's better to start by choosing an appropriate alphabet and learning to letter it with broad-point pen and India ink *before* going out after that first assignment.

You also should read up on the rich history of hand-lettering at the public library . . . or see your favorite art supply shop or bookstore for Alexander Nesbitt's comprehensive *History and Technique of Lettering* ($3.00 in paperback from Dover Publications).

Besides giving you a perspective on the art of lettering and a wealth of curious information (why we dot the "i", for instance), such research will help you find the right alphabet to learn. Although you'll eventually want to master several, one good basic set of letters will see you through at first.

Your best choice is a variation of what was the major hand in Europe centuries before printing (Gutenberg chose a closely related face for his earliest work in the mid-1400's). This dignified, ornamental style—with its strong vertical down-strokes—had a "woven" appearance on early manuscripts and, consequently, was named *Textur*. Derivations of the face are called *Text* alphabets and include Old English, Old English Script, Black Letter, Gothic Style, Cloister Black, Cloister Text, Spire Gothic, etc.

Begin by choosing one Text alphabet and learning its majuscules and miniscules (capital and small letters). As you begin to master the forms, you'll discover that they lend themselves to certain liberties . . . and your personal style will begin to emerge.

At this stage—if you're hard up and had to borrow the copy of MOTHER you're reading—all you really need for equipment is a bottle of black India ink, a penholder, and a point (say a Speedball size C-4). Later you'll want to make further investments, as suggested in the list with this article or in the books you run across during your research. These volumes will also tell you how to prepare and carry out your work . . . and you can get further hints from Ross F. George's compact

---

A FEW EXAMPLES OF HAND LETTERING

ABCDEFGHI

Modified Old English

Florida Straits

Wallau

Manchester City

Jessen

A Babdefg

Script

Speedball instruction book, published by the Hunt Pen Company for about a dollar.

One skill you should practice carefully is correct spacing and centering. Nobody likes cramped or irregular lettering placed lopsidedly on a certificate! When you're working on translucent parchment or light paper, you can save yourself the trouble of measuring each word if you slip a guideline sheet under the page. For heavier stock, I use a primitive light table made by laying a piece of thick glass across the arms of a child's chair and putting a gooseneck lamp underneath.

Once you've got your alphabet down pat and a sample or two prepared, you're ready for business, and you've got to give some thought to how much you're going to charge. In general, it's best to go by the prevailing market price. Call up a couple of local printers and find out their rates . . . and if possible get a look at their products too, just to see how you measure up.

It's best to establish a minimum fee of, say, 40¢–50¢ a name . . . mainly as a safeguard against that small persistent group which specializes in wheedling volunteer labor from the

BASIC HAND-LETTERING EQUIPMENT

Drawing board	$5.00	Can be held in the lap and leaned against a desk or table. 16" X 21" is a good size.
Ruler	.45	Cheap wooden.
45° triangle, 6"	.50	
T square, 18"	2.00	This and the triangle are used for marking guidelines.
Drawing pencils, 2	.50	H and 2H.
Sandpaper pad	.20	For pointing pencils.
Eraser	.30	The kneaded kind leaves no residue.
Ink, 1-ounce bottle	.65	Use black India ink, which is waterproof and opaque. Later on you may want to try colored drawing inks.
Pen points, 1/2 dozen @ 25¢ each	1.50	Assorted oblique style, flat. They last a long time and are also available "left-handed".
Penholders, 4 @ 25¢ each	1.00	They never wear out.
Crow quill pen points (4 @ 15¢ each and holders (2 @ 15¢ each)	.90	Don't go hog-wild with embellishments, even though the Text alphabets invite them. You will, however, sometimes want minor flourishes best wrought with crow quill pens. The points are less long-lived than regular nibs.
Drafting tape	.70	A 10-yard roll of 3/4-inch tape will last months . . . at least.
	$13.70	Prices, of course, vary locally. Additional future costs will include only refills of ink and an occasional replacement of pencils, erasers, and pen points.

innocent. (If you've ever done posters, you'll know what I mean!) Possible factors for price adjustment will be your speed and skill, deadlines, size and number of certificates . . . and perhaps your feelings toward the soliciting organization. (Also, possibly, how broke you are at the time.) Be flexible at first, like any young business. Your rates will eventually stabilize.

Do you feel a little nervous about launching this venture? Never mind . . . start anyhow. Don't pass up any opportunity to make your availability known. Valuable contacts can be made through campus and local newspaper ads, printers who handle certificates, and officers of various organizations. If your work is good and your price reasonable, most groups will prefer your fine hand-lettering to poorly rendered or mechanical substitutes. With a minimum effort on your part, work will start coming in . . . with a maximum, it won't ever stop! ☒

The above article originally appeared in THE MOTHER EARTH NEWS® NO. 24 . . . along with a great deal of other live-better-for-less and self-sufficiency how-to information. For further information about the magazine—and other books and periodicals devoted to home businesses, self-sufficiency, and related subjects—please see page 367 of this handbook.

HOW TO BE A CARTOONIST

INTRODUCTION : JOHN SHUTTLEWORTH

Now look, gang, don't get us wrong: We're most certainly not suggesting that half the readers of this book are gonna run out and become freelance cartoonists immediately after reading the following articles. A few, yes. The great majority, no.

We've gone pretty deeply into the how of this particular work-at-home dodge, though, for several reasons: [1] it's a fascinating field, [2] it's part of the communications/persuasion industry which plays an increasingly important part in our lives, [3] like writing, commercial art, and various other skills and crafts, cartooning does offer a way out of the 9-to-5 rap for a certain number of talented and determined individuals, [4] it's mainly a mail-order operation, which means it neatly sidesteps race, color, creed, and most other excuses we all use for putting bad trips on each other, and [5] successful freelancing—whether as plumber, cartoonist, cake baker, baby sitter, candlemaker, or whatever—depends on a certain life-style—a way of looking at things—all its own. The products (skill, drawings, pastry, mere presence, decorator items, etc.) may differ but the ground rules are always the same: You're either your own man, work when, where, and at what you like and successfully exchange your output for what you need and want ... or you go back to pumping gas on the corner.

So, even if you think you have no drawing ability and you couldn't care less about trying to sell funny pictures to magazines, come on along. You're going to learn how to get a highly specialized art—or other—education for very little money (maybe even free), you'll find a definite step-by-step drop-out-and-do-your-own-thing plan used by one successful

*cartoonist, and Carl Kohler's section, in particular, should [a]
turn you on to some immediate moneymaking angles if you
are, or want to be, a cartoonist or [b] just generally turn you
on if you're not a tooner but need some inspiration from a
sassy, successful practitioner of an alternate lifestyle.*

So you wanna be a cartoonist? . . . Great! But why?
Why?

Yes, why . . . because if you're just looking for an easy way
out, this probably isn't it. Cartooning, like most other
endeavors, can be brutally hard work . . . and, like most other
endeavors, it can be deliriously wonderful play that you just
happen to get paid for.

Let's stop and lay down some ground rules right in front: We
presently live in a society that puts a price tag on virtually everything, right? Right. And that can be a real drag, right? Right.
Because you always wind up having to put in your time on a job
you hate just to get the necessities of life, right? Wrong!

It doesn't *have* to be that way, gang. It's all in how you look at it. Remember, we said, "The society puts a price tag on virtually everything." OK. There's no reason why you can't make that work *for,* rather than *against,* you.

It's easy. First, decide what you really want to do; second, start doing it (as long as you're not putting a bad trip on someone or something else); and third, figure out some way to exchange what you do for what you want and need.

If you're hung up on horses and hate office work, in other words, you'd be damn foolish to work all week as a secretary just so you could pay the rent, put food on the table, and-maybe-have enough left over to ride an hour or two each weekend at some expensive stable . . . yet, that's exactly what an awful lot of women do. But not my clever little wife. She loves horses, so she teaches riding, trains, shows, and judges horses . . . and, incidentally, makes twice what any desk job would pay her.

Rule Number One in Successful Living, then, goes something like this: Get yourself together, find out where the action is for *you*, go there . . . and start making it happen. As Thoreau said, "Build your castles in the air . . . and then put foundations under them."

So, for the sake of argument, let's say that cartooning is your thing. You're fascinated by the idea of communicating with hand-drawn pictures, you dig the ego trip of being a successful artist, or cartooning just appeals to some artsy-craftsy element in your nature. It doesn't matter. Don't analyze it. All you have to know is that cartooning is Your Thing.

Fine. Now, how are you going to start? With ten years of art school or an expensive home study course and a fancy studio with all the trimmings? Not on your life . . . or, I should say, not *with* your life. You haven't got that much time. You're interested in beginning right here and now. And, just so you can walk away from that factory job (work) and start cartooning (play) any time you feel like it, you're gonna want to make it begin paying off just as soon as possible. Here's *how*:

Every field of endeavor, every sport, every industry, every special interest group—it seems—in the country has one or two or seven or twelve or more magazines, papers, or newsletters published just for it. If the publication covers the field, it's called a trade journal. If it's put out by one company or subgroup within the field for "their own", it's called a house organ. TJs and HOs are what you look for whenever you want to get inside a field or a special interest group, quickly and easily. As a cartoonist, these publications should doubly interest you because a couple are going to teach you *how* and the others are going to buy a lot of your finished work.

Forget the shysters who exaggerate the opportunities in the field while selling you an overpriced art course or a truckload of fancy equipment. Forget the dilettantes who always flutter about the edges of the action. Go right to the heart of whatever field interests you by getting your hands on current copies of the working trade journals of that field.

There's no faster, easier, better way to pick up inside language, check out the economics, get filled in on the latest methods, spot developing trends, and learn "who's who" in the particular establishment or power structure that interests you.

When I decided to break into cartooning—back in the mid-50's—Don Ulsh's *New York Cartoon News* and George Hartman's *Information Guide* were the two "bibles" that showed me the way. Through them, I learned very quickly that, while my cartooning was less than professional, there was definitely a market for the gags I was writing. So I switched to writing for *other* cartoonists (whom I often found listed in *NYCN* and *IG*) and used the money I earned that way to finance the improvement of my drawing. Within six months (while I was still an ignorant 16-year-old Indiana farm boy) I had had gags, drawn by other artists, published in *Collier's, True,* and lesser markets, and I was selling cartoons of my own. I had never had (still haven't) an art lesson, I owned no expensive drawing equipment, and I definitely wasn't a genius. I had just used the cartooning papers as a magic carpet to get me where I wanted to go.

I've since used my cartoon experience as a springboard into some nice public relations and writing jobs, and I've kind of drifted away from the field. If I wanted to get back to the drawing board today (or if I were just starting out), however, my first move would be to get my name on the mailing list for the *IG*. It's now called *Cartoon World* and is published from P.O. Box 30367, Lincoln, Neb. 68503 for $20.00 a year. *New York Cartoon News* is no longer around but, for an annual $25.00, *Gag Re-Cap Publications* puts out a regular cartoon sheet from P.O. Box 86, East Meadow, N.Y. 11554 . . . and I'd get it. And then, of course, *Writer's Digest* carries a regular-cartooning column and ads for many market directories, cartoonists' newsletters, supplies, etc.

I'd also, maybe, invest $3.50 in *Careers in Cartooning* by Lawrence Lariar and $4.95 for Jack Markow's *Cartoonist's and Gag Writer's Handbook* if I couldn't find them in a library. That, plus the following articles by Kohler, would give me (and should give you) enough marketing information to make it.

And remember, whether you're trying to make it *inside*, or *outside* the present establishment, the key to success is *marketing*. If you don't somehow swap what you have too much of (beans, fenceposts, cartoons, ripe fruit, or enthusiasm) for what you need (shoes, bananas, and automobiles), you ain't gonna make it.

But what about drawing . . . isn't that important too? Yes, but not as important as you may think. A poorly drawn cartoon with a strong gag that hits the readers of a particular magazine right between the eyes will always sell before the beautiful rendering that isn't really relevant. This is no excuse for lousy artwork, understand, but it *does* explain why—contrary to what most cartoon course peddlers tell you—you don't need to go to any art school or take any course on the market to become a cartoonist.

As a matter of fact, I feel very strongly that—unless you're really a lazy lout who needs to be pushed, and pushed hard, to start a gag or finish a drawing (and what are you doing in cartooning, in that case?)—you'll find most instruction in the field (and most other fields, too) vastly overpriced and largely irrelevant.

You don't *really* want all those pre-packaged assignments, pen-pal letters, and a $500 diploma to hang on the wall, do you? Maybe so, maybe not. As for me, I was more interested in kicking the 9-to-5 job . . . and that meant *selling* cartoons.

If you're determined to squander your hard-earned loot on a cartoon or commercial—or even fine arts—course, I *will* give one company a left-handed recommendation: Any of the Famous Artists courses is a bargain . . . at about one-sixth the current asking price of, I believe, over $500 each. I made the rounds, one week, with a Famous Schools salesman, and I know about what everything from the salesmen's commission and district manager's override right through the triple-page ads in the glossy magazines costs the company. After all the hype, there isn't much left for art instruction. No worse than other firms in the field, you understand, but not a lot better either.

Besides, there's literally tens and tens of thousands of courses from that one company (and as many, if not more, from each of the others) gathering dust on bookshelves throughout this country. A two-line classified ad in any big city paper should get you a lot of answers and at least one course for $75.00—which is what I paid for mine—or less.

A good course, used as a reference, can be valuable to you, but it's only worth what you take out of it. The most important thing for you to do if you want to be a cartoonist is to draw every chance you get. And don't take the lazy man's way out and only draw the things that are easy for you. You're only fooling yourself if you do. Draw, and keep on drawing . . . from life, from memory, from imagination.

You don't need fancy drawing pencils and pads either. Ordinary notebooks and regular pencils (whatever number you prefer) are plenty good enough. The really important thing is developing coordination between your hand and eye.

And here's a fact that should surprise you . . . the best teachers in the world are all set to help you for *free*. That's right, the cartoonists who sell their work for the highest prices today are ready to teach you to draw.

All you have to do is leaf through any magazine or newspaper that prints cartoons. If you don't have any lying around, go out and ask the neighbors for back issues . . . or make a trip down to the nearest wastepaper firm. Get yourself a big stack of magazines with cartoons in them.

Then go through all the publications and clip out all the cartoons you find. Keep it up until you've got drawings by every artist whose work you can get your hands on. These cartoonists are the best teachers in the world. Why? Because these are the guys who are *selling* their work, right now, today.

Forget all the two-bit teachers who never sold a drawing in their life. Forget all the dated artwork in the cartoon courses. Study what the *selling* artists are doing. They're the ones who really know what cartooning is all about.

Notice how they place their characters. See how they vary the lines in their drawings. Study their methods of shading. Compare the different ways they draw people. Look at the way they sketch the backgrounds. Soak up every detail of every drawing you can get into your file.

Then try to draw that way yourself. Use every trick you can steal to make your drawings sparkle just like the professionals. Gradually, you'll pick up one idea from one artist, something else from a second, and another wrinkle from a third. Pretty soon, you'll be cranking out clean cartoons in a style all your own.

If you don't think you can learn about drawing this way, let me tell you something: The pros do this all the time . . . it's the way it's *done*. So go to it.

Some skills, such as learning to draw perspective, you'll probably have to learn from regular art books because it is hard to acquire such knowledge merely by looking at finished artwork. In the main, however, you will find that the best cartoon instruction in the world is only as far away as the nearest printed cartoon.

THE TOOLS OF THE TRADE

As for supplies needed to begin cartooning . . . here again you can forget the sharpester who want to sell you everything from hand-engraved sketch pads to chromed drawing tables.

Essential, of course, is a pencil. Ordinary everyday pencils are plenty good enough for a start. When you think you need something better, you will probably want a few real drawing pencils, since you can specify their lead hardness much more exactly. They're graded from 7H (a very hard lead that makes a light line) through F (medium) to 7B (the softest, blackest lead). I usually wind up using a 2H and 4H most of the time. You may find other grades more suitable to *your* touch.

Paper is another primary must. Professional cartoonists use regular typing paper for the most part, and there is no reason for you to buy anything any more expensive. For rough drawing and just doodling, use a cheap 16-pound paper. Inked cartoons that are submitted to editors should be done on a good grade of 20- or 24-pound, 25% rag content paper.

Only a few artists who regularly do complicated cartoons with tints and washes (colored or black ink mixed with water and used like watercolors on a finished drawing) for the top-paying markets (*Esquire, Playboy*, etc.) ever use expensive drawing papers or illustration boards . . . and, then, only after submitting a rough idea on typing paper, usually.

Another essential tool (at least for me) is a good eraser. Again, you can start with pencil erasers. But sooner or later you'll want a good "Artgum" and a kneaded rubber eraser.

Cartoons used to always be done in ink, but that is changing rapidly now, and it's not at all uncommon for a drawing done in black pencil and spray-fixed to be bought and reproduced in a middle or minor (or even major) magazine. Still, you should learn to handle ink ... because you *will* be called on to produce an "inker" once in a while. As a matter of fact, while you're starting you'll make a much better impression on editors if you submit all your cartoons in ink. Later, when you're "in" with a few magazines, you can start sending in penciled roughs (rough drawings) or even typers (typed gags for an editor to read so that you only have to draw the particular cartoons he wants to buy). At any rate, black is the only color ink you'll need, and most artists seem to prefer the Higgins brand.

Some artists use only brushes, others like pens, and still others prefer to use a combination of the two for inking. You'll just have to find what is best for you. I've heard of cartoonists using brushes from no. 00 to no. 7. A few popular pen points are Esterbrook 356 and 358 and Gillot's 290, 303, and 404. Gaining in favor are some of the new mechanical pens—particularly the Rapidograph—which are made in various sizes.

A drawing board is pretty much standard equipment. Here again, you can save a lot of money by using a standard breadboard or a piece of plywood for a starter. Prop it up on a table and you're in business. Later, when you have the loot rolling in, you can buy a regular drawing table (there's some great bargains in used tables floating around) or make one from a flush door.

Fancy light boards (which make tracing finished cartoons from a penciled rough much easier) are expensive, so I made my first one from an old window pane and some scrap lumber. A mimeograph stencil light board also works well at very low cost.

A ruler, some paper clips, a few thumbtacks, and a small piece of cloth for a pen wiper come in handy. For correcting ink mistakes, some opaque white is useful. Your local stationer's store probably has "showcard" or "poster" white.

As you progress you can pick up all kinds of stuff such as paste, T squares, a compass, triangles, blotting paper, colored ink, etc., but paper, pencil, black ink, rules, drawing surface, and eraser are all you really need to start.

Remember, it's the finished cartoon you get paid for ...

not the equipment you used while drawing it.

WRITING THE CARTOON IDEA

Now that you're all set to draw, where will the ideas come from? Well, you can use one or more gag writers who will mail typed cartoon ideas to you. You then return the ones you don't like and draw up the others. When you sell one of the finished cartoons, you pay the gag writer 25% of the price you received for the drawing.

Let's save the gag writers for your first dry spell. Here's how you'll think up your own gags:

Start a morgue. All cartoonists have one, and it's not as gruesome as it sounds. An artist's morgue is just a collection of pictures, cartoons, funny remarks, jokes, sketches, and a thousand and one other things. A cartoonist generally keeps two morgues: one of cartoons and drawings to refer to whenever he needs help while drawing and a separate collection of jokes, gags, etc., to prime the pump when he's writing gags.

Organize your morgues any way you like . . . in old shoe boxes, cardboard cartons, filing cabinets, albums, notebooks, or whatever. But *do* use a system so you can find what you want when you want it. Add new material constantly. Your morgue is your most valuable tool.

Whenever you need fresh material, you'll start digging in the morgue and letting your imagination wander as you filter various bits of material through your brain. Pretty soon you'll come up with a combination you think is funny. You'll even begin to surprise yourself by suddenly thinking of a situation entirely different from the original idea you used to prime your creative process.

This is just a variation on the way most writers work, and the magic word is cram. Cram yourself full of life. Use it all as your gag writer. Watch TV (if you can stomach it), listen to the radio, go to the movies, read, read, read, and keep your eyes open. Soak up every impression you can absorb.

Then, when you sit down to shape up usable gags, you will never have any trouble pulling ideas out of the air. Some of your best gems will pop out of your subconscious when you least expect it: while you're reading a good book or carrying out the ashes or just as you drift off to sleep.

Once you train your mind to think up humorous ideas, you'll turn out material faster than you can use it.

SELLING BEGINNING WORK

Carl Kohler's excellent pieces which follow this diatribe are really gonna open your eyes to the marketing possibilities in cartooning. If you think you can only sell single panel gag cartoons to magazines, in other words, you're going to have your mind pleasantly stretched. Carl's underlying philosophy should prove quite valuable to *anyone* trying to make it outside the system with *anything*. Roughly translated, he's saying, "Life is just exactly what *you* make it."

Although I kinda started at the top and worked down (my gags were published in slick, national magazines first. I next began selling the middle markets . . . and wound up doing local stuff last of all), most beginning cartoonists do best if they concentrate on digging the gold in their own backyard. Every top cartoonist in the country (the world, it seems) is trying to crack *Playboy*, for instance, but you are probably the only artist knocking on the door of your hometown newspaper.

Prepare a sample kit of your very best work. Make it neat and as attractive as you can. Make two or more sample kits, and you'll have one to show and others to leave with interested prospects.

Now visit local printers and stress the fast, customized nature of your work. There's a blue million "mat" and clip-art services . . . but there's no way for them to customize their art the way you'll be able to.

Stop in at the local newspaper with some editorial or feature cartoons slanted especially for your town. Newspapers have access to more syndicated artwork than they can use, but most editors are always interested in something with a local flavor.

Offer to do an editorial cartoon or a sports feature about local athletes . . . on a regular basis, of course. Maybe the paper is ripe for a feature reporting upcoming community projects. If you like to do caricatures or portraits, you might work up a regular weekly panel featuring an outstanding citizen: the mayor, industrial leaders, local celebrities.

Merchants can always use good, eye-catching cartoons in their newspaper ads, posters, store windows, handbills, and all the stuff they give away free, such as blotters, mailing pieces, etc. You just have to be enough of a go-getter to sell them on using your stuff.

Do you know the comic strip *Tumbleweeds*? It's drawn by a fellow named Tom Ryan. Tom lives in Muncie, Indiana, and

I've known him a long time. When he was a beginning cartoonist (and that was just a few years ago), he sold one newspaper in Muncie on the idea of using a little cartoon character, *Benny Beans*. This little guy was featured in the paper all the time: When the United Fund was having a drive, *Benny Beans* would be shown holding a poster or a collection can. During the yearly Paint Up/Fix Up/Clean Up campaign, *Benny Beans* would be seen sweeping the streets with a broom . . . and on and on and on.

Tom was too clever to stop with that. He sold a local hardware store the idea of having another cartoon character, *Jiffy Jackson*, in all their ads. And, eventually, Tom landed a sydicate for *Tumbleweeds* and graduated into the Big Time . . . but his local cartoon work helped keep his family eating until he finally made it.

You might think that Tom had the cartoon business around Muncie all sewed up when he was doing the local work. Not so! A number of sign painters were doing the usual cartoons on trucks, billboards, buildings, etc.; another cartoonist occasionally contributed an editorial drawing for a second paper in town; I did some cartoons for WLBC-TV in Muncie; and a housewife successfully launched herself into a seasonal business decorating store windows with watercolor cartoons of Santa Claus and other Christmas scenes. I understand she still has a long list of regular customers for this service, and she earns several hundred dollars every December this way.

About all that this work involves is chalking the basic layout on the outside of the plate glass windows of a store . . . and then going inside and doing the finished artwork in show-card colors. This is a little tricky because you're working backward . . . but, if you do the finished art on the outside of the window, rain and small boys will soon mess it up.

One of the best ways to sell your work in the beginning is to offer to take your pay out in trade from the merchants you do work for. They like the idea and will often use your stuff this way when they won't pay for it in cash.

George Hartman, publisher of *Cartoon World*, says he always had 1,000 cans in his pantry throughout the depression just because he took goods in trade in return for printing a small town "shopper" on a mimeograph machine.

Approach the chairmen of various clubs and offer to dress up their programs and announcements when they are planning special events. Maybe you can land a job designing a calendar showing the year's important meetings for a club or lodge.

Richard Riley, writing in the August 1969 *Cartoon World* (just in case you think the above won't work), says: "Our town has an annual rodeo each spring, and, since I do a great deal of rodeo-type cartoons, I talked to the program manager of the Jaycees. After they had their dummy made up, they gave it to me and I did cartoons in the white spaces. The Jaycees told their customers about me as they sold the ads, and I not only picked up a nice check from the Jaycees but from the ads too. Also, my cartoon book, *Lil' Wrangler*, will be sold at the rodeo . . . and I got ten free tickets, too!"

Get a big pad of newsprint or drawing paper and teach yourself to give interesting chalk talks. A 2' X 3' pad is a good size for this, and you'll find charcoal crayons handy to work with. One subject you can use is "How cartoonists think up gags and make their drawings". Clubs and other groups will use you as entertainment for $10.00–$20.00 a throw with, usually, a meal for good measure.

A lot of people will pay very good money for a custom mural done on playroom or den walls. These are generally colorful scenes done in opaque watercolors and varnished over when well dried. Better practice this one first! Banks and restaurants also go for these.

A well-drawn replica of a new home will sell to the proud homeowner. Merchants will pay for good drawings of their stores. They hang 'em on the walls and use 'em on letterheads and in advertising.

Most factories print a small paper or magazine for employees. Offer to do artwork or a cartoon for them.

Teach yourself to do a nice job of lettering . . . and learn to use transfer lettering. You'll find a lot more jobs coming your way.

Drop in to the local TV station with a portfolio. Local stations can always use locally drawn "spots". Some cartoonists have even landed a cartoon TV program of their own.

MAGAZINE CARTOONING

OK. We started telling you about magazine cartooning, so it's about time we got back to the main subject.

There are thousands and thousands of specialized publications printed in this country. You know about *Playboy* and *Newsweek* and other national magazines . . . but have you ever heard of *Boot and Shoe Recorder* . . . or *Pure Milk News* . . . or *Printing Impressions*? Probably not . . . but all three use cartoons.

Go to the local library and look through the directories of business and trade magazines. One is *Gebbie's* and another is published by N.W. Ayres and Sons. They'll open your eyes and give you enough names and addresses to keep you busy for a long, long time. But you'll be submitting your work a little blindly if you only use such directories.

As I mentioned earlier, subscribe to the cartoonists' tip sheets. They'll keep you advised of buying action in the middle and minor magazines. So will *Writer's Digest* and *Author and Journalist*. They all list cartoon markets and, if you submit to the magazines listed, you should gradually build up a list of editors that will regularly buy your work, assuming it is of professional quality.

These little magazines are actually pretty easy to work with and, if your gag sense is sharp and you can slant ideas to the readers of a particular publication, your artwork can actually be a little rough.

One word of caution: *Stick to the fields you know.* Since I lived on a farm when I was doing my heavy cartoon work, I drew mostly farm and dairy cartoons and had no trouble selling them to the smaller farm publications. I was also hung up on aviation and developed a secondary market around that interest.

No matter what magazine you decide to submit to, *give the editor what he wants for his readers.* Not what *you* want them to have. This is called *slanting* your work. You send farm cartoons to farm magazines, girly cartoons to girly publications, and supermarket cartoons to magazines for supermarket managers.

If you run across a new market and you don't know exactly what kind of cartoons it uses, get a copy of the magazine and study it. If you can't find a copy, write the editor, tell him you're a cartoonist, offer your services, and ask for samples of his publication. If he's interested, he'll send you a few copies. If he's not interested . . . it's better to find out right in front.

Most editors are honest and hardworking, but you'll find a few that won't return drawings or who use your stuff and never pay for it. Forget them . . . they don't last very long, anyway. There are more good markets than you can cover. Concentrate on the good ones.

SUBMITTING CARTOONS TO MAGAZINES

After you've drawn up a good batch of ten or twelve cartoons (or five or six for a very specialized market), address a 9 X 12 manila envelope to yourself and a 9½ X 12½ envelope to the editor. Stamp *both* envelopes with sufficient postage, put the cartoons into the smaller one, and put it into the big envelope. A cardboard stiffener is also a good idea. Seal the large envelope and mail. It's now becoming increasingly popular to make a very light fold across the center of the batch of drawings and use half-size envelopes. They seem to stand up a lot better in the mail.

You can seal cartoons, according to the post office regulations, and send them third class as long as you don't include a written note. If your local post office gives you a hard time on this, write to the Postmaster General in Washington, D.C.

Always include return postage and a return address on the envelope in your submission.

Sooner or later, you'll have to set up some kind of system so you can keep a record of the drawings you have in the mail, the ones that have already been to a particular editor, and the ones that haven't. You'll want to put your name and address on the back of each cartoon, too. Editors sometimes get several batches mixed up together, and this will help to keep everything straight.

PAYMENT FOR A BEGINNER'S WORK

The usual rule for a beginning cartoonist is, *"Get as much as you can, but get the job!"* As you start doing work for local businessmen and newspapers, you'll find that many of them can't—or won't—pay a lot for the work they use.

Don't be discouraged. The experience acquired on these first jobs is worth a great deal to you. As you improve your work, you'll gradually slide up from, maybe, $5.00 a drawing to $15.00 to $50.00 or more. Some of the TJs even go over $100 to their regular contributors.

A good artist who keeps at least ten batches of cartoons in the mail at all times should average $100—$200 a week. A part-timer with only a batch or two out at any one time can generally pick up $10.00—$20.00 extra spending money each week. That's not great, but cartooning worked that way can be looked upon as a hobby that pays its way . . . and I've seen a lot of times when that $10.00 came in very, very handy.

Naturally, since you *want* to be a cartoonist, you're going to make every last drawing your very best .. whether it's a paid-for-in-advance $100 cartoon or a $5.00 spot.

Cartooning is no bed of roses but it *can* be a very fun way of making a living and—if you make it to the top with a syndicated strip of your own or as a regular artist for, say, *Playboy*—you'll be in the big money, indeed.

Now, for a detailed, step-by-step plan for dropping out of the rat race to start cartooning on very limited means, read on. Carl Kohler is the fascinating guy who did just that . . . he also has originated many, many ways of selling cartoons, and he will generously share some of them with you.

And, I'll say it once more: Carl's section should inspire a lot more people than just the would-be cartoonists among the readers of this book. ♣

THE LONELY WORKER
CARL KOHLER

NOTE: The following series of high spirited articles originally appeared in Information Guide *(now* Cartoon World*) during 1957-1959.*

For an unbroken succession of seven years I freelanced—full time—drawing and marketing advertising and magazine cartoons and—later—writing and marketing humor pieces for various publications.

Now get the picture: I lived through seven years of obtaining an income *solely* through my alleged efforts at the drawing board and typewriter. I'm speaking singularly on the basis of that experience, and what follows is based entirely upon it. When I first quit a paid job (illustrator/editor for an aircraft company's technical book department), I was 28 years old and in good health and had one wife, one son, $145 cash on hand, about a year's experience at selling magazine cartoons (totaling about $225 worth of sales), a lot of illusions regarding full-time freelancing . . . and a huge dissatisfaction with *any* way of earning a living other than drawing cartoons.

Seven years later (presently, in fact) finds me with one wife (the same one), three sons, still in good health, and 35 years old, with less hair, more wrinkles, a hell of a lot more cash on hand than I started with, a definite disinterest in cartoon freelancing, a good job (four days, weekly) with a magazine, and three days weekly in which *everything* I write sells . . . a happy fact that could not be, had I never learned how to make it happen through freelancing.

For me then, freelancing has been a transitory period: For you, it may be a hoped-for future. I am going to offer a suggestion which (while certainly not the only way for a promising beginner to start freelancing), if followed to the letter, will keep you: [1] eating, [2] out of the cold, [3] freelancing, and [4] from the necessity of giving up the whole idea and going back to a time clock.

Perhaps I'd better add: These points are guaranteed only if you are a type-churl who really wants to freelance and whose family is given to adjusting reasonably easy to new situations.

You understand, I am not advocating the following method of *getting into* full-time freelancing for anybody who cannot change their present paid-employment standard of living . . . nor for anyone whose wife does not implicitly believe in their chances of eventually making the so-called grade.

THAT OLD DEVIL, OVERHEAD

Get your affairs in order, tabulate your bank account (if any), and move to the nearest, *smallest* town located on the edge of a river, lake, or (better) an ocean.

Remember, I said the *smallest* town. Here, despite general

opinion to the contrary, you will be able to rent a house or cottage (and don't look for luxury) for around $35.00 monthly. I've even lived in some places—rather on the order of elaborate chickenhouses—that rented for $25.00 with utilities included.

The farther away from industrial areas your town is, the lower the available rentals will be. I know of one cartoonist who rents a cabin with ten acres of ground for $10.00 monthly. Fabulous? Nope. The joint has an outhouse and no running water . . . but I told you: If you want to cut that overhead to your freelance pocketbook size, *forget your present standard of living for a while!*

CHOW AND STUFF

Okay. You've moved. Your wife's relatives, your relatives, and your mutual friends think you've lost your mind . . . but you *have* moved. Fine.

Now, as soon as you've unloaded your gear (I always rented unfurnished places, bringing a mere minimum of furniture of our own), hand your wife a hoe, grab a shovel, and put in a vegetable garden. *And do this right away!*

Next, investigate the fishing in the area. I mean, *study it factually.* Remember, the fishing you'll be doing is primarily to put fish on the table. And I don't care how inexpensively fish are selling in the markets . . . you get your own and save those seemingly absurd few cents. It'll make quite a difference over a year's stretch.

If your frau doesn't know how to feed a family of, say, four or five on $20.00 a week—and feed them an enjoyable variety of food on that sum—this is a swell time for her to learn how. It's been done. I know wives who are presently doing just that, and it will be possible years from now. But *only* if you supplement that $20.00 worth of store chow with vegetables from your own garden and fish caught, netted, or speared yourself.

Within six months you should be able to get by with as little as $15.00 weekly for purchased food items . . . and eating grandly. Naturally, this doesn't include steak regularly.

SPENDING

Aside from occasional items of clothing, art supplies, stamps, and medical costs . . . I suggest you keep all spending (for the first three months) to a miser's range. In short, no wild splurging just because you discover (as you will now and then) that you've made four or five—or even six or seven—hundred dollars in one month.

Assuming you've decided to freelance from an area not visited by heavy winters (and I do not see how anyone could make this particular method work outside of Florida, the Southern States along the Gulf, or California), forget all previous notions about what you must wear to be presentable. A clean shirt, clean washable britches, and tennis shoes are fine. To hell with public opinion and convention, too . . . for this first freelancing year, anyway.

If your wife simply cannot be happy in cotton dresses and inexpensive sandals, you're licked before you start. My clever little gal actually *made* sandals for all of us, using old inner tubes and secondhand leather . . . and those sandals outlasted anything we ever purchased in a shoe store.

It's a tasty notion to keep $100 in the bank against the time (and it'll happen often) when every editor seems to be slow in issuing those checks. Secondary measures include friends who can and will loan you money until the checks finally arrive . . . or a landlord and grocer who understand the time element in your profession and don't mind waiting for their money while extending credit to you. I've used all three of these methods. I heartily endorse all three. Maybe *you* will, maybe you won't.

AND THEN WOT HOPPENS?

Without touching upon any particular method of marketing (several varieties work beautifully), I will underline the advisability of writing *thank you* notes *every time* you make a sale. Editors like this. It even (although many selling cartoonists don't realize it) makes quite a difference in many extra sales.

Within a reasonably short time you should be selling a certain amount of cartoons on arranged terms, regularly. Today's freelancer—if he has halfway decent ability and common sense—does not entirely rely on total speculation sales. It just isn't necessary.

Somewhere there are, at least, three editors waiting who will like your work sufficiently to buy from you regularly, give you assignment work, and, in some cases, offer you cash advances against work to be done. The last, of course, holds only if you don't snow them about being a wealthy-type success and you honestly let them know when you can really use some advance loot.

This money in front is not theory. It's fact. As of this writing I am into one book for better than $300 . . . strictly because the editor knows I *can* and *will* produce exactly what he wants for that magazine, when he wants it. Frankly, this isn't the best practice in the world, but—given time, experience, and accumulated skill—you'll be working the same deal occasionally.

Those three editors mentioned above should be able to give you a total of $200 monthly in assured sales. If you have a distinctive style (such as Tupper, Thaves, Harley, or Pete Millar), I would feel safe in saying that—within six months of launching your freelance career—you should have something like $275 to $400 in assured monthly sales.

That's assuming your particular method of marketing includes getting editors interested in your availability . . . and *keeping* them interested. Same thing goes for any and all commercial cartooning. There just isn't (in my opinion) a very big difference between magazine editors and advertising purchasers.

IN CLOSING

I know there are a thousand ways to punch a million holes in what I've suggested . . . and only somebody with a better method will try it. You've got to want to freelance very much to do it the way I started and have outlined here.

This same system has been worked with other variations . . . and there are undoubtedly still *more* ways to make it give a guy his start in freelancing. It would take a book to give you all the tricks, and I don't have the time to write that book. I'll leave it to you. I used the system exactly the way I've outlined it on these pages . . . and it worked fine.

And why did I leave full-time freelancing if things were so good? You may be silently asking that question, and I'll be happy to answer: [1] I simply became disinterested in drawing cartoons full time, [2] I wanted to cut down the amount of hackwork necessary to earn a better-than-average living in order to try writing something other than pure magazine humor, and [3] a magazine—*Skin Diver*—offered me a very

fine four-days-a-week position. Since I have been a skin diving enthusiast for years, this has proven to be both fascinating *and* profitable . . . and I have the satisfying knowledge that I've learned enough about freelancing to go back to it, full time, *anytime* I find that either desirable or necessary or both. Now if Mel Millar, Charlie Dennis, Bob Tupper, or Peter Millar (who only recently began freelancing) could be coaxed into writing down their opinions, methods, and reasons for freelancing, the younger, less experienced cartoonists would have the information it took me some fifteen years to obtain.

In other words, don't imagine for one minute that the entire behind-the-scenes story of freelance cartooning and humor writing has ever been fully told.

Because it hasn't. ◖

The above article originally appeared in THE MOTHER EARTH NEWS® NO. 1 . . . along with a great deal of other live-better-for-less and self-sufficiency how-to information. For further information about the magazine—and other books and periodicals devoted to home businesses, self-sufficiency, and related subjects—please see page 367 of this handbook.

EARTHA:
FLOWERS
FOR
FRAMING
AND FUNDS

Every spring and summer, not so long ago, I'd grub daily in the earth . . . weeding, mulching, coaxing my flower patch to bloom. By July there would be buds, by August blooms, and by September death: the growing season over and a lot of work and beauty lost. No more! Now, with the seedlings just popping out of the ground, I'm looking forward to turning those fleeting delights into long-lasting, attractive floral "pictures" . . . and a handy source of extra cash.

I got started in this profitable craft almost by accident. One day I picked a few cosmos blooms, brought them inside, and placed them between the pages of an old magazine (remember the orchid from the high school prom?). Two weeks later, I returned to find the flowers dried and still perfect in shape and color. Inspired, I dug out an old picture frame and was on my way. Here, for all you other flower freaks, is the technique I've worked out since that beginning.

First, the flowers. I've included with this article a list of beginner-proof species, and you'll soon find other good kinds near you . . . probably right outside the kitchen door. Pick them on a sunny day around noon, when there's a minimum of humidity and dew on the petals.

Indoors, away from breezes and the kids, lay your treasures on two thicknesses of paper toweling. Press each bloom flat with your fingers. The center part can be removed if it's too bulky, and the stem either snipped off or left, depending on whether you like its looks. Space the prepared materials half an inch apart on the sheet. When the page is full, cover it with two more layers of toweling and several open facial tissues. Then carefully place the "sandwich" between the pages of a magazine. (Use an old, discarded periodical—not a MOTHER—so you won't mind if the paper is discolored in the process.)

Lay the closed magazine on a hard, flat surface (the attic floor is low in humidity and out of harm's way). Bring out the heavies—bricks, dictionary, etc.—and place them on top of the improvised flower press. The blossoms will be dry and flat in a week or two.

Meanwhile, you can be collecting the rest of the materials.

FLOWERS FOR DRYING

The following are good materials for beginners, guaranteed to dry well. Some of my pictures made from these ingredients are now two years old and haven't discolored, faded, or deteriorated. Flat-petaled blooms are best . . . petunias, roses, dahlias, etc., are no good unless you pull apart the flower heads and rearrange them after they've dried (a challenging project).

COSMOS	Orange, yellow; pink. Excellent!
WILD VIOLET	Blue, purple. Also called Johnny-jump-ups.
AFRICAN VIOLET (indoor)	Use blues and purples . . . the white may turn yellow.
GREENHOUSE FERN	Good for background. Very inexpensive and goes a long way.
IMPATIENS	Pink, reds. Excellent!
WAX BEGONIA	White, pink, reds.
BUTTERCUP (wild)	Yellow.
CORNFLOWER	Blue.
FORGET-ME-NOT	Blue and white, small. Excellent in clusters.
PHLOX	Pink, white, red.
HYDRANGEA (Snowball)	White, good picked green before the petals mature. Also purple.
FOUR O'CLOCK	Red, blue, white.
WILDFLOWERS	Any that are flat and look workable.

FIELD-SIDE MEMORABILIA

Larger weeds (one to two feet high) tied together in bunches and hung upside down for a few weeks make great centerpieces . . . and bring in more dollars. Spray-paint the dried plants or leave them natural.

For handmade Christmas ornaments, gifts, and novelties: Collect opened milkweed pods in the fall. Pull the two sides apart and let the pieces dry a few days to make sure they're brown and free of moisture. Glue three half-pods together to make a dove, or use just one segment as a fish shape. Sew a single loop of thread in a central position and spray-paint or hand-decorate designs.

Buy or find inexpensive black velvet (short, flat nap is the best and least bulky to work with). Frames can be bought complete in local discount stores—at a cost of 69¢ to 90¢ for three-by-five-inch or five-by-seven-inch sizes—or picked up at roadside flea markets for next to nothing. Look for those with the glass intact. Missing backings don't matter . . . cardboard taken from laundered, folded shirts or cereal boxes is ideal in weight and stiffness. The finish of a frame, too, is unimportant. Sandpaper and a can of spray paint work wonders for a quick refurbishing.

Cut the cardboard 1/4 inch smaller all around than the opening at the back of the frame. Next, prepare a piece of velvet about 1/2 inch larger than the backing and glue it over the cardboard, clipping and trimming the corners to reduce the bulk. Dried ferns and flowers can then be set on that background in any desired arrangement. Just place the materials . . . don't glue them, or the petals will be discolored. Each picture is unique and the variations endless. Simple designs, though, are best.

Clean the glass well, *dry* it, and place it over the flowers. With the covering well pressed to the velvet, turn the creation over (backside up) and slide the whole works slowly into the frame. As long as the glass is held firmly, the blossoms won't slip out of place. Practice will enable you to do this fearlessly and well.

Then glue kraft paper (the brown grocery bag kind) over the back of the frame, clean the glass in front, and the picture is finished. My first attempt took my beginner's thumbs half an hour to assemble. Now I need only 15 minutes for each floral ornament.

My craft began as a means of keeping all the beautiful life

of summer for my own pleasure . . . but soon grew into a source of gifts which I gave friends and relatives on all occasions. Even so, it took a lot of convincing from Ron—my husband—and other fans before I was ready to try marketing my craft. The first time out, I felt most comfortable approaching a nearby community store that specialized in the sale of homemade articles (and particularly local goods). From there I went on to more commercial shops. I shouldn't have been reluctant . . . my pictures were welcomed.

We live near a populous center, so access to my market was relatively easy. If your place is out in the backwoods, get together 15 or 20 pictures and make a day of it downtown. Go anywhere, from super-straight gift boutiques to real head shops. There's no need to make a special sales effort. Just be sincere and honest, and your genuine local handcraft will practically sell itself. Most likely you'll find—as I did—that people are really interested and friendly from the start.

Almost all shops will take articles on a consignment basis (that is, you leave four or five and when they're sold you get the cash). Be sure to tell the proprietors what you think your pictures should sell for . . . you'll probably be asked anyway. My five-by-seven-inch size goes for about $3.00, and the store generally takes 10% of the price as commission. The exposure is certainly worth 30¢!

Give the storekeeper your name, address, and telephone number, if you have one, and don't leave the shop without a receipt to show that the establishment has so many of your pictures. Although I've found no rip-offs yet, it's best to be on the safe side. File the paper carefully should you need it in the future.

Then sit back and wait . . . but keep busy making more pictures and trying new places to sell. Usually you'll come across a real business doer who will make a special effort to display and talk up your goodies. Also, don't forget any exhibits of local crafts in shopping centers and community fairs.

Original work really goes over. The more effort you put into the venture, the higher the return. Just use your eyes and imagination, create, enjoy . . . and keep those extra funds rolling in. ●

The above article originally appeared in THE MOTHER EARTH NEWS® NO. 27 . . . along with a great deal of other live-better-for-less and self-sufficiency how-to information. For further information about the magazine—and other books and periodicals devoted to home businesses, self-sufficiency, and related subjects—please see page 367 of this handbook.

LIFESTYLE LIVELIHOODS

This should be considered one of the real focal points of this manual . . . because the section you're now getting ready to read was written by people who've found ways of combining business so closely with play that it's sometimes hard to prove they "work" at all.

The life enjoyed by Don Melvin, his wife, and sons is a good example. Can any family that gets paid for living in such a satisfying and close-knit manner actually be said to "labor" for its daily bread?

Or what about Greg Siple . . . who is given money every summer just for taking a vacation? Or Marty Bessenbach, who receives regular payments plus free rent for doing what most of us do anyway (taking care of minor repairs and cleaning up around the place where he lives). Or Merrill Sanders, who makes good money by introducing people with problems (work which must be done) to other people anxious to solve those problems . . . and who picks up extra cash by "hiring" herself whenever she personally feels like helping to solve those problems too!

And for all you footloose young men who would like to mix a little travel and adventure into any work you do, a special treat: the secret methods Charles Zabielskis has used to land a job on a freighter when everyone was assuring him that no such job was available.

We call this section, for obvious reasons, "Lifestyle Livelihoods". ●

DON MELVIN:
BUILDING THE GOOD LIFE

For years I dreamed of a way to stay at home, be my own boss . . . and earn enough to adequately support my family. The several most unsatisfactory and unrewarding jobs I held during that period of time did much to inspire my desire for independence: I tried many forms of employment and—having never been satisfied with any of them and having never satisfied anyone else with them—I knew there must be a better way. Work, for me, was becoming more a "life sentence" than a job. However, in attempting to set myself free, I only became more enslaved by systems and people.

In my desperation, I considered all kinds of self-employment, from raising rabbits to raising cain! . . . but the many "how to do" books didn't do for me. All the advertised home businesses required too much money, and many of them—I later learned—were pure "con" outfits.

To cut the moorings and launch out into the deep, I knew, could only come through some original effort on my part. Going against the tide and being an up-the-streamer would cost . . . but the loss of my freedom was costing even more.

My life would have been different, I'm sure, if only I had had the "herd instinct" ... but when you can't join the ranks of the rat race—or beat it either—then you just have to be a lone rancher.

In 1961 I gave up teaching school (it was giving my ulcers ulcers) and started working door to door as a Rawleigh Products salesman. Although my parents thought this was a disgrace for a man with a Bachelor of Fine Arts degree, I enjoyed selling fairly well. At that time, it was the living in the same house with my parents that was beginning to really bug me. Since we were right in the center of town my two little boys didn't have much yard to play in. I wanted my own house as dearly as I wanted to be my own boss. I was only one step from Clay County over these two goals!

Then a nice lot just outside the city limits was offered for sale. The price was $1,250, and I didn't have the full amount, but I was determined to buy that lot and pay cash for it. The property especially appealed to me because it had no building code to worry about. Taking the money I had on hand—and getting my mother to go on a bank note for the balance—I purchased the lot and took possession. I wasn't letting any grass grow under my feet.

Then came the major problem of building a house. A mortgage was definitely out: We would build our own home somehow. There would be a way if I had to make one out of no way. Money, naturally, was still the number one mountain to scale: I was paying off the note at the bank, making car payments, and doing my best to survive the money changers.

It was six months before we could start on the house. Finally I had a man with proper tools lay off the foundation, and I dug ditches for the concrete footing. Next, Solite blocks were ordered (along with some reasonable brick masons), and we lifted the walls up to floor level. Then ... nothing happened on the little house for many months. It's no sin to be poor, just terribly inconvenient!

At last my father-in-law presented us with a check for $500 and the walls went up to the roof. I was wonderfully blessed in locating some used, heart pine lumber from an old house being torn down nearby, and my father-in-law, a friend, and I used the wood for an A-roof.

A neighbor (who volunteered his services and wouldn't accept any pay) and I wired the house for about $65.00, and two men dug a well with a hand auger at a price that I could—

if I cut some other corners—afford: $60.00. The plumbing was the final hurdle, and we solved that problem by letting Montgomery Ward do the job for $715, payable over the next two years.

On June 14, 1962 we borrowed my father-in-law's red Ford truck and, with much excitement, moved into our new home. The total cost was just a little over $3,000, and we paid that off during the next three years by using notes at the bank. There was never a mortgage on the property, and there never will be!

In passing, I'd like to point out that some items—usually regarded as luxuries—can not only be enjoyed on a limited budget . . . but can also go a long way in helping to stretch that budget. We built a nice fireplace into our house, and the whole family loves the open fire and finds it very relaxing. An added bonus, since wood has always been freely available in our area, is the good deal of money the fireplace has saved on our fuel bill.

We soon found that—even with a house to our good—we still hadn't quite mastered our own lives. There always seemed to be urgent bills to pay, and we were constantly in need of some additional income. One day my wife—Lou—feeling the money strain said, "I wish there were something I could stay at home and do to bring in a little extra money."

I seriously began to think about Lou's comment. I knew she was very good at sewing and handwork, and I had often heard her say she wanted to learn to weave. Somehow, thinking about Lou's artistic and creative yearnings brought back memories of my own desires as a child: I had always wanted to learn to play the piano. At the time I wondered what childhood longings could possibly have to do with the problem at hand. A few months later I would see the connection.

Once I had again started thinking about a piano, I couldn't get it out of my mind, and I asked the little wife what she thought of my getting an old upright for $100. "NO!" she said, "there's no room for a big, old piano in our small living room." I knew she was right . . . but her refusal still made me mad! And, lucky for us, my getting mad at this point ignited a series of events that completely revolutionized our lives.

"OK," I thought, "if I can't have a piano, how about one of those old-fashioned, parlor organs that you have to pedal with your feet? It won't take up nearly as much space as a piano."

Once my wife had agreed to the organ idea I began a three-month search for one. Finally, an old gentleman gave me a tip that led me to an oak organ out in the country. The owner sold it to me for just $5.00.

Again borrowing the red Ford truck, I brought the organ home and placed it in the middle of the living room floor. I was so excited I couldn't think about going to bed, and, late that night, I began to take it apart. I just had to see what made it work!

At 4 o'clock the next morning everything was an oblong blur, I was exhausted, and I went to bed. Lou, rising early, saw nothing but organ parts scattered all over the living room. "He's ruined it," she said. "He'll never get it back together again."

Well, it did take me quite a few months to restore that organ, but only because I was learning the art of organ rebuilding well.

I first refinished the case before tackling the bellows and inside work. We had heard somebody say that household ammonia would take the old varnish finish off antiques, so I got a half-gallon at the A & P for 35¢ . . . and found it to be a cheap source of paint remover. I also found that boiled linseed oil will darken wood and bleach will lighten it; chewing tobacco makes a pretty good stain, and a beautiful stain can be made by putting green walnuts in a gallon plastic container

and pouring ammonia over them.

As I was learning these tricks of the trade, friends and neighbors—who saw how well the refinished organ looked—kept asking us to do little refinishing jobs for them. I began to see we could earn extra money with antiques and refinishing, and, besides, I really enjoyed this work that could be done with very little equipment out in the fresh air and sunshine.

To increase business, I decided to invest $3.85 for a ten-word ad in the classified section of the local newspaper. We didn't have a telephone at that time, so I gave my mother's number and asked her to handle the calls for me. She did and, much to my delight, the business began coming in.

My wife had made me mad and started a career for me . . . now it was my turn to start one for her.

One day an elderly man drove up with an oak chair to be refinished. The chair's old cane bottom needed redoing, and he asked if we did that kind of work. "Oh yes," I said, "my wife can do anything."

The man left the chair. I carried it in to Lou, set it down, and announced that she had to cane it. She announced right back that she couldn't . . . and, furthermore, she wouldn't cane it. So I reminded Lou of her earlier wish about making money at home and—realizing the opportunity—she agreed to learn the ancient art of caning.

An antique dealer had given us a Home Demonstration Club instruction sheet which Lou studied carefully. The seven steps in caning were Greek to me, but she seemed to understand what it was all about. We ordered a hank of cane, and the first chair was begun and completed. We were in the caning business.

Later, Lou took a rush chair, turned it upside down, looked at it, and started doing rush bottoms. An old craftsman helped her master split bottoming.

When the message got around as to what we could do, we were well on our way to doing it. My refinishing business picked up, and the boys, Jonathan and Joel, helped me with it. Their mother taught them how to do caning and split bottoms, and they helped her too.

Our caning, rushing, refinishing, and organ rebuilding had now become well established, so I decided to give up the Rawleigh products and settle down to the new business at home. I continued to run the newspaper ad from time to time, and it always seemed to work. Besides that, our patrons were advertising for us, and this word-of-mouth publicity was really the most effective. Our business was generally good, but sometimes in the year we would have a slump. We needed more exposure.

Realizing the power of television, I had a brainstorm. I wrote to the hostess of a local television show and offered my services free in exchange for a chance to display my organ work. She immediately phoned and extended an invitation to appear.

A year or so later, I did the same thing with another TV personality on a station in Durham, North Carolina. This time the whole family was invited, and we demonstrated our various abilities. When we arrived back home we were greeted by several long distance calls for information about our work. Many of our friends considered us very important to be invited on television. Little did they know that I had engineered the whole thing!

Then another wonderful opportunity came to us. A distant relative connected with a local Arts and Crafts Fair invited us to participate in a show at the mall of a large shopping center. This was just the exposure that could put us on the map.

We were advised to have business cards to give to passers-by, so I went to a print shop and ordered a rubber stamp made.

Words can't express what this little stamp did for our business that first year in the fair. A card, stamped in red ink (to make the information really stand out), proved to be an eyecatcher, and, after four years of giving away cards at the show in the mall, we're getting business from Washington, D.C., the eastern shore of Maryland, and many other Atlantic coast states.

Our primitive crafts have certainly come alive. To date, my wife has done over a thousand chairs, I have rebuilt the bellows of 158 organs . . . and they still keep coming.

Almost all we know about our skills is completely self-taught. The home business—after five years—appears to be well established. We're completely out of debt, and we hope to save a little money at last. It's especially satisfying to feel our present degree of independence. At times our work load even gets so demanding that we have to turn down business; the telephone rings so much some days that we're forced to take it off the hook.

Little did we realize that our childhood dreams could do so

much for us. Not only did I learn to rebuild the reed organ but I was able to teach myself—with simple beginner books—to play the instrument. I've now performed on two television programs and played and spoken on the subject to many women's clubs . . . all without ever having had a professional lesson. In addition, the family now owns twenty-four of these beautiful old antique organs, which I mostly picked up for five and ten dollars apiece.

One good thing just seems to lead to another. About a year ago I started wood carving as a hobby. It all began because of the organs. Many of them are hand-carved with rosettes and beautiful designs, so I figured I could do simple animals, letter openers, and things like that. Then, last Christmas, people started popping in and buying them, and a whole new business was opening up.

We've found our home businesses to be more than we ever expected, and it's wonderful to know that "we can't be fired 'cause we've never been hired". It took a lot of self-discipline to make a way out of no way . . . still and yet, we feel much more secure in our setup than we ever could with a job. If we get tired, we take a nap; when we want to go fishing or camping, we go.

Of course, we can't say that our lot has been entirely a bed of roses or a cross of sunshine. We've had some hard days like many of our peers, but I doubt we could stop our way of life now if we wanted to. It's extremely satisfying when visitors come long miles to see our organs and other work. To be happy in one's work is the real test.

I've been able to give my family more of myself and my philosophy of life during the past five years. When I was teaching school and holding down a job, I couldn't be relaxed enough to really communicate with them. I can only wonder what would have happened to my central nervous system if I had stayed in the classroom chained to a system which so many teachers—who love to teach—hate.

We've found such joy in our work and have been so honored by it that we sincerely long to see others launch out into the deep where the fishing is good. We're committed to encouraging all arts and crafts around and about us.

If you're interested in learning caning just write to Peerless Rattan & Reed Co., 97 Washington Street, New York, N.Y. 10006. They will be glad to send you a free instruction sheet

and prices on caning materials. Your library is a fine source for books on rush work and split-bottoming, and the librarian can order books on these subjects if necessary.

Refinishing can be done with very little equipment and know-how. Experience is the best teacher, and you'll pick up many little tricks as you go along. I've found, for instance, that box lye—cost, 25¢ a can—will make a gallon of paint remover when mixed with water (always neutralize with an application of vinegar to prevent damage to the wood). I use this mixture to take five or more coats of paint off old chairs.

A very practical refinishing solution can be made by thinning shellac half-and-half with denatured alcohol. If you wipe this solution into wood with an old nylon stocking (a trick I learned from an antique dealer), you'll have a beautiful hand-rubbed finish. Twenty coats can be put on a chair in just an hour.

Your library can, again, be a good source of other refinishing information.

If carving—the most ancient of all the arts—interests you, then just get a utility knife (like they use in grocery stores to open cardboard boxes) and start carving. I never buy any wood because there is always an abundant free supply.

You can carve letter openers from the slats on the ends of grape crates. Melon boxes furnish enough wood for small animals. I like to carve larger cats, so I go to the mills around here, get big crates, and cut between the nails of the 2 X 4's.

Taking a piece of 2 X 4 six inches long, I drill a hole in the top and proceed to carve out the cat. The hole makes a holder for pens and pencils.

A very good income can be realized by visiting every trash and dump pile you can find. In such places, I constantly find valuable chairs, brassware, glassware, old iron items, and many, many other treasures.

I can't emphasize strongly enough the extra money we make on things found at the city dump. Many of the antiques in our house were picked up there. I once found a very valuable round oak table in the dump . . . not to mention an oak dresser, the oak case of a pipe organ, two ladder back slipper chairs, an iron kettle, a pair of andirons, and some much-sought-after, blue clamp-top canning jars. These are only a few of my great finds. Many people will also give you all the stuff in the attic if you'll just haul it away. I've been in more attics than a thief.

On Sunday afternoons, the family goes out for a walk. We observe wildlife, dig sassafras root, and have a good time. As we meander we pick up pop bottles, put them in a big supermarket bag, and bring them home.

The bottles are stored in crates (easily obtained from the supermarket), and—every six months or so—I take them to the bottling companies and collect the deposit. The take is usually about $10.00. That's $70.00 a year for helping to clean up the landscape, keeping the heart young, and taking off extra pounds.

Two years ago we started gardening organically as real "homesteaders". This summer we canned and froze over fifty quarts of tomatoes, and the freezer is full of corn, beans, squash, pumpkins, okra, and apples.

We're trying to learn everything there is to know about living off the land, and we're particularly interested in free wild foods and preserving by sun drying. We're simple people wanting the simple life.

I've had the most fun telling "you all" about our home business and way of life. As a matter of fact—since starting our work here—I've thought of several other home occupations, but I'll save those for another time.●

The above article originally appeared in THE MOTHER EARTH NEWS® NO. 6 . . . along with a great deal of other live-better-for-less and self-sufficiency how-to information. For further information about the magazine—and other books and periodicals devoted to home businesses, self-sufficiency, and related subjects—please see page 367 of this handbook.

MARTY BESSENBACH:
FREE RENT

Trying to get out of the city, or just scraping together enough cash to do what you really want right where you are . . . either one can be hard when you have to cope with the cost of urban living. I've been there myself: struggled along in town for a few years, got nowhere with my savings, and wound up frustrated. How was I supposed to put by any money when—on top of paying for food, transportation, and other needs—I had to hand out a big chunk of my income for rent and utilities?

Then, one day, a casual glance through the classified section of the local newspaper showed me an answer I now wish I'd thought of long before: I could care for an apartment house and live there rent-free.

Once I was on the lookout for caretaking jobs, I found no lack of openings. A good Sunday edition of our Cincinnati paper generally lists half a dozen positions available (under the headings "Janitor", "Apartment Manager", or "Couple Wanted"), and I've never failed to see at least two such ads. The larger the town, the more opportunities. In fact, now that I'm used to earning my lodging this way, I'm surprised that most people would rather pay cash for shelter than work for it directly.

OK, there were plenty of jobs going . . . but at first my longish hair and beard made me hesitate to apply. I needn't have worried. Any city is packed with apartment houses, and most such buildings have at least some freaky tenants. Why shouldn't one of those longhairs sweep out the hallways and drag out the trash instead of paying rent?

If you scan the "Caretaker Wanted" ads you'll find, as I did, that some list phone numbers, but more are write-ins. Don't avoid the second kind . . . they're often the better openings. Which is more hassle: to hand over hard-earned cash every 30 days or to sit down and write a letter?

Whichever ads you decide to answer, you may want to try a few pointers I've used with success. For example: Exaggerate when necessary! Don't be afraid to build yourself up a little. In particular, always say that you're handy with your hands.

Most caretaker deals require a small amount of maintenance work, but almost never a job you won't be able to handle. Just because you've never done any simple repairs doesn't mean that you can't. Changing fuses, replacing leaky washers, plunging a stopped-up toilet: These are all minor problems which anyone can set right if he tries. Most things go back together the same way they come apart.

You won't normally be expected to do any but trivial jobs. Most real estate companies have crews to maintain their property, and if real trouble comes up the management calls in a professional. (If you *are* thoroughly qualified at any trade, by the way, be sure to mention the fact. You may be able to pick up some extra income.)

I've personally discovered hidden talents just by tackling some everyday household repairs for the first time, and you can do the same. A fix-it book will help you learn by doing: My own bible is a *Better Homes and Gardens* guide that shows the basics of just about everything I'll ever have to try.

Remember, in general, that getting the job you want requires salesmanship. Convince the management you have enough assets, and they'll buy. Just be confident and assure them that you can handle the whole situation.

By the time you've talked to a few potential employers you'll be amazed at the variety of caretaking positions. Some are full time and require you to handle the rentals along with building and grounds maintenance. Jobs in large complexes may demand 30–40 hours of work per week, *but may also bring you $200–$500 a month in addition to your no-cost apartment*. Other openings offer free living space only in exchange for light duties ... and there are all sorts of in-between deals.

The spot to look for is the one that fits in well with your personal situation. If you have a good job now and like it, you can still be a part-time caretaker and at least live rent-free. One way or another, you have to work for shelter ... but it seems that the effort that goes into getting free lodging is usually much less than the equivalent required to earn rent money at another job.

The facts of your private life don't limit your employability as much as you might think from looking at some of the ads. For instance, those "Couple Wanted" notices don't necessarily mean that one of you will be stuck in the building at all times. The management may have chosen that wording because they consider a pair more stable and reliable than a single person, or because the job includes a variety of duties which a man and a woman could share. If you're single, try for those positions anyhow. On the other hand, an advertisement that specifies a male or a female doesn't have to mean that a couple won't be considered. It's worth applying even for jobs you don't get, just for the tips you pick up.

Maybe nothing offered in the papers will appeal to you ... in which case I suggest that you go around and ask all the local realtors about upcoming janitorial openings which haven't yet been advertised. (The early bird and all that.) If the owners can't use you as a caretaker right then, they may still want you to clean and paint an apartment, haul away trash, or whatever. Impress them as a hard worker and they'll most likely remember you when they do need a building tended.

The first caretaking job my wife and I took—about three years ago—was also the first we applied for. Getting hired was easy, even though we weren't legally married at the time (it's probably best, in such a case, to say that you're wed).

Our building, a big old place with twelve apartments, also happened to be one of the most beautiful and famous

landmarks in this part of town. The duties consisted of
sweeping and mopping the hallways, looking after the garbage,
and doing a little yard work or snow removal as the season
required. For about ten hours of effort a month we received
free rent, utilities, and $50.00 in salary. Not bad!

Our new job also gave us a great deal of freedom: As long as
the work got done we didn't have to be around at set hours.
And, like most such situations, this one had its unadvertised
fringe benefits. Each floor of the building contained about a
dozen rooms and one apartment which had once been quarters
for a live-in maid. Since we had the entire top story to
ourselves, we expanded our living space into most of the
unused rooms on that level . . . and furnished our "mansion"
with some nice junk which had been left there and which we
found in the tenants' trash. One way and another, the two
years and three months we spent at the "Netamora" were very
enjoyable.

That period of our lives was profitable, too, because I used
my ample free time to start a side business of roofing,
painting, hauling, etc. The building's large basement gave me
storage space for my materials. (If you get into such a sideline,
by the way, remember that your own employers may need

help on some of their other pieces of property.)

When we quit our first caretaking job several months ago, Nancy and I still weren't ready to settle down. We thought we'd do some traveling . . . starting with a winter in Florida. Within one week after our move south, we'd landed a position as managers of an apartment house located just four miles from the beach. It's set in a big yard that's loaded with fruit trees. (Living in the city doesn't have to cut you off from nature. Many owners of urban buildings will let their caretakers plant gardens on the surrounding land.)

A tip to remember when you leave a janitorial position: Ask your boss for a letter of reference. If you've done a good job he should be glad to oblige you, and you'll find that testimonial very handy later . . . especially if you move to another town.

Finally, anyone who wants to get into the caretaking business should keep in mind that all the jobs aren't in apartment buildings . . . or even in the city. Some friends of ours found a good deal taking care of a beautiful country estate, where they have their own house and large garden (and access to a 16-acre lake), keep chickens and bees, and produce enough extra food to stock a roadside stand. Their duties—two days' housework a week plus the care of the yard and garden—bring the couple a good salary along with the pleasure of living in such mellow surroundings.

If it's a rural position you're after, watch your local paper for a few days to get an idea of the possibilities in your area. I've seen advertisements for people to take care of horses, feed cattle, or merely occupy a country place and look after it for an owner who prefers to stay in town. It's a fine chance to live and learn if you're planning your own homestead . . . and, with your former rent money going into a land fund, you'll be able to afford the place you want a lot sooner. Then, if you start slowly with your own property—maybe work it only on weekends for a while—you'll find when you're ready to make the move that everything falls into place.

City or country, caretaking can be a good way to live . . . and a good moneysaving start for a new life. Good luck and happy job hunting.◗

The above article originally appeared in LIFESTYLE! NO. 7 . . . along with a great deal of other live-better-for-less and self-sufficiency how-to information. For further information about the magazine—and other books and periodicals devoted to home businesses, self-sufficiency, and related subjects—please see page 367 of this handbook.

GREG SIPLE:
HOW TO GET PAID FOR TAKING A FREE VACATION

If you enjoy outdoor life, cycling, all-expense-paid vacations, and the company of young people . . . you should know about a program originated by American Youth Hostels, Inc. Each year, AYH pays dozens of men and women to lead small groups of teenagers on one- to two-month bicycle excursions in forty countries. This coming summer the organization plans to double the number of these trips in the United States and Canada, which means that qualified leaders are in short supply. This could be your big chance! . . . but first, as they say, a word about the sponsor:

WHAT IS AYH?

American Youth Hostels, Inc., is a non-profit, service

organization that was established in 1934. The association maintains a system of simple, low-cost overnight accommodations for young people (generally 15 to 35, although older "youngsters" are always welcome) who prefer to travel alone or in small groups on inexpensive public transportation, by sharing rides or—and especially—by hiking, cycling, canoeing, skiing, sailing, riding horses, or otherwise "using their own steam".

AYH is a member of the International Youth Hostel Federation, and membership in AYH entitles an individual to admission to any hostel in the forty-six other nations in which IYHF affiliates are located. Young adults who join AYH, then, can travel throughout large sections of the civilized world on a people-to-people basis at rock-bottom expense.

Yearly dues for AYH members under 18 are only $5.00, and AYHers over 18 pay an annual membership fee of just $10.00. Hostelers are required to carry along their own personal eating, sleeping, and washing gear and pay a small overnight charge for the use of bed, mattress, blankets, and cooking facilities at each stop.

WHAT IS AN AYH "TRIP"?

Although hostelers may travel alone, with one or more friends, or with their families, many prefer to pay a set fee and join an AYH-sponsored tour lasting four to eight weeks. These excursions are carefully mapped in advance on out-of-the-way and scenic routes and are led by qualified individuals who are responsible for the safety and well-being of the group.

Each member of the tour is expected to furnish his own bicycle, pack, and personal gear and share cooking, cleaning, and housekeeping chores along the way. The fee he pays ($330–$760 for a domestic trip, $1,000–$1,400 foreign) entitles him to round-trip transportation with the group, all meals and accommodations, personal accident and sickness insurance, approved leadership and organization of the outing, and such miscellaneous extras along the way—budget permitting—as visits to museums, concerts, and theaters.

WHERE DO AYH OUTINGS GO?

Forty-two AYH groups traveled through parts of the United States and Canada last year and thirty-three expeditions were sent to Europe. There is also a special two-month tour of Japan. Separate domestic itineraries cover the Rockies, Hawaii, New England, the Pacific Northwest, the Great Lakes, and other regions. Overseas swings are usually limited to the Scandinavian countries and northern and central Europe.

WHO MAY TAKE AN AYH TRIP?

In general, any AYH member who has been certified by his family doctor to be physically and mentally fit and who is at least 14 years old by July 1 of the summer of the excursion is eligible for a hosteling expedition in the U.S. or Canada. Minimum age for trips to most other parts of the world is 16 by July 1, although applicants only 15 years old are sometimes accepted for such excursions if they have certain previous AYH experience. All participants must enjoy the outdoors, get along with others, and be willing and prepared to "put themselves" into the undertaking to make it a success.

WHO MAY LEAD AN AYH EXCURSION?

Leaders must be over 21, young in heart, members in good standing of AYH and their communities, and in good physical health. Anyone who meets these qualifications will be considered, although applicants are often graduate students, teachers, and group workers looking for an interesting "job" during their long summer vacations. AYH plans its programs months in advance, and wise aspirants apply early.

Every applicant is required to attend a one-week National Leadership Training Course conducted by experienced AYH leaders. The course costs $75.00, is informal and fun, and covers the following subjects:

Philosophy of Hosteling	Menu Planning
Budgeting	Public Relations
Bicycle Safety	Bicycle Repair
Packing	History of Hosteling
Hosteling Customs	Group Relationships
Problem Trippers	Trip Emergencies
AYH Policies	First Aid

Health Problems

Leadership courses need not be taken the same year that a trip is led. I attended the training program in 1967 and led my first outing in 1969. My wife took the course in 1968 and didn't lead until 1971.

Married couples are eligible for leadership assignments together if both individuals have completed the training course. The assistant spouse then pays the regular price of the excursion, less leadership and organization fees.

WHAT DOES A LEADER DO?

An AYH leader is not a travel guide. His primary responsibility is the well-being and safety of the group, and he rides behind the others when cycling and watches for trouble. The leader also delegates responsibility for meal preparation and campsite and hostel clean-up (as well as doing his share!) and coordinates the flock's decision making. He is further required to dispatch a weekly letter to AYH headquarters and keep a daily record of expenditures, roads traveled, and overnight conditions.

AND WHAT IS HE PAID?

In return for his services, an AYH leader receives an all-expenses-paid vacation plus a modest amount of spending money. That is, he is given—free of charge—all the meals, accommodations, insurance, and extra group activities (concerts, plays, etc.) enjoyed by the members of his flock plus a basic allowance based on the length of the excursion plus an extra allowance based on the total number of trips he has led in the past. In addition, the leader receives an allowance for the distance he must travel from home to the expedition's departure point and return.

IS IT WORTH IT?

I've now led two AYH tours. The first was a six-week swing through eastern Canada in 1969 and the second—co-led by my wife—a one-month cycling jaunt down the Atlantic seacoast last summer.

In both cases, most of my trippers were from middle- or upper-middle-class homes in the New York-New England area. All (there were nine youngsters in each troupe) were well-educated kids who quickly adapted to hosteling and enthusiastically accepted the hardships of bicycle touring.

On the Canadian excursion, we stayed overnight in youth hostels, YMCA's, a jail, a church, one motel, and some camp facilities. We also spent nights in three youth hostels, a tourist home, a church, and a motel on the East Coast trip . . . but, for the most part, camped out in the tents we carried along on that expedition.

On both outings, each tripper carried all his own equipment and belongings plus a share of the group's cooking utensils and food. We averaged about 40 miles a day and only used supplemental transportation (such as the AYH-arranged-for truck that carried us across the Chesapeake Bay Bridge-Tunnel) when necessary.

Neither trip was entirely free'n'easy. On the East Coast venture—for instance—we weathered two or three rainstorms, had a bicycle stolen in Atlantic City (the kids voted to buy a new one with group money), ate burned dinners, sometimes found ourselves stranded with a bent wheel, and suffered other large and small mishaps that I had to find some way to turn into jokes.

For the most part, though, life as an AYH trip leader is great. The duties are slight when compared to the month or more free vacation, opportunity to see some country at a leisurely pace, special companionship of bicycle touring, and general satisfaction that you receive in return.

All that and spending money, too! As an AYH tour leader, you just can't lose.◒

TYPICAL AYH TRIPS

PACIFIC NORTHWEST—$580

6 Weeks

Clean fresh air awaits you in the Northwest . . . camp on a bed of pine needles in the shadow of Mt. Rainier . . . stand on the deck of a ferry winding through Puget Sound to San Juan Islands and Vancouver Island . . . see the famed gardens of Victoria, authentic totems, and old English towns . . . swim on beaches laced with evergreens or hop a logging train to visit a forest museum. Cycle around the Olympic Peninsula, stopping off to view the rain forest or dig clams . . . visit the logging and lumbering center of Aberdeen and cycle down the coast to the mouth of the Columbia River . . . stand where Lewis and Clark stood in 1805 . . . follow the river into Portland for the ride to the California wilds, culminating in a 6-day raft trip on the Klamath River. This is a rugged camping and cycling trip, starting in Seattle and ending in San Francisco. HIGHLIGHT: Raft trip on Klamath River with experienced guides.

EUROPEAN EXPLORER—$1,145
London, Belgium, Germany, Austria, Italy, Switzerland, Paris, Amsterdam

This trip has been especially planned to accommodate those who dig "FYOP" (find your own place) itineraries. From London the group crosses to Belgium, visiting Ghent, Bruges, and Brussels. Castles on the Rhine carry you south to Heidelberg and then to Munich. Here the group is free to explore Bavarian Germany and Austria for two weeks, finding all of its own accommodations in out-of-the-way hostels until it resumes its scheduled reservations in Salzburg. The group covers Vienna, Venice, and the major Italian cities, and then to the Swiss Alps, Lausanne, Geneva, Paris, and Amsterdam. Sleeping bags and an adventurous spirit are a *must*. ♣

For information on AYH trips here and abroad, the leadership program, and hosteling in general, write:

AMERICAN YOUTH HOSTELS, INC.
Travel Dept.—National Headquarters
Delaplane, Va. 22025

1975
NATIONAL LEADERSHIP
TRAINING COURSES

(You must take one of these courses before you'll be allowed to lead an AYH trip.)

Western Region	Hemet, Calif.	March 22–29
Midwest Region	Porter, Ind.	May 30–June 7
Midwest Region	Bowling Green, Ohio	Aug. 30–Sept. 6
Eastern Region	Bushkill, Pa. I	June 14–21
Eastern Region	Bushkill, Pa. II	June 22–29

The above article originally appeared in THE MOTHER EARTH NEWS® NO. 14 . . . along with a great deal of other live-better-for-less and self-sufficiency how-to information. For further information about the magazine—and other books and periodicals devoted to home businesses, self-sufficiency, and related subjects—please see page 367 of this handbook.

CHARLES ZABIELSKIS:
HOW TO GET A JOB ON A FREIGHTER

I'm here to tell you that—contrary to popular belief—you can still work your way to almost anywhere in the world on a freighter. You don't need money, short hair, experience, or references. You won't even have to fill out an application! All you'll need is a passport and a vaccination certificate.

There are two good ways for the complete novice to get a job on a freighter. One is by going from ship to ship and asking each captain if he needs [a] a *deckboy* or [b] a *workaway*. A deckboy is part of the crew and gets paid (although very little), and a workaway gets no wages at all but swaps labor for his passage. Although few companies now accept workaways, some captains will still take one in place of a paid crew member.

Don't waste your time with United States vessels when

going from ship to ship unless you're already in the American union (in which case, you probably wouldn't be using this method of locating a job anyway). If you're not a union member, don't bother trying to join; they'll just put you on a waiting list. I was about No. 200 when I first applied and, one year later, they had taken only ten people into the union. Now that the war in Asia has wound down, there are a lot of unemployed sailors . . . and too many union members. So concentrate on foreign vessels.

The second easy beginner's entry to a freighter job is through the Scandinavian Shipping Office. There are only two of these offices in the United States: One is on Pier 29 in San Francisco and the other is at Hansen Place in Brooklyn. When the captain of a Scandinavian ship in our waters needs crew members he calls one of these two offices, and the chances of getting a job this way are probably better than by going ship to ship.

The Scandinavian Shipping Office in San Francisco, where I hired on, gives out jobs at 10 a.m. each weekday. Members of the Scandinavian unions are given first preference, experienced non-union people get second choice, and anyone else present can then apply for jobs still unfilled on a first come, first served basis.

This puts you on the bottom but, if there's a deckboy opening, you stand a good chance of getting it. A deckboy is usually a non-union crew apprentice, and his pay ($100 a month) is about one-third of a seaman's wages. Only rarely will a Scandinavian union member or an experienced non-member take this job.

Have your passport with you when you go to the shipping office. If you get called, they'll want to see it. If you're aiming for a particular place and plan on staying, ask at the U.S. passport office if you'll need a visa. That visa, by the way, will be issued by the foreign country involved and *not by the U.S. Government*. Most countries have consulates in New York and San Francisco (and, sometimes, other cities as well), and it only takes a day for most consulates to visa a passport. The proper visa can really save a lot of hassles if you decide to quit ship in a foreign port.

If you're hired at the shipping office you'll be sent for a physical before you board the freighter. In San Francisco, the examination is made at a place called the Overseas Medical Center, and it's nothing to worry about. The whole thing takes an hour and is not very rough (I flunked my draft physical but passed this one easily). You'll be given a vaccination and any other shots you'll need for where you're going, and it's all paid for by the shipping company.

OK. What are your chances of getting a freighter this way? That depends . . . on luck, timing, and persistence. I caught a vessel the second day I went to the shipping office . . . and I've met a fellow who tried every day for a month (in the fall, the slowest season of the year) before there was an opening for a deckboy. The best time to try is in the spring or summer. Christmas is also good because many sailors want holiday leave and there's a big turnover in personnel then. For what it's worth, the New York Scandinavian Shipping Office is a lot busier than the one in San Francisco . . . so your chances might be better in the east coast port.

It's important to be at the shipping office when the assignments are given out (10 a.m. in San Francisco). If you're there at any other time your chances of getting a job are practically zero. And don't be discouraged if you get little information and much run-around from the office personnel: They want to spend as little time as possible talking to inexperienced non-union job seekers. The day I was hired they had told me there probably wouldn't be an opening for another eight months. The sailors are the people to talk to if you want straight information.

The ship I worked on was a 10,000-ton (average size) Danish freighter sailing between the west coast, Australia, and New Zealand. It was a fairly new and completely modern ship with a crew's lounge, tiled and paneled passageways, and carpeted and individually air-conditioned cabins. Deckboys were bunked two to a cabin, and there was a desk and individual closets in each room.

Deckboys work either in the pantry or on deck with the crew, and I did both for a while.

Working in the pantry is terrible. At 6 a.m. you start cleaning the bathrooms and scrubbing passageways outside the crew's cabins. You also set the tables, bring the food from the galley (which is far away), serve, clear the tables, and wash the dishes for all meals and coffee breaks . . . for about 16 people. There's a thousand little hassles and a lot of running involved because the crew wants their meals on time, but the cook won't fix chow until the last minute because he doesn't want it served cold. The day isn't finished until after 7 p.m., and it's a seven-days-a-week grind. Even with an hour or two free every afternoon, this is a hard job.

Working out on deck with the able seamen is a lot better. The night watchman wakes the crew at 6:30 a.m., and they meet in the messroom for coffee and start work at 7. Breakfast is served at 8 o'clock and there's a coffee break at 10. Twelve to one is lunchtime with another half-hour break at 3. The workday is finished at 5 o'clock, Saturdays and Sundays are free, and you're entitled to two extra days off each month.

The work on deck is sometimes dirty (cleaning up oil or greasing cables), sometimes heavy (putting away hardware that secures the deck cargo), and most of the time menial (scraping rust and painting). But there are consolations. For one thing, you're out in the sun and clean sea air working more or less on your own and, for another, you're doing something different every day.

A job on a vessel beats most work situations in this country (where workers hate their grind, do the minimum, and can't wait for the day to end). On a ship the crew knows what has to be done, they do it right, and they take pride in their labor. The situation is very relaxed, everyone works at his own pace, no one is pushed, and there's no time clock to punch. It's *what gets done*—and not time put in—that counts.

"Good, working people" is the best way to describe sailors. The crew I joined was really great . . . not at all like the hard, rough cutthroats I'd imagined. Working on a ship is sometimes dangerous (you can easily get hit by the huge hooks that swing from the cranes or have your fingers squashed in machinery), so crew members always watch out for one another. I was really surprised at the way we all stuck together, especially in port.

Although none of the able seamen had long hair, they

accepted mine from the beginning. Apparently, most people making just one trip on a vessel do as little as possible, and the other hands liked me because I did my work and did it well. I found it much easier to keep busy than to stand around—bored—doing nothing.

Gradually the crew accepted me as one of their own, and we did a lot of rapping (they all spoke good English, and one could talk fluently in five languages). Most hands were Danish (one was dodging the draft in Denmark), but the ship's complement also included a Chilean, an Australian, a Swede, an Irishman, a French Canadian, and a Greenland Eskimo. They all had interesting stories of the places they'd been.

Life aboard the freighter was good, but the routine did get a little boring. We spent our evenings playing cards, reading, writing letters (all postage was paid by the ship), or just sitting in the messroom talking. A movie was shown twice a week while we were at sea. Some of the films were good, most were bad, and a few weren't even in English. The chief steward opened the ship's stores twice a week also, and we bought things like soap and candy against our pay. Everything was duty free, and some of the items were really inexpensive (a carton of cigarettes cost $1.75).

The food was excellent and plentiful and the variety served at each meal was amazing . . . within limits. The Scandinavians are meat, cheese, and bread eaters, and they don't have much of a sweet tooth. Dessert during the week was fresh fruit, with Danish pastry served only on Sundays. Still, even though I ate no meat on the trip, I never once left the table hungry.

Working on a ship, I found, is not at all like being in the Navy. Ours was more of a boss-worker than an officer-enlisted man relationship. There were no "orders", "regulations", rank, uniforms, or inspections. In warm weather most of the crew—including the captain—went without shirts and wore either shorts or cutoffs. There was practically no tension between officers and crew . . . in fact, we rarely saw the officers during working hours. After work, the seamen and officers treated each other as good friends.

Another major difference between working on a freighter and being in the Navy is the fact that you can always quit in the next port if you don't like the vessel. All you have to do is give the captain notice one week before you enter the seaport where you plan to leave ship.

By the way, if you have only limited time for your voyage,

don't trust the shipping company's docking schedule. According to the timetable, my round trip was supposed to take six weeks . . . it actually took twice that long. Anything from bad weather to repairs to harbor strikes can and will delay a ship.

In case you're wondering . . . yes, the first day out nearly everyone gets at least a little seasick. It's a nasty feeling, but even old salts have it after spending some time ashore. Most people get used to the ship's motion in a day or two and are OK for the rest of the voyage. I was never in a big storm but, from what I've heard, they can be pretty miserable.

Nobody on our freighter even mentioned those supposedly famous initiation ceremonies held for people crossing the equator the first time. I don't think that ritual is observed on many other cargo ships either. It doesn't seem to fit the peaceful live-and-let-live atmosphere of a working vessel.

To me, that peaceful life is the best part of being at sea: spending the whole day out in the sun, eating good food, getting plenty of sleep, never having to rush or run around, and not having to cope with radio, television, newspapers, or uptight people.

Instead, there is the sky and the sea. The horizon stretches for three hundred sixty degrees, and the sunrises and sunsets near the equator are fantastic. There are waves, porpoises, flying fish, seagulls, and albatrosses but—two thousand miles from land—virtually no pollution. The stars shine so brightly they're like holes in the sky, and their light is so strong that it actually reflects from the waves.●

The above article originally appeared in THE MOTHER EARTH NEWS® NO. 9 . . . along with a great deal of other live-better-for-less and self-sufficiency how-to information. For further information about the magazine—and other books and periodicals devoted to home businesses, self-sufficiency, and related subjects—please see page 367 of this handbook.

OCCASIONAL JOBS

And here, to close out our book, are two short reminders that—if you'll just look around—you'll often be able to pick up a few extra dollars doing things that you might have thought you weren't even qualified for.

Ever try to apply for a few weeks' work as a camp counselor? Or consider yourself a candidate for self-employment as a freelance substitute teacher?

Well, give these—and related ideas—a whirl if you're looking for a way to make a little "side" money. Deb Sillers and Chris and Kathy Cooper have found such jobs open even to people without "proper" credentials. Which means that opportunities *really* abound for anyone ambitious enough to organize his or her own night classes in art, auto repair, wild food identification, or any other in-demand subject. Classes that can be run right out of a city apartment or country living room.

In other words, seek and ye shall find. Knock and the door shall be opened to you. There are absolutely uncounted ways in which you can operate your own little home business. This book only hints at a *few* of the possibilities. Look around and you're sure to see many more.

And, if you don't find anyone already engaged in what you personally feel is the ideal self-employment enterprise for *you* . . . then get busy and pioneer that brand-new business on your own! ⬤

DEB SILLERS:
HOW TO BE A
CAMP
COUNSELOR

I was once skeptical of camps . . . till I found out how nice talking to an eight-year-old about turtles can be. Now I know that a summer job as a counselor can be just the right first step (especially for a girl) back to the land. It's a way to believe those Earth Mother dreams into reality and certainly beats sitting mournfully in a dorm while reading books on life in the wilds.

A summer spent among children can be an educational, joy-filled experience. There are other valuable benefits:

[1] It gives you some confidence in living with nature. This is especially important for those who have lived with wall-to-wall carpeting and motel vacations all their lives.

[2] It gives you a definite starting point for beginning your move back to the simpler life.

[3] It starts you with some money. Lots of camps pay from $300 to $500 a session.

[4] It gives you time to be quiet and to think without being totally alone (a lot of girls are scared out of the forest by solitude when they try to "go it alone" all at once).

[5] It puts you in contact with other people who dig the woods and gives you a basic feel and knowledge of woodcraft.

[6] A summer spent in the mountains (or wherever) gives you a real opportunity to get in touch with what is happening out in the hills: not the people wandering through them . . . the hills themselves.

Staying in one area the whole season will give you a chance to get to know the land . . . to learn what the woods have to say. If you can begin to understand just one creek or one ravine, you'll have the key to understanding the land wherever you finally settle.

One word of warning: Camps are definitely not for everyone. If you don't dig being with kids a lot, *don't go*. Most camps give their counselors ample free time, but you'll be living with children. Some of these children will be away from their parents for the first time, and others have problems accepting the fact that they are always sent away to camp all summer. All these children need a lot of love. If you go, be ready to give: to the kids, the other people there, the animals, and the land. You'll get it all back.

I'm off this summer to a camp in the Adirondacks to hunt for things that other people haven't looked at, watery places in the forest, and quiet spots under the pines.

Here are a few agencies to contact for a counseling job. The first two are especially helpful:

Association of Private Camps
55 West 42nd Street
New York, New York 10036
(must be 19 and have 1 year
  college)

American Camping Association
Directory of Accredited Camps
Bradford Woods
Martinsville, Indiana 46151
Cost $5.95
(317) 342-8456

Black Diamond Girl Scout
  Council
708 Bigley Avenue
Charleston, West Virginia 25302

New England Camping Association, Inc.
29 Commonwealth Avenue
Boston, Massachusetts 02116

Girl Scouts of the USA
National Branch Office,
  Region II
1911 North Fort Myer Drive
Rosslyn, Virginia 22209

New York State Department
  of Labor
Division of Labor
Professional Placement Center
444 Madison Avenue
New York, New York 10022

Saginaw Valley Council (Camp
  Fire Girls, volunteer only)
107 South Washington Street
Saginaw, Michigan 48607

Camp Counselor Placement
  Service
Box 188
Tuxedo, North Carolina 28784 ●

The above article originally appeared in THE MOTHER EARTH NEWS® NO. 3 . . . along with a great deal of other live-better-for-less and self-sufficiency how-to information. For further information about the magazine—and other books and periodicals devoted to home businesses, self-sufficiency, and related subjects—please see page 367 of this handbook.

CHRIS AND KATHY COOPER :
HOW TO GO BACK TO SCHOOL... AT $5.00 AN HOUR

If you walked into your first college education course a few years ago (and walked out just as briskly)—or if you sat through one or more semesters of Ed. Psych., Ed. Foundations, or Ed. Whatever before you jumped ship—you may still be able to enjoy some of the benefits of teaching, yet escape most of the horrors which turned you away from that profession in the first place.

We've found that our own alternative, substitute teaching, brings in an adequate amount of money and calls for a minimum of compromise with our consciences. If you can meet a few basic requirements (one of which is the ability to live on a modest and erratic income), you're in a position to discover the job's satisfactions and benefits for yourself.

REQUIREMENTS

You probably need not be a college graduate, and certainly need not hold a teaching degree or state certificate, to be allowed to substitute in your local primary or secondary schools. In general, anyone who has completed two or more years of college can figure on being seriously considered as a stand-in instructor in most areas.

If you have the requisite background and decide to get yourself listed as a possible substitute teacher, you'll need—first and foremost—a phone. Its expense will be minimal as long as you resist the temptation to use it for other than business purposes (i.e., receiving calls to work).

An automobile is also a necessity, unless you live within bicycling or walking distance of several schools (or one large one) or can get to work by bus.

The last requirement—a reasonably presentable suit or dress—is probably moldering in your closet right now. Your attire doesn't have to be stylish (although it and your person should be clean), and you won't need the varied wardrobe of a full-time teacher. It's quite acceptable to wear the same outfit two days running, or to use a shirt until it's actually dirty . . . particularly since each day may find you in a different school before a different set of eyes.

Chris' teaching gear consists of two shirts, both of his ties, and a couple of sports jackets and pairs of pants he's had for years. No one objects to his use of new workshoes in place of oxfords. Since he's sometimes called upon to teach shop or conservation classes, or to supervise recess or sports, heavy footwear is both practical and comfortable.

Your job prospects will be improved if you're willing to keep your normal personal appearance in line with community standards. We don't mean that you must compete with the crewcut-and-Cadillac set: Chris has a beard and drives an old jeep. But we both wear rather conservative clothing at all times (mostly because, in the good old days when we last bought dress clothes, hippies hadn't been invented yet and everyone looked about the same).

We don't try to be anything but ourselves. On days when we're not teaching, the school bus will pass our house when we're digging in the garden, cutting wood, or sleeping in the sun with our cats. The students, teachers, and administration all seem to accept our habits.

If asked, we admit to being vegetarians . . . and we aren't ashamed of believing in George McGovern. We don't argue or proselytize on school time, however, nor do we seek to advertise our opinions and lifestyle. In this way we can operate without compromise in a world which doesn't allow for much independence of thought or action. We're looked upon as perhaps a little strange, but not as a threat.

INITIATION

To become eligible for replacement teaching jobs, simply contact the office of the superintendent of schools or a local principal's secretary. Either source will tell you what educational background you must have and how many established substitutes are already available. You'll also be given an application form, which can be anything from a fairly involved questionnaire to a simple blank for your name and address.

You may, if you wish—or if required to do so—indicate a preference for a particular grade, school, or subject. In our own case, we've found it best to take whatever is available on a given day. Since our combined skills include carpentry, English, American studies, elementary education, conservation, and the natural sciences, we've never felt ourselves unable to handle any assignment.

The next move is up to the schools . . . but if you're acquainted with a teacher, secretary, principal, or janitor in the system, cultivate that friendship! As in any other job, *whom* you know is important. Also, occasional mention of your name might keep it in circulation. We didn't get a call for weeks after signing up as stand-in instructors until our neighbor, who teaches in a local school, recommended us when she knew an opening was available. That got us into the building, and we must have made a favorable impression because we've been called back frequently since.

Which just goes to prove, I suppose, that you're more likely to be called upon once the secretary or principal has become aware of you as a person rather than just a name on a sheet of paper. Most schools develop a list of substitutes they like and draw repeatedly from that pool. This makes it relatively difficult for a newcomer to get established, but does offer some security once you become known.

DUTIES

First, always be on time... and second, if there's any doubt about whether you're required to do a certain task (hall duty or lunch count, for instance), *do it.*

Beyond that, you'll find that some of your employers expect you to be little more than a baby sitter. This is boring and frustrating, but may allow you to be paid for taking attendance and then reading a book for the rest of the day. Most schools, however, appreciate your at least making an effort to discuss the subject you're supposed to be dealing with.

Any attempt at actual teaching has to be based on the current work of the class... and you may have some trouble finding out what that is. Teachers usually call in sick just before school starts, so you can expect little help in the way of notes from the instructor you're replacing. But—since that person completed all those education courses you dropped out of—you'll most likely find on or in the desk a daily plan book that lists the textbooks, pages, and problems to be covered. Although the students aren't necessarily doing what that journal says on any given day, you can at least get a general idea of what they *should* be doing.

Asking the pupils themselves for information about their studies may get you some help... or, especially in junior high, may initiate a horrendous pack of lies. Try to question a studious child, or one who seems unpopular, awkward, or shy. More often than not such youngsters will not only tell you what the class has been working on, but will also be happy to help you take attendance and collect milk money or run messages to the office or the janitor.

When you collect papers, assign homework, or cover work in class—especially in the lower grades—you may hear an anguished (or even menacing) groan of "That isn't the way our teacher does it!" As much as a seventh-grader hates "mean old Miss Gillespie", he'll defend her method of operation to any substitute who tries to change the routine.

The first time this happens, growl back, "This is how *I* do it, and as long as I'm teaching this is how it's going to be done!" We're not saying that you should arbitrarily change a teacher's ritual if you're aware of the manner in which he or she normally operates, but neither should you let a gang of unruly preadolescents run the classroom.

It's much more difficult for a substitute to maintain order and discipline than it is for a full-time teacher. You must be prepared to be strict and, on occasion, even unfair if necessary. Recently one of us put a whole class on detention, although three members out of twenty were innocent of wrongdoing. The group had been warned that the next infraction—no matter who was responsible—would result in exactly that punishment, and the threat had to be carried out.

Your pupils will tromp on you as soon as they detect a note of indecisiveness in your bearing . . . and if you're faced with a high school automobile mechanics class, that can even mean physical assault. Call the office if you don't feel that you're in control. It's much better to admit you need help than to struggle foolishly with a situation beyond your abilities.

Of course, the job isn't usually as grim as all that. You'll always have troublemakers, but peer pressure will keep most of them more or less in line, and threats of detention (or whatever penalty the school allows) will give you the edge over the rest. Unless matters are almost out of hand, your voice—coupled if necessary with a book slammed on the desk—will quiet a class. (If you're permitted to use physical force, do so with caution. Only as a last resort should you feel it necessary to touch a child.)

If we've dwelt at length on the subject of discipline and order, it's not because we're authoritarians or think that's the most important part of education. It's simply that students—and again, those of junior high age seem to be the worst offenders—will naturally try to get away with whatever they can when a substitute teacher is in charge. And much of what they try to get away with is injurious to them, to the school, or to you.

Finally, we suggest that you decline any request by your pupils that you chaperone a dance or special event. Though the school might allow you to serve, you wouldn't be paid for a possible three hours' work (plus the time and cost of transportation) . . . and you could get into trouble. At a recent local junior high dance, an enterprising group of youngsters gang-raped a girl in the bushes near the building while a number of parents and teachers supervised inside. It's natural to want to be a friend to the students and to go a little out of your way to help them, but we feel that volunteering for tasks beyond normal school hours is taking on too much responsibility for the position.

REMUNERATION AND OTHER BENEFITS

Here in Maine, we get $20.00 for a day of substitute teaching (about four or five hours' work, not counting lunchtime and free periods). A friend of ours in central New York State can earn $27.00 a day in his hometown and $30.00–$32.00 in nearby schools. We're not among those (usually teachers themselves) who think that the profession is overworked and underpaid . . . in fact, we consider even our own rate more than the job is worth. All the same, we're glad to accept the money.

Though your pay as a substitute is less than that of a full-time teacher, the disadvantages are also fewer. You're free to refuse any job . . . and when you do work, you remain essentially an outsider: You can be friendly with everyone but needn't engage in the petty politics and personal rivalries common to schools, offices, and work crews everywhere. Also, you aren't required to sign a contract or a loyalty oath (a condition of employment in New York State, where one of us taught full time for a year). Nor are you in any way beholden to a school board. If you can keep a classroom full of students reasonably quiet—and maybe teach them a little while the regular instructor is gone—you fulfilled your obligation.

Work as a substitute doesn't just free you from the hassles of full-time teaching . . . it also offers you many of the same benefits. You'll enjoy those generous vacations during the year, for one thing, and you'll have the whole summer to do with as you like. (Our market garden gives us another source of income during that period.) There's even a fair degree of security in this field, since you can expect an ever-increasing number of jobs once you're established in a school system. We know persons who've had to withdraw their names from some lists because they were turning down too many offers.

Finally—though the fifth grade isn't exactly the Harvard library—it's pleasant to be involved, in some way, with books and ideas and group learning. The substitute feels just as much satisfaction as a regular teacher when a grubby little girl hands over the "I like you, Mrs. Cooper" card she's made . . . or when that slack-jawed senior finally raises his hand and has, of all things, the right answer.●

The above article originally appeared in LIFESTYLE! NO. 7 . . . along with a great deal of other live-better-for-less and self-sufficiency how-to information. For further information about the magazine—and other books and periodicals devoted to home businesses, self-sufficiency, and related subjects—please see page 367 of this handbook.

MERRILL SANDERS:
TEMPORARY WORK CAN BE A PERMANENT CAREER

You'd like to go into business for yourself but have no capital to invest . . . and you don't want to be tied down by a full-time enterprise, since you need one or two weeks off every month.

If your thoughts have been running along the above lines, you might consider becoming a self-employed temporary worker.

A little over a year ago I started a job as typist for a temporary help agency. I liked the freedom of more or less coming and going as I pleased but found it hard to get ahead on the low wages my employer paid.

Then, while I was toying with the idea of taking a full-time job, a friend mentioned that a temporary who had once worked in her office now contacted companies on her own. I had seen copies of agency bills and realized that by pocketing the service's fee as well as my own I could make more as a substitute than as a regular employee. So, that afternoon I made my first phone calls ... and the next day I was earning $5.00 an hour instead of the $3.00 I had received from the temporary employment bureau.

People with clerical skills who live in or near big cities are in the best position to get temporary jobs. However, almost anyone living anywhere can find work. All businesses—stores, farms, small manufacturing plants—have busy periods and times when the regular staff is away. More and more, employers are turning to stand-in workers to fill these needs.

How do you get your own temporary employment business started? If you've had special experience as a legal secretary or medical technologist, look under "Attorneys" or "Hospitals" in the Yellow Pages of the phone book to find your list of potential clients. If you have no specialty, turn to "Travel Agencies", "Hardware Stores", "Feed Dealers", or any field that interests you and start calling.

The responses you get will vary. Some companies never use temporary workers, and a few big ones have exclusive contracts with agencies. But most office managers will be interested in the idea of a self-employed person and will ask you to send them a résumé.

If a company sounds like a good prospect, it's a good idea to offer to go in for an interview. Most people will take your word that you can type 60 wpm or have driven a forklift, but they're often a little reluctant to hire a total stranger over the telephone. Don't be surprised, however, if—after a five-minute meeting with an office manager—he or she asks if you can start work immediately.

In densely populated areas you can pick and choose, selecting jobs which pay particularly well or offer a chance to learn something. If the closest town is a settlement of 754 people, on the other hand, your approach will be different. You might want to make some business cards and visit every place of possible employment in the region. Try to arrive at a slack time of day when the person in charge will have time to talk with you.

Keep records of all your contacts with organizations. Operating in the city as I do, I've found that a simple way to do this is to cross off in the phone book the names of companies that don't seem interested and to prepare index cards on places that look promising. A typical entry from my file reads:

> XYZ Designers, 851-9000. Personnel Director, Jane Doe. Phoned June 15, 1973, went in for interview June 16, résumé submitted. No openings now, but three secretaries going on vacation in August. Call back last week in July.

After you finish a job, write down any information you want to remember. For example, you could add to the above card:

> Worked as secretary for Bob Green August 1 to August 15. Pay, $5.50 an hour. John Blue's secretary leaves for a month starting October 10.

To decide what to charge for your work, phone temporary agencies in your town and ask about their rates for a person with your skills. You can then set your fee 50¢ lower. Be willing to negotiate . . . when you first start out you may have to accept less than you would like in order to get jobs. Later, after you've worked for a company a few times, you'll be in a position to raise your charges substantially. Most organizations will pay a premium rate for a worker they know to be reliable, efficient, and familiar with their business procedure.

If you want short-term jobs, contact small companies . . . but if you prefer working for months at a time in one outfit, call only large organizations (where as soon as one job ends another will probably open up). If you're not familiar with the businesses in a city, by the way, you can learn a lot about them from their phone numbers. Large companies usually have easily remembered numbers like 863-1200, while small ones have irregular numbers such as 863-9247. Yellow Pages ads also can give you a clue to a firm's size.

There's a certain amount of bookkeeping associated with having any business of your own, and this one is no exception. Companies do not put temporary workers on their pay-rolls . . . they will expect you to bill them for your services, as agencies do. This is a simple matter: On a sheet of white paper type your name, your address, the date, the company's name and address, the hours worked, your rate of pay, and the total amount due. Some companies will ask for weekly bills, while others will give you a check the day you leave.

As your own boss, you are also responsible for making your own income tax and social security payments. If you expect to earn more than $500 a year from your temporary help business, ask the local IRS office for Form 1040-ES, "Declaration of Estimated Tax for Individuals". This is essentially an income tax withholding method for self-employed people and must be filed quarterly. The federal government doesn't expect you to be very exact in your calculations on these preliminary forms, but you'll be charged 6% interest if you underpay by more than 20%. Schedule SE, "Computation of Social Security Self-Employment Tax", must be filed with your yearly return, and state income taxes may apply to your business too.

On the bright side, business expenses such as upkeep of your office at home, stationery and mailing costs, and part of the telephone bill may be deductible from your taxable income. Consult, if you like, an accountant or IRS office for specific information on your particular case.

After you've been working for a while and have a number of satisfied customers, companies will begin to contact you. Your friends will probably be calling you too, asking if you have any extra jobs to hand on to them. At this point you'll be in a position to do one of two things: You can start your own temporary agency, charging commissions on work you find for other people . . . or, if friends with similar skills are interested

in working with you, you can form a cooperative.

Temporary employment is easy to handle on a cooperative basis because you'll often be offered two jobs at the same time, and you're sure to hear of extra positions in the larger companies at which you work. As a member of a collective you can give any of these jobs you don't want to your friends, and they can return the favor. If you want to get really organized, you can share the costs of an answering service to keep track of calls from firms, or you can send out a mailing advertising your services. A smoothly running co-op will provide a pool of jobs you can dip into as you need money. And, if your group is large enough, you can arrange benefits for yourselves . . . for example, by applying for a low group rate on health insurance.

The temporary employment business is very adaptable. You might start out working steadily in the city to save enough money to buy land. Then, after moving to the country, you could supplement your income by taking over as manager of the local general store whenever the owner's gout started acting up. However you decide to run things, being a self-employed temporary is a satisfying job that offers good pay, the liberty of taking off when you want, and the satisfaction of being your own boss.◕

The above article originally appeared in LIFESTYLE! NO. 6 . . . along with a great deal of other live-better-for-less and self-sufficiency how-to information. For further information about the magazine—and other books and periodicals devoted to home businesses, self-sufficiency, and related subjects—please see page 367 of this handbook.

PUBLICATIONS DEDICATED TO INDIVIDUAL INDEPENDENCE

If you've enjoyed the self-employment, work-at-home, and do-it-yourself business ideas in this book, you're sure to be interested in the following magazines:

FREE ENTERPRISE
800 Second Ave.
New York, N.Y. 10017

This bi-monthly periodical is always packed with franchise information, articles on self-employment ventures, and home business ideas. A 10-issue trial subscription will cost you $9.95.

THE MOTHER EARTH NEWS®
P.O. Box 70
Hendersonville, N.C. 28739

MOTHER always contains one or more do-it-yourself business articles. In addition, this bi-monthly periodical is jammed with firsthand reports from folks who've constructed their own ultra-low-cost homes, raised organic gardens, moved from the city to the country, kept cows and pigs and goats and chickens and other homestead livestock, built solar and wind and water and methane and other "alternative" energy systems, and—in general—"busted out of the rat race and taken life into their own hands". A one-year subscription (6 issues) costs $10.00.

NOTE: LIFESTYLE!, from which several articles were taken for this book, is no longer published. Back issues, however, are available from THE MOTHER EARTH NEWS®.

A SOURCE OF "GOOD LIFE" BOOKS

If your local bookstore doesn't stock the home business and other books devoted to self-sufficiency that you want, you can obtain a free catalog of such titles from:

MOTHER'S BOOKSHELF
P.O. Box 70
Hendersonville, N.C. 28739

INDEX